PR   Charlton
        Shakespea   ragedy

FEB 14 1995

SHAKESPEARIAN TRAGEDY

SHAKESPEARIAN TRAGEDY

BY

H. B. CHARLTON

HON. LITT. D. (LEEDS)
DOCTEUR DE DIJON

*Professor of English Literature in the
University of Manchester*

CAMBRIDGE
AT THE UNIVERSITY PRESS
1971

PUBLISHED BY
THE SYNDICS OF THE CAMBRIDGE UNIVERSITY PRESS

Bentley House, 200 Euston Road, London, NW1 2DB
American Branch: 32 East 57th Street, New York N.Y. 10022

ISBN 0 521 08104 1

First edition 1948
Reprinted 1949
1952
1961
1971

First printed in Great Britain at the University Press, Cambridge
Reprinted in Great Britain by
Lewis Reprints Limited, Port Talbot, Glamorgan

TO THE
SODALITY OF THE UNIVERSITY OF DIJON
IN TOKEN OF ENROLMENT THEREIN
AS ONE OF ITS HONORARY
DOCTORS

PREFACE

THE HONOUR of being invited to be the Clark Lecturer to Trinity College, Cambridge, may well go to any man's head, swell his presumption and inveigle him, in choosing his subject, to fly well beyond his capacity. Obviously, I have done this in choosing Shakespearian Tragedy as my theme. In mitigation of such presumptuousness, I have but one decent motive to plead. It is a matter of professional morality. For the whole of my adult life, I have earned my living as a teacher of literature. It is a profession which Plutarch put third in a list of the most desirable and worthy occupations (though he somewhat spoils the compliment to such teachers by putting at the head of his list a form of livelihood which it is hard to describe as other than sponging on a monarch). The academic world does not appear to be hostile to Plutarch's appraisement of professors of literature; at all events, almost every university has founded chairs of literature. The motive for this must lie in a belief that literature as such has its own special contribution to make to the moral or spiritual well-being of mankind. Even for a sojourner in an Epicurean garden, 'l'œuvre la plus haute n'a de prix que par ses rapports avec la vie; mieux je saisis ces rapports, plus je m'interesse à l'œuvre', as Anatole France put it, and he was not thinking of a Marxian world. If this belief be well-founded, then the greater the literature, the greater must be its potential spiritual or moral worth. From this it follows that, however much for their private hobbies the stipendiary teachers of literature may rightly revel in intriguing by-ways and in exhumations of *poetae ignoti* whom the world has willingly and wisely let die, yet in their public office they must not skip lightly over the giants of literature. It is the duty of every professor of literature to say his say on Shakespeare and on what Shakespeare means to the world. To shrink from the task is immoral: to face it, is, you will perceive from these lectures, to expose one's own unworthiness.

Committing these lectures to publication, I wish to thank the Master and the Fellows of Trinity College for electing me to their Clark Lectureship for 1946–7, and for making the holding of the lectureship a delightful experience. I am also grateful to the Fellows of the British Academy, and to my colleagues on the Council of Governors of the John Rylands Library, for permission to include in this series of lectures material previously published under their auspices.

H. B. C.

AUGUST 1948

CONTENTS

Chapter I	Introduction	*page* 1
II	Apprentice Pieces: *Titus Andronicus, Richard III* and *Richard II*	18
III	Experiment and Interregnum: *Romeo and Juliet, King John, Julius Caesar*	49
IV	*Hamlet*	83
V	*Othello*	113
VI	*Macbeth*	141
VII	*King Lear*	189
VIII	Conclusion	230
Index		245

INTRODUCTION

In the forty-odd years of my own addiction to Shakespeare, the progress of Shakespearian studies has been marked by an increasing divergence between the interests of Shakespearian scholarship and those of Shakespearian interpretation, although, of course, the wiser exponents of either sort have always been conscious of the interdependence of both these forms of 'criticism'. In the field of scholarship, concerned as it is with consolidating, extending, and authenticating our knowledge of the objective facts about Shakespeare and his plays, there have been great gains. Particularly in the new science of bibliography the historico-textual scholars have produced palmary results: it is to-day more than ever possible to know with large probability what in fact were the words which Shakespeare wrote, and the interpreter of Shakespeare can start with greater confidence in the material of which his own task is to find the meaning.

In the field of interpretation, the most striking trend of the last generation has been the assault on Andrew Bradley. On the one hand, we are told, he is too little of a historian and too much of a philosopher; he lifts Shakespeare out of his Tudor theatre, making no allowance for Elizabethan stage conventions, and assuming in his innocence that words and scenes mean what they seem to mean. On the other hand, he is assailed because he takes Shakespeare's dramas as plays and not as poems; he accepts the persons of them at their face value as semblable men and women, and not as plastic symbols in an arabesque of esoteric imagery, nor as rhythmic ripples intoned in a chromatic ritual. The position of these neo-Shakespearians perturbs me because I cannot understand it. Much of it is

Cantabrigian in origin, or in orientation, though perhaps less so in quality. I cite a few characteristic passages without naming their source, well knowing that a Cambridge audience would recognise them. When, for instance, I read that *Hamlet* 'so far from being Shakespeare's masterpiece...is certainly an artistic failure', I feel that English is a language which I do not know. When I am told that to attain the 'soul-experience' of a Shakespeare play is 'a process which forces us to cut below the crust of plot and character, and to expose those riches of poetic imagination too often buried in our purely unconscious enjoyment of Shakespeare's art', I applaud the recognition of the mystery of poetic genius, but I ask whether the crust has not itself some meaning, whether in fact it is not the means to meaning chosen by the poet, whether it be not indeed part of the form which has attained identity with its substance. Moreover, I feel entitled to demand whether the values of these treasure-troves from the unconscious should not be expressed in a recognised coinage of critical currency. Again, I am told how to approach Shakespeare if I am to participate with the elect in their mystic rites. 'We start with so many lines of verse on a printed page which we read as we should read any other poem. We have to elucidate the meaning (using Dr Richards' fourfold definition) and to unravel ambiguities; we have to estimate the kind and quality of the imagery and determine the precise degree of evocation of particular figures; we have to allow full weight to each word, exploring its "tentacular roots", and to determine how it controls and is controlled by the rhythmic movement of the passage in which it occurs.' All seems as systematic, as precise, and as rigorous as a measurement in the Cavendish Laboratory. But how does one estimate 'the kind and quality of imagery'? By what test does one establish that it has been 'truly' estimated? What instrument measures the 'precise degree' of evocation and on what principles does one determine how a word 'controls and is controlled by the rhythmic movement of the passage in which it occurs'? Are not critics of this school using the façade of the Cavendish to hide a conventicle of impressionist anarchists? The abracadabra apparently most potent in all these neo-Shakespearian conjurations is some such phrase as 'organic poetic structure' or the even more gnomic 'objective correlative'. These presumably can be recognised infallibly, and are sufficient warrant for distorting the plain sense of the words of the text and for discarding the apparent meaning of the incidents of the scene. *In excelsis*, the doctrine asserts that Shakespeare can mean nothing to us to-day unless we happen to hold the peculiar tenets of a relatively small theological sect, and have withal a peculiarly idiosyncratic intuition for chromatic and tonic values. 'The difficulty is for a modern dichotomised mind to comprehend the organic functioning of minds free from our own pathological division.' The terms of the diagnosis suggest what may well be the mainspring of the new creed: the resurgence of the cult of the Middle Ages. The doctrine is formulated by one of the most recent neo-Shakespearians somewhat like this. Culture has declined with the decline of Catholicism since the Middle Ages. The Renaissance gave rise to rationalism and experimental science: rationalism and the growing prestige of science debased reason by exalting it over the speculative intellect, whilst in effect it was limiting it to the mere ordering of physical fact. Hence the growth of materialism and of intellectual submission to the dictatorship of meaningless physical phenomena, culminating in the philosophic naturalism of Darwin and Spencer and Huxley: hence, at the next stage, the prevalent agnosticism of our times, with the result that, as the naturalist is blind to Christ in the universe, we moderns miss Shakespeare in the theatre.

Such seems to be the metaphysic of the neo-Shakespearians. It is a comprehensive dogma, and the most characteristically dogmatic articles of it are the assertion that it is we who miss Shakespeare, and that it is they alone who have caught him since he passed from the bodily presence of his contemporaries.

Who was it then that was seen by Dryden and Johnson and Coleridge and Goethe and Hazlitt and Arnold and Meredith and Bradley and uncountable hosts of normal sensible men throughout the last three centuries?

For my own part, I am a devout Bradleyite. I was bred on him, for his *Shakespearian Tragedy* appeared in the year in which Shakespeare began to mean something vital to me. He opened a door, and, in the forty-odd years between, I have found no single volume which seems so securely to admit one into Shakespeare's tragic universe as does his. He comes to the plays as a psychological naturalist, or rather as a natural psychologist. He sees the men who move through them as if they were real human beings struggling through a world which seems in moral substance very much like our own. He finds that the sequence of action by which they move to their destiny appears as the intelligible outcome of the particular impulses and motives which give to each of them his distinctive personality, and which operate within these characters as mankind's accumulated experience of humanity has found them tend to operate in real life. So Bradley is preoccupied, though not exclusively occupied, with Shakespeare's portrayal of his hero's character as an autonomous dynamic element, forging that man's future in its interplay with fate and circumstance. He finds this the most palpable clue to Shakespeare's power of infusing into his tragedies the sense of universality and inevitability, and, of course, he finds it by remembering that the literary means by which Shakespeare achieves this supreme impression of tragedy are his mastery, not only of words and of verse, but of all the other components of dramatic poetry. Bradley's method was not new, and, indeed, particularly in phrase, or at times even in diagnosis, it may not be approved by the particular psychological doctrine of to-day. But it is essentially the method of our greatest Shakespearian critics, and is none the worse for having been traditional for over two centuries.

It is with what, I hope, is a Bradley outlook, lamentably defective, however, in his philosophic equipment, that I come to Shakespearian Tragedy. I fortify myself for this defect by two of Dr Johnson's aphorisms: 'the merit of Shakespeare was such as the ignorant could take in, and the learned add nothing to', and 'the common voice of the multitude uninstructed by precept, and unprejudiced by authority, which, in questions that relate to the heart of man, is, in my opinion, more decisive than the learning of Lipsius'.[1] From this starting-point I make, I hope, none but simple and commonplace, or easily justifiable, assumptions. In pagan and in Christian times, tragedy has been accepted as probably the noblest of poetic achievements. Amongst other races who have not known the artistic form which is now called tragedy, there is in the noblest of their poetry a sentiment essentially similar to that which gives to tragedy its own nobility. Shakespeare is, and has for long been held to be, the world's greatest dramatic poet; and his tragedies have almost invariably been taken as his greatest achievement. His repute has been established in the minds of men of widely varied race, epoch, religion, culture and social standing: there is, then, something universal in the nature of his tragic appeal. Many approach his plays through the theatre; many more enrich that reception from recollections of performances springing to memory as they read the text; still many more are their own stage-managers, seeing the play enact itself in the theatre of their own minds, hearing the unspoken words in the silence of their own imaginations. Fashions in this theatre of the mind are infinitely varied, from the extreme bareness of a surrealistic or allegoric décor to the realistic visualisation of scene and dress and gait in all their detail—for even those who read the play 'purely as a poem' must sometimes forget themselves into remembering that words do not drop from heaven but fall from the mouths of men. Yet all these uncounted

[1] J. E. Brown, *Critical Opinions of Samuel Johnson* (Princeton University Press), pp. 469 and 206.

spectators and readers—play-goers, play-readers and poetic text readers—find in Shakespeare something which they count as a sign of his supremacy. This may be because Shakespeare is a supreme tragic dramatist, or it may be because he is something in poetry which is independent of drama. But even if it be the latter, it is plain fact that he set out to be a dramatist, went on writing pieces which were called plays, and sought and won the foundations of his fame in the applause of a theatre audience; and a theatre audience is mankind in epitome, representative humanity of all kinds, all creeds and all complexions.

The public by pleasing whom Shakespeare lived, the public which is still pleased by Shakespeare, is sufficiently agreed in knowing what it means by a play. To them it is a theatrical and literary (often poetic) creation which represents action on a stage. The actors representing it look like men and women; they talk and speak like men and women; they encounter predicaments and respond to them variously, but more or less as such men and women as they shew themselves to be would respond in that sort of predicament. Moreover they exist in an imaged but visibly presented world not alien in essence from our own, and one in which the compelling forces, human and non-human, are not different in nature from the operative powers which we take to be the arbiters of our own human destiny in this our own world. A play, in fact, appears to be a representation of the impact of man and circumstance, wherein circumstance, as in familiar human experience, may be the casual constituents of man's own inner or outer person, or the characters of other men, or the ways and institutions of society, or the powers of nature, or the strokes of chance or fate, or the very might of the gods themselves. As drama, the presentation of this impact grips our attention and excites our interest in its issue; for such conflicts have shown themselves in the long stretch of human memory to be the crucial moments of man's mortal experience. Hence the outcome, the ending of the play, to be acceptable to us, must in some profound sense be satisfying to our excited intelligence of it. When, in the conflict, man wins, the dramatic *dénouement* is easy for the dramatist; it is in fact, too easy: for the eagerness of the rest of men in the audience to see poetic justice done will not strongly resent the arbitrary imposition of a happy ending on a plot which in itself has generated no dramatic force to compel such *dénouement*. The eighteenth-century version of *King Lear* springs to mind at once. But in tragedy man is overcome by the powers opposed to him; and hence the problem, why does mankind find pleasure in tragedy?

How indeed can tragedy provide pleasure for man? That it does so is long-established fact. But how and why does it do so? Tragedy is a form of poetry and, like all poetry, it came into being to gratify certain of the deeper instincts of human nature: it exists, as Aristotle pointed out, to provide its own particular kind of aesthetic pleasure. No one compels us to read or see tragedy: we choose to do so for our own gratification. Maybe the gratification is an austere and exalted enjoyment. Pleasure, however, it certainly is. But wherein lies the pleasure of a tragic spectacle? Consider what, at a cursory glance, seems to be the general run of a tragic play. The curtain rises; the audience is introduced to the hero, of whom hitherto it is usually ignorant and towards whom therefore it has no more sentimental ties than those which bind the whole human race together. But the dramatist uses his two hours' traffic deftly, stirring admiration and exciting sympathy or even affection for his hero. Then, remembering that he has promised a tragedy to his audience, he steals up slyly behind his hero and stretches him out dead, just as the audience has been moved to its most cordial sympathy or most reverent awe for that hero. On the face of it, it would seem that a tragic audience finds pleasure in maimings and slaughters, and, even further, that its pleasure is made more exquisite when the victim to be mangled and destroyed is one whom it respects, admires and loves. But if this were a true diagnosis, then the Romans who flocked to Nero's circus to see Christians torn by lions were decent moral beings compared with a modern audience of tragedy, for they at least thought that Christians were enemies of the state and of the gods. Clearly, the diagnosis is faulty; and the evident proof of this is the outcry of the woman in the gallery as, awe-struck, she watched Romeo in the Capulet tomb lifting the vial of poison to his lips in the belief that Juliet was dead. 'Stop ! Wait a minute !', she is alleged to have shouted, for she knew that Juliet was shortly to awaken from her deathlike trance. Her protest is human nature's resentment at the callousness and inhumanity of the powers, be they God's or the dramatist's, which seem to wanton in needless sacrifice of human life.

The cry from the gallery is the voice of Aristotle's *to philan-thropon*, the cry of what Bacon called 'the secret inclination and motion in man's nature, towards love of others...which maketh men become humane and charitable',[1] 'the affecting of the weal of men which is what the Grecians called *philanthropia*, and the word humanity as it is used is a little too light to express it'.[2] It is the instinct which prefers to see other men happy rather than unhappy. It is a sentiment which suggests, as it did to Aristotle, certain grounds of criticism in tragedy.

Tragedy ends in death; but its fatal ending must not appear as an exhibition arbitrarily contrived by the dramatist. The tragic author must exonerate himself completely from all complicity in his hero's death: the hero's fate is not at the author's choice; it springs irresistibly from the ultimate nature of things, from the final compulsion, from ἀνάγκη, the last all-powerful Necessity. The dramatist is not devising a spectacle. His imaginative vision has caught glimpses of the ways of destiny; he simply reveals his hero's death as the inevitable outcome of primary universal law. That is, indeed, the fundamental note of tragedy, a sense conjured in us by the miracle of

[1] F. Bacon, *Essays*, 'Of Love'.
[2] *Ibid*. 'Of Goodness and Goodness of Nature'.

poetry, convincing us that the action we are watching must sweep irresistibly to its inevitable end. The inevitability is primarily impressed on us, not precisely, and not purely, as an intellectual conviction. It arises from a state of induced feeling in which intellectual satisfaction is only one element, often, too, an element which afterthought alone makes conscious to us. Indeed, intellectual acquiescence is all that is immediately required; one is aroused to feel that the action is inevitable, but reason cannot formulate the ultimate principles which make it inevitable. The riddle of the universe remains; and mystery is still one of the major threads in the web of human destiny. But the tragic dramatist has a larger awareness than ours, and the profit of it to us is not so much that he diminishes the ultimate mystery, but that he enables us to grasp the knowable and the mysterious as elements in a potential universe, a cosmic system whose laws in the end are inscrutable, but indisputably are laws. In the greater Shakespeare tragedies, man enthrals the attention more than does his universe, for Shakespeare's world is moral rather than metaphysical; humanism and humanity hold him far more passionately than theology and religion, men more than angels, earth more than heaven. The philosophic pattern implicitly adumbrated in his imaginative presentation of life is that of morality in emergence. In the earlier tragedies, man accepts morality easily and conventionally as the law of God. Then, in later ones, he begins to discover it in nature. In the end, Shakespeare watches nature-in-man, or human nature, visibly making morality, shaping it in the creative mind by some ultimate and mysterious impulse in him for which the name may well be God.

This is the ground-tone of Shakespeare's greatest tragedies. But as its heroes wring out of life its meaning, they succumb, and inevitably succumb, to its strain. They die, but the inevitability of their death is itself the mightiest force by which the truth which their life has revealed is driven home in us with absolute conviction. In some sort, then, the most direct and the simplest way in which to begin appraising the tragic value of a tragedy is to ask, 'Why does the hero die?' From great tragedy the only answer is, 'Because, such being the nature of things, he inevitably must': and part, but part only, of the grounds for this conviction of his inevitable end, will it be possible to state in reasoned form. The scope within which such ratiocinative sanction contributes to the necessary absoluteness of final conviction is very different in modern tragedy from what it was in Greek tragedy. All turns on the extent and the nature of a common religious belief. Broadly speaking, the Greek conception of Nemesis as the ultimate Necessity, in the last resort the arbiter of the universe and all that is therein, gods and men alike, is a magnificent philosophic back-cloth for the tragic scene. The inherent force of the moral order of the cosmos exerts itself to redress distortions of its nature, and to restore the stability by which it endures. Hence purely personal problems of individual motive are insignificant compared with the outcome of the deed done. Man, trusting to his own judgement, may determine to dispense himself from one obligation in order to fulfil what he regards as a higher good. Prometheus, for the benefit of mankind, steals fire from heaven. But, despite the motive, his act is an infraction of the highest good; his conscious motive was worthy, but his unconscious motive was *hubris*, pride. So he suffers the tragic doom. Or Oedipus also sins, but in sheer ignorance. Still, the offence has come, and woe even to the unwitting offender through whom it comes. Here, then, is the inevitability of Greek tragedy. This doom must follow this act, because all religiously believe that such is the course of destiny.

But when modern tragedy started in the sixteenth century there was no such universal agreement about the ways of God with man; and above all, the one common and dominant element in Europe's religion was apparently far less apt to the idea of tragedy. Christianity seemed to remove the foundations of the whole tragic scheme. Seeing life on earth as a mere moment in eternal immortality, it took finality from death; and it made sin mainly a matter of personal responsibility. The doctrine of redemption promised salvation for all except the worst of the wicked; and death on earth, for all but these, was but a gateway to everlasting bliss. So, a really tragic doom is reserved alone for the entirely reprobate: the evil man is destroyed by his iniquity. But is this really tragic? On the contrary, is it not a gratifying assurance of the Christian hope?

Whether these speculations on the apparent incompatibility between the traditional groundwork of tragedy and the tenets of Christianity are sound or not, one thing is certain: the tragedians of the new tragedy, Shakespeare and his fellows, seem to have thrust the Christian articles of current belief far into the background of consciousness. There is, for instance, in all Shakespeare's greater tragedies no admission of the Christian conception of immortality. In *Richard III*, a murderer, grue-somely consoling the man whom he is about to murder, tells him that death is a deliverance 'from this world's thraldom, to the joys of heaven';[1] but the occasion of the utterance and the substance of it are part of that quality in the play which makes it inferior to the greater tragedies. In them as in *Hamlet*, after death 'the rest is silence'. Perhaps it is the sheer imaginative potency of the artist which stirs instincts buried more deeply in us than the feelings grafted on to a comparatively new faith; maybe he liberates primitive sensations of the early man which we all inherit from the time when death was a final extinction. However that may be, the result is that, in essence, whereas the foundation of Greek tragedy was religious, that of Shakespeare's tragedy is not. Elizabethan tragedy had perforce to explore other sources of the indispensable inevitability, the ultimate Necessity. The most effective one that it found was in the newly discovered wonder of human personality. What a piece of work is a man! Here, in the hidden resources of will, the

[1] *Richard III* I. iv. 255.

unmeasurable strength of passion, the uncountable vagaries of impulse were the powers which patently participated in the shaping of destiny, though, of course, they did not finally determine it. So in Elizabethan drama, character becomes the smith of fortune, if not entirely of fate: and tragic drama finds its *ultima ratio*, its spring of inevitability, in the interplay of man and the world, in which the subtle though elusive link of psychological cause and effect gives to events sufficient appearance of a cosmic order. The mind of the reader is moved to acquiescence, his imagination sweeps him into the total acceptance which is for the moment absolute conviction.

For this reason, most inquirers into Shakespeare's tragic genius have occupied themselves with his instinct for characterisation, and expositions of his tragedies have been largely given to an analysis of the character of his tragic hero.

But our argument is passing well beyond its immediate purpose. It started merely to put forward a few assumptions which seemed commonplace enough to be axiomatic, and has led itself into propositions more fitted for a concluding estimate, to follow only when the tragedies have been duly surveyed. One advantage, however, such perfunctory anticipation may have had. It may have made clear the structure which it is proposed to give to the treatment of the theme.

Summarily these are its main principles and its main lines. On the whole Shakespeare is taken to mean what he seems to mean. His meaning is public for all sorts of men. His plays are plays: as other plays, they show human beings engaged in human action in a world which is the world of all of us. His tragedies depict men and women struggling with life and brought by it to death. In the dramatic execution of such a momentous action, the death of a great human being, a 'hero', the dramatist must evoke from the stuff of his play the force of powers sensibly compelling the course of incident to its inevitable ending. The source of these powers in Shakespeare is his intuitive sense of personality and his intuitive vision of the ways of mortal destiny, the cosmic arbiters and universal laws of human life. To be admitted to such imaginative insight into truth and reality is for the spectator itself a pleasure. But a more intimate and personal gratification alleviates the painful sense of destruction: there emerges through the grief a growing sense of the immeasurable spiritual potentiality within man. Pessimism is banished by the revelation of desperate trial and loss as the main circumstance which brings forth and even creates deeper and deeper spiritual resources. The nobility of man triumphs over tragedy through tragedy. For Shakespeare, tragedy becomes the stern, awful but exalting picture of mankind's heroic struggle towards a goodness which enlarges and enriches itself as human experience grows longer and wider through the ages. Shakespearian tragedy is the apotheosis of the spirit of man.

It is generally agreed that the most consummate expressions of Shakespeare's tragic art are to be found in the four great tragedies, *Hamlet*, *Othello*, *Macbeth* and *King Lear*. In them the conflict between man and that which is hostile to his well-being is most intense. It is of profounder significance because, on the one hand, the man in them embodies richer or more fundamental or more vivid or more universal traits of permanent human character, and, on the other hand, the powers in them alien to man's good are in their turn more intimate or more elemental or more universal or more ultimate. Between them these four tragedies exhibit the depredations of the tragic fact at receding levels of human evolution, in different spiritual epochs; they seem like pictures of human life at great stages in the past history of its spiritual progress. With *Hamlet*, we are in the complex, elaborate, even sophisticated civilisation and culture of to-day's moral world, just as in Hamlet himself there are the full development of mind and the completed articulation of those multitudinous elements of spiritual sensibility which make man what he now is. In *Othello*, two worlds clash. The drawing-rooms of the delicate and refined children of an exquisite modern culture open their doors to one in whose blood runs the more primitive traditions of African tribal warrior-princes. But the ultimate tragic fact is lurking no less certainly in Othello's character than in Hamlet's. Man has not always had in his nature that capacity for intellectual subtleties which is part of Hamlet's native endowment; indeed, mankind which had not yet grown to the possession of it, must have been immune from the particular strokes of tragedy which destroy Hamlet. But passion is older than thought, nearer to the animal: and it is even more liable to stir tragic consequences when, lacking a restraining counterpoise in intellect, it finds itself moving in a more intellectual world. Even in its setting, *Macbeth* reflects nothing peculiar to the modern world. Its hero is in some ways even more primitive than Othello, for in Macbeth it is the moral sense which is but dimly beginning to recognise the faintly articulated imperatives of the still small voice; in his guilt, Macbeth manifests not so much the awakening of conscience as a stage in the process of its emergence. In *King Lear* the wheel comes full circle. The world of it is shorn of all its acquired circumstance and most of its cultural trappings. The tragic situation, though it enmeshes a king, is not the outcome of a social order even so far developed as to have organised a simple monarchical system. The tragedy of it springs from the simplest and the primary social entity, the family, and from the human relationship which is the absolute beginning of all and every human society, parenthood, the relation of father to child and of child to father. Like the setting and the circumstance, the people of *King Lear* mark the backward reaches of symbolic human time. Man is near indeed to the animal, sometimes in sheer simplicity of innocence, but more often in worse than animal bestiality, his intellectual sense serving only as craft to add a finer edge to his cruelty. With such people as its persons, and parentage as its sole plot, *King Lear* bares the tragedy of human life to absolute simplicity and to almost absolute universality.

Bradley surely was right in building his *Shakespearian Tragedy* on these four great tragedies, for it is in them that the dramatist's tragic insight is deepest and most sustained. Though the same four will be our main concern, their predecessors will be cursorily looked at. There is the first group comprising *Titus Andronicus*, *Richard III* and *Richard II*, in which, although Shakespeare the poet is Shakespeare's unique self, Shakespeare the tragedian is as yet no innovator. He expresses conventional tragic patterns in his own idiom. Then comes a real innovation in tragic idea, *Romeo and Juliet*, but, superb as it is in lyrical poetry and promising in some of its characterisation, it was, as tragic drama, stillborn. Perhaps a sense of frustration prompted Shakespeare in *King John* to divert a conventional tragic pattern from tragedy towards what later was to realise itself as the Shakespearian history or chronicle play. In any case, after *Romeo and Juliet*, Shakespeare turned from tragedy to the more congenial domain of comedy, for comedy was giving him an inward sense of growing mastery. But in due course, amongst the figures and the themes of *Julius Caesar*, which in essentials belongs not with Shakespeare's tragedies, but with his history or chronicle plays, there are component parts sufficiently tragic in their nature to bring Shakespeare back to tragedy and, as by immediate inspiration, to the four great tragedies. After their exhausting toll, come *Antony and Cleopatra*, *Coriolanus* and whatever of *Timon* is Shakespeare's. These are great achievements in drama and in poetry, authentically Shakespearian too, in both. Yet they are the products of a Shakespeare whose hand has lost none of its cunning, but whose inward eye is dimming. His imagination ranges widely as ever over space and time; but it dwells more on the surfaces and no longer thrusts to the utter depths. The two Roman plays, apart from their Shakespearian poetry, are remarkable more for the artistry than for the genius of the dramatist displayed in them. The wide diversity between the ultra-romantic structure of *Antony and Cleopatra* and the almost classical formality of *Coriolanus* suggests rather their author's exuberant revelry in his theatrical skill than a profound upheaval in his imaginative experience. Though they are forms of Shakespearian tragedy as only Shakespeare could write it, they will not enter into our argument, mainly because they are Shakespearian tragedy falling away from the peak of it, and also because they fit better into the theme of Shakespeare's Roman political plays, and one therefore to be deferred for some later occasion.

To this introductory or anticipatory indication of the way in which the argument will be pursued in the following pages, a final statement may be added. The Bradley attitude towards the plays is accepted throughout, together with his conviction of the place of characterisation in Shakespearian drama. It has not, therefore, been thought necessary to go over again the psychological analyses which are the main substance of his argument. At times, of course, one's own assessment of the psychological import of this or the other manifestation of personality is different from that of Bradley; and sometimes, where this difference has seemed important enough, it has been made explicit. But throughout there has been no conscious swerving from Bradley's sense of the dramatic function of character. In formal method, more attention than Bradley gave has been given to the cosmic framework peculiar to the stuff of each particular play, and to the things other than man which constitute man's universe. In that way, more emphasis has been put on one of the means by which Shakespearian tragedy secured its effect of inevitability. Even in this, however, one hopes that the argument is an implication of, and not a departure from, the Bradley tradition. Lastly, a traditional aid of scholarship has frequently been sought for the purpose of supplementing deficiency in critical intuition. A mere scholar seldom has the gift of perceiving directly what are the distinctive traits of artistic genius. He needs all the pointers and sign-posts which he can find. Hence, wherever there is a non-Shakespearian source of a Shakespeare play, it has generally been called in to help. It has, one hopes, never entered merely as a fact of erudition. Its function has been purely critical. If one can see the specific and concrete raw material which a genius had on his table while he was transmuting it into a masterpiece, one may be able to catch glimpses of the way in which his mind was working. One may even venture to speculate on the conscious or unconscious motives for the changes by which the sublimation came.

CHAPTER II

APPRENTICE PIECES

TITUS ANDRONICUS, RICHARD III & RICHARD II

1. *Titus Andronicus*

Though in none of the three plays which will occupy this chapter does Shakespeare achieve the tragic idea which gives their characteristic form to his great tragedies, one can nevertheless trace progress in his experiments. The progress is generally a positive gain in matters of the many techniques which together comprise the art of tragic drama: the adaptation of poetic to dramatic utterance, the balancing of speech and dialogue, the intensifying of situation, the cementing of plot, the animation of characters, and the disposing of action to run to a cumulative intensity of thrilled suspense—in all these accessory dramatic techniques, Shakespeare's apprenticeship moves quickly to expertness. But in grasp of inner design, in visual projection of the tragic idea, in the plastic patterning of poetic tragedy, in all these deeper reaches of the art of tragic drama what progress there is is mainly negative, producing a series of apprentice or experimental forms tried and found wanting.

Titus Andronicus is melodrama, the crudest of Shakespeare's tragedies, magnificent only in this, that its language is always adequate to its own dramatic and theatrical demands, crude or low, spectacular or sentimental, as on varying occasion they may be. But as drama it can never disguise its own quality. It is a rudimentary type of tragedy. It appeals only to the eye and to the other senses. Response to it is confined to the nervous system. Its thrills and throbs are not transmissible to the mind in forms more intellectual than mere sensation. They induce a nightmare of horrors. As sensations of horror, if they are felt as such at all and not laughed off by man's sense of the ludicrous, they strike so heavily and so frequently that the mind is incapacitated from attempting to translate them into its own discursive idiom. So great is the weight of horror that the response of the senses themselves is finally stunned to stupor, and the disabled sensibility is deprived of the power to prompt mind and imagination to cope with such tremendous issues as are the essence of tragedy, the ultimate mysteries of human destiny. 'Those who employ spectacular means to create a sense not of the terrible, but only of the monstrous, are strangers to the purpose of Tragedy.'[1]

As a piece of serious drama, *Titus Andronicus* has little of worth except its theatrically stirring situations. Even these occur in isolation. A momentary spectacle can be given as much conviction as is needed for the achievement of its stage effect by craftsmanship of no higher order in the art of poetry than is the stage-carpenter's in the art of drama. But a sustained representation of human action in a continuous dramatic plot makes greater demands. As Aristotle put it, what happens must happen according to the law of the probable and the necessary. As human action, it must be intelligible. The men and women in the play must act as human beings do act. When their action seems to be spontaneously prompted by passion or by instinct rather than by considered choice, those passions and instincts must be shown to be of that sort which in our experience of life seems likely to break out in that way. When the doers of such deeds plead also the sanction of deliberate choice, the systems of conduct to which they appeal must appear to have impetus vital enough to make their compulsion inevitable. However, a qualification must here be made. Sanctions, like the systems of law and morality which give them their warrant, are but rarely eternal and are often flagrantly ephemeral. *Omnia mutantur, nos et mutamur in illis.*

[1] Aristotle, *Poetics* XIV, 2 (Butcher).

Autres temps, autres mœurs. But in drama, sanctions which are pleaded as constraints to a decisive course of action must have something more than a merely historic warrant to give them effective dramatic force. The compulsion must be felt by the audience as a power which might well compel human beings to such deeds.

It is in respects such as this that the greatest French classical drama seems to an Englishman less universal and therefore less tragic than Shakespeare's tragedies. Their preference for pitting love against honour in the tragic conflict appears, to a modern, to commit them to a contest between unequally matched opponents. The dictates of love may vary from era to era; its nature may swing through a whole range between lust and the lyric-love which is half-angel: but love is a passion, an affection deeply rooted even in the physiological genes of spiritual man. There is no limit to its potential urgency as an impulse to action. On the other hand, honour is a code of human construction, and the course of its formulation can be easily watched through a relatively short stretch of historic time. Its taboos and its injunctions are the patent outcome of particular forms of society at particular periods of history. Hence its content embraces manners as much as, and often more than, morals. Its edicts tend therefore to seem arbitrary and even factitious; and as imperatives they have but temporary and local authority. They lack the absoluteness of a universal tragic sanction. Sometimes one of the opposing stresses is formulated in a phrase which seems a limitedly localised or a dialectal idiom; but often this is only the accident of phrase or of manner, and the real significance is clear. Antigone must bury her exiled brother; but the burial itself is only the ritual action symbolising the real compunction by which the act itself is categorically imperative, the absolute obligation of fraternal duty. Contrast Racine; though the surge of his Phèdre's love can sweep us into conviction of its fury, and, on the other hand, the obligation on her to suppress it or to die can be felt as the command of a code of honour with foundations firmly based in the depths of morality, yet the momentousness of such contending and mighty opposites suffers a sharp collapse on our discovery that the honour of Phèdre, whilst permitting her maid to make wicked charges against Hippolyte, can recover itself by laying all the blame on to this poor servant whose only motive was devotion to her mistress. Often, to drive his action forward with the sense of irresistible compulsion, the dramatist will invoke an impetus from sources outside the will, blind or deliberate, of his persons. At worst, he may allege any extraneous and intrusive determinant as a mere chance, relying on his audience superstitiously to identify chance within some pattern or other of purposive destiny. No great tragedian, however, fails to introduce amongst the operant powers which direct the stream of his plot those cosmic forces which lie beyond human personality and outside the established formularies of human cognition. In the dramatist's summoning of these great mysteries as actors in his drama, his tragic genius is revealed in its deepest qualities. His greatness as a tragedian depends on the extent to which he can invest these superhuman arbiters with the absoluteness of ultimate Necessity. In Shakespeare, this dramatic ultimacy inheres in and also exists outside his characters. For him the stern necessity of character and the resistless compulsion of circumstance are a form of what John Morley called 'the modern and positive expression for the old Destiny of the Greeks'.

With a mind conscious of these considerations, turn to *Titus Andronicus*, and enquire how far its action is autonomously and organically propelled. Very soon, its nominal hero, Titus, is a comparative pawn in the theatrical game, and the real protagonists are the villains, Aaron and Tamora. The incidents of the play, and especially the more theatrical of them, proceed in the main as the deliberate purposes of the villain's evil designs. These purposes are those of sinners whose prevalent passion is lust, than which no passion is more deeply seated in the human animal, none more primary nor more insatiable. The dramatist can therefore permit to them the extremest of enormities; the law of human probability can be pleaded for suspending for them its own normal requirements; as Aristotle says, 'such an event is probable in Agathon's sense of the word: "it is probable", he says, "that many things should happen contrary to probability."'[1] Moreover, with such human devils as these for the outstanding figures, other characters and episodes in the play can be stretched to extravagant limits. Titus in his turn can execute his own son. In these ways, the dramatist is easily provided with a string of melodramatic incidents in unbroken sequence. But it is merely the sequence of succession, each item owing its occurrence not to what has gone immediately before, but as the accidental next in the cumulative outcome of the bestial passions of the main contrivers.

There is, however, some attempt to give to this succession a specious appearance of causal sequence. Action is sometimes expressed, not as the spontaneous consequence of passion, but as the recognisable manifestation of some sort of world-order.

The first scene sets up the façade of the universe in which its action is to occur. The 'righteous heavens', 'the gods of Rome' preside over it; priests minister at their solemn services, sometimes with 'holy water', sometimes with 'sacrificial rites'; its men lift up their 'vows to heaven', and 'sumptuously' maintain the sacred 'monuments' in which their dead are solemnly interred. But it is a mere façade. The moral system which would give such a universe a credible substance manifests itself as an incoherent chaos. There is talk of 'virtue' and 'nobility', yet they appear to comprise nothing but a primitive valour in martial enterprise. 'Piety' is named; but it gives nothing beyond a moment's historic authenticity to a Roman father's right to kill his son, and such historic authentication may even be an obstacle to dramatic plausibility: 'the poet should prefer probable impossibilities to improbable possibilities'.[2] In *Titus*

[1] *Poetics* xviii, 6 (Butcher). [2] *Ibid.* xxiv, 10.

Andronicus the standard of moral currency most in use is 'honour'. The word occurs a score of times in the scene in which Titus kills his son; it is made more prominent by another half-score instances of its opposite, 'dishonour'. But it is utterly impossible to define the content of the moral concept implied, and quite impossible therefore to assess its potency as a moral agent in motivating action. Titus is 'dishonoured' because his sons do not immediately obey his edict, and no less 'dishonoured' because Bassianus, with what appear to be highly honourable intentions, marries Titus' daughter. Saturninus is 'dishonoured' because someone has revealed the flagrant truth that he is a scoundrel, and even more 'dishonoured' because others have helped him to secure the throne instead of recognising his right to it without help. The audience, with more justice than Falstaff, may well enquire 'what is this honour?' The play gives no answer, for nothing consistently recognisable as 'honour' animates its action. Hence its incidents sink to melodrama. There are crucial examples in this first scene.

Take one which relies on an alleged ancient practice: the noblest prisoner taken must be sacrificed to appease 'the groaning shadows of the slain'. Tamora's son is the victim chosen by Titus' sons, and they will 'hew his limbs and on a pile *Ad manes fratrum* sacrifice his flesh'. Tamora appeals, with far less ancient terms and with more intelligible instinct, for the exercise of the 'sweet mercy which is nobility's true badge'. But Titus is placidly unmoved: for 'their brethren slain' his sons 'religiously ask a sacrifice'; they have marked her son for this, and 'die he must'. He is haled away by Titus' sons with fervent zeal, and in a twinkling they return to tell that his 'limbs are lopped',

> And entrails feed the sacrificing fire
> Whose smoke, like incense, doth perfume the sky.

As a mere record in human archaeology, such a scene can doubtless be freely paralleled; but its persons have not here inspired the psychological resuscitation which would give them dramatic personality. Their motives, therefore, implicit and explicit, are dramatically inert; the 'must' of 'die he must' is merely arbitrary and void of all power to excite in the audience a willing concurrence in its compulsiveness. Or take the incident in which Titus, exercising the Roman *jus patrium*, slays his son Mutius for a single act of sudden disobedience. Mutius' action is completely intelligible in common sense and in the simplest psychology; moreover, it commands enough moral sympathy to make it instantly credible to the audience. So, in despite of assurances from historical record, it is impossible for the audience to slip into a requisite and subconscious understanding of Titus. For them he is a lay-figure, humanly, and therefore dramatically, unreal.

As in its first scene, so throughout the whole play. There is no inner world to it. Hence its plot is factitious; its people are mechanised puppets wearing masks of human faces, but seldom reacting even with a faint semblance of humanity except when their deeds are crimes which are prompted by a primitive human passion, crimes such as are still occasionally committed by the more bestial members of the human race. It is sheer melodrama and not tragedy; for, as *The New British Theatre* even as long ago as 1814 distinguished them, 'in tragedy and comedy, the final event is the effect of the moral operations of the different characters, but in melodrama the catastrophe is the physical result of mechanical stratagem'. And melodrama, lacking an inner world, can have none of the philosophic significance which is the peculiar function of tragedy; it can throw no light on the great mysteries of human fate.

2. *Richard III*

Richard III is Shakespeare's first dramatic attempt to weave the stern necessity of character and the resistless compulsion of circumstance into a tragic idea of human destiny. For the first time the two sources of dramatic energy which sweep the plot on its course, man on the one hand, and, on the other, the extra-human powers prevailing in the play's climate, are set in the grip of mortal conflict. But the dramatist is as yet more adept in the projection of man than profound in his apprehension of cosmic energies. Richard is his first great tragic figure; but Richard's universe is not universally tragic. The result is a flaw in the dramatic organism of the play. At a decisive moment in the stream of Richard's progress, the current of it turns its direction from the open water of triumph to the rapids of destruction; and there is nothing in the nature of the stream itself, nothing in the momentum of the action of the play inevitably to compel the change.

It is a commonplace that Marlowe first of all made human character the main agent in our serious drama. His Renaissance mind was intoxicated by glimpses of the seemingly limitless resources of spiritual power in man; excited to an ecstasy of awe, he was conscious of personality as the mightiest mortal instrument in man's universe. Shakespeare felt no less zestfully the marvel and the mystery of mere man. Richard is his first embodiment of the stupendous stature of the human atom. The characterisation of Richard is psychologically simple; he is an incarnate idea, an ideal rather than an individual: humanly he is only an individual in the sense that he is unique. He embodies absolute and deliberate evil. Impelled by his character, and deploying the resources of his personality, he seeks triumph: the plot shows him achieving mighty successes, and yet in the end brought to ruin, the victim of his own character. But when the end comes, has it the conviction of absolute inevitability? What, in the full circumstances of the play, and of the play alone, does in fact necessitate Richard's death? This is the crucial question. But the answer must await further exploration.

The actual characterisation of Richard, that is, the technique of translating into dramatic media the particular character meant by Shakespeare to be Richard, is superb. There is dramatic intuition in devising the scene of the wooing of Anne, and it is one of the few scenes of the play for which Shakespeare had no copy in the chroniclers. It was a superb stroke of dramatic art to make it herald the play. On the face of it, it is a scene which flouts all human probability. The recently widowed Anne, caught at the very funeral of her husband's father, suspecting, too, Richard's remote or direct complicity in the death of both husband and father-in-law, is wooed by Richard, hideously ugly, misshapen and notorious for a bloody mind which dreams on naught but butcheries. Yet Richard woos and wins: and he revels with grim delight in such monstrous departure from all likelihood:

> Was ever woman in this humour woo'd?
> Was ever woman in this humour won?

It is indeed an incredible achievement. But it has to be believed, or at least it is thrust at us for belief, as a precondition of all that is to follow. Lest we should fail to seize its dramatic significance, Richard himself fixes our attention on its flagrant incredibility and the consequent flouting of usual dramatic requirements:

> What! I, that kill'd her husband and his father,
> To take her in her heart's extremest hate,
> With curses in her mouth, tears in her eyes,
> The bleeding witness of her hatred by;
> Having God, her conscience, and these bars against me,
> And I nothing to back my suit at all
> But the plain devil and dissembling looks,
> And yet to win her, all the world to nothing.[1]

It is Richard's diploma-piece, his warranty that henceforth as the play moves on, no limit can be set to the capacities of his genius. From this chartered beginning, he moves from triumph to triumph, brushing obstacles aside with a flick of his little finger, taking an artist's joy in the cunning perfection of his evil stratagems, and always renewing his zest for devilries by the sardonic humour which they inspire within him. Nothing can stand in the way of this master-mind and master-hand: his opponents are as pygmies in the path of a giant. So

[1] *Richard III* I. ii. 231.

it goes on through three acts of the play. But in the fourth, the tide turns; from that point, the plot of the play has to show Richard in decline, and the dramatist is expert enough to make the course of the descent psychologically appropriate. The fall starts with Anne's confession:

> For never yet one hour in his bed
> Have I enjoy'd the golden dew of sleep,
> But have been waked by his timorous dreams,[1]

an exaggerated tale, obviously, but conventionally throwing into backward time the beginning of Richard's collapse. When Richard next appears, his acts betoken a weakening of his assurance and self-control. He is irritable at Buckingham's reluctance to kill the princes: 'I will converse with iron-witted fools and unrespective boys', and lookers-on are struck by his inability to mask his anger: 'the king is angry; see, he bites the lip.'[2] He admits a lack of confidence—'Uncertain way of gain'—but resorts to a courage of desperation though not yet of despair:

> But I am in
> So far in blood that sin will pluck on sin;
> Tear-falling pity dwells not in this eye.[3]

He confesses to Tyrrel that his 'rest and his sweet sleep' are disturbed. His grip on circumstance is loosening. He lets Buckingham speak without paying heed to him; and if this is through policy, it is patently bad policy; it is, however, more obviously out of distraction, for his mind is running on prophecies which are ominous for him. The symptoms become more marked; his irritability increases, his power of decision wavers from moment to moment, recovering only the peremptoriness of tone but nothing of the clarity of direction which hitherto had made him equal to all emergencies. His commands change and lose definiteness as orders; yet he rates those who are naturally confused by them as villainous blockheads: 'Dull, unmindful villain, why stand'st thou still?'[4] He

[1] *Ibid.* IV. i. 83. [2] *Ibid.* IV. ii. 27.
[3] *Ibid.* IV. ii. 64. [4] *Ibid.* IV. iv. 444.

devises plans and immediately countermands them: 'my mind is changed, sir, my mind is changed.' He affects momentarily a jocular hilarity on hearing bad news, and becomes serious only to fling groundless charges of treasonable intention against the nobleman who announces them. When heavier news is brought by a mere messenger, he loses all control of himself; he strikes the messenger in passion, and makes the unreason of it even more flagrant by adding:

> I cry thee mercy,
> There is my purse to cure that blow of thine.[1]

This lack of control increases rapidly; it destroys his confidence in his own power. His appetite fails: 'I will not sup to-night';[2] to nerve himself for the next day's battle, 'give me a bowl of wine', for somehow he feels downcast:

> I have not that alacrity of spirit
> Nor cheer of mind that I was wont to have.[3]

He seeks rest in sleep, but his dreams are haunted by avenging ghosts, and he awakes with cold fearful drops standing on his trembling flesh. A knock on his door causes him to start, and he confesses that shadows have struck terror to his soul. The end is near. In the excitement of impending battle, he can pull himself together to defy both prophecy and conscience:

> Let not our babbling dreams affright our souls:
> Conscience is but a word that cowards use.[4]

His recovered confidence inspires his rousing battle-speech to the troops, and re-invigorates his own spirit: 'a thousand hearts are great within my bosom'. But the fight goes against him: all he has left is the grim determination of primitive and pagan valour, what Holinshed called 'a great audacitie and a stoute stomacke':

> I have set my life upon a cast,
> And I will stand the hazard of the die.[5]

---

[1] *Richard III* IV. iv. 515.   [2] *Ibid.* V. iii. 48.
[3] *Ibid.* V. iii. 73.   [4] *Ibid.* V. iii. 308.
[5] *Ibid.* V. iv. 9.

Shakespeare does not display the scene of Richard's death: but the chroniclers record that 'manfully fyghting in the mydell of his enemies he was slayne'.

So Shakespeare's Richard lives and dies. But the outlines of the portrait are not of Shakespeare's creation. He found them all in the chroniclers; Polydore Vergil, More, Hall and Holinshed were all in substantial agreement about what Richard was and what his life portended. Thomas More had made current the general impression of Richard's character, a dynamic embodiment of evil power, a satanic figure whom More could easily fit into his theological universe as an example of the sinner destroyed by the inescapable justice of God. He sees God's hand directly working divine justice and exacting condign punishment from Richard and his associate evil-doers, even to the mere executants of the sin planned entirely by Richard himself. Thus of Tyrrel and the two murderers whom he suborned, he says:

which thinges in every part wel pondered, god never gave this world a more notable example, neither in what unsuretie standeth this worldly wel, or what mischief worketh the prowde enterprise of an hyghe heart, or finally what wretched end ensueth such dispiteous crueltie. For first to beginne with the ministers, Miles Forest at sainct Martens pecemele rotted away. Dighton in dede yet walketh on a live in good possibilitie to bee hanged ere he dye. But Sir James Tirel dyed at Tower hill, beheaded for treason.[1]

Hall adopted More's portrait, and told a fuller story without materially altering the outlines of it. In general, too, he fitted Richard into a universe not different in substance from that of More. When Richmond made his abortive attempt to invade England, landing was prevented by a storm which scattered his fleet, but Richmond himself was spared to return to France for further preparations; this was secured, says Hall, by 'a prosperous and strenable wynde and a freshe gale sente even by God to delyver him from that perell and jeopardie'.[2] His

---

[1] More, *The history of king Richard the thirde* (1557), p. 69.
[2] Hall, *Chronicle*, ed. 1809, p. 396.

comment on the last phase of Richard's reign runs thus: 'In the mean ceason Kyng Richard (whiche was appoynted nowe to finyshe his last laboure by the very devyne iustice and providence of God which called him to condigne punyshmente for his scelerate merites and myscheveous desertes)....'.[1] It is true that Hall does not frequently advert with such directness to the immediate interference of God. But, as Mr Tillyard has pointed out in an acute assessment of the distinctive qualities of our chroniclers, Hall's chief importance was that he first showed in all its completeness the new moralising of history.[2] He gave to history a sense of the concatenation of great events, a concatenation which Mr Tillyard calls a 'moral' concatenation, though a better word might be 'theological', for here, as in Mr Tillyard's distinction between 'moral' and 'psychological' drama, 'moral' seems to require some special definition. Hall undoubtedly accepted all the implications of the contemporary Christian universe. But, in general, he is content with a vaguer sense of the divine providence which somehow controls the confused and complex actions of human beings. 'This I leve to God his judgemente', he says of the speculations about Richard's coming forth into 'the worlde the fete forwarde':

whether that menne of hatred reported above the truthe, or that nature chaunged his course in his beginnynge, which in his life many thynges unnaturally committed, this I leve to God his judgemente.[3]

Setting forth the possibilities that Richard had contrived Clarence's murder, he weighs the plausibility of opinion, and concludes: 'but of these poinctes there is no certentie, and whosoever divineth or conjectureth, may as wel shote to fer as to shorte'. He has, however, no moment's doubt that God in his providence determines human fate; and that Richard was 'brought to his death as he worthely had deserved'. It was Holinshed, however, on whom Shakespeare mainly relied for

[1] Hall, *Chronicle*, ed. 1809, p. 413.
[2] E. M. W. Tillyard: *Shakespeare's History Plays*, p. 42.
[3] Hall, *op. cit.* p. 343.

his history, and Holinshed was a simple-minded fellow of average intelligence untroubled by and incapable of obstinate metaphysical questionings. His hobby, and his main preoccupation, was his passion for England's past; and as a story-teller rather than as a critic, he took over from his forerunners in the making of chronicles anything which read like history. He gave to Shakespeare the English myth; that is, the tale of England's past as it had cumulatively crystallised itself in the English mind: it was history and legend as much as Homer's myths were Greek history and Greek legend. Like Homer's too it incorporated the nation's theology as it seemed to the man in the street: Holinshed's explanations of the course of events are generally borrowed from his favourite chroniclers, but they propound nothing repugnant to the common sense and the conventional beliefs of his readers. Though Holinshed is Shakespeare's historical bible, he certainly knew some of the earlier versions which Holinshed also had on his shelves; in particular, he must often have had an eye on Hall when the Holinshed story was running through his mind.

So, when Shakespeare took the figure of his Richard from the chroniclers, he took also the universe with which the chroniclers, and especially Holinshed, had surrounded Richard. Shakespeare's universe, like theirs, is the conventional cosmos of the current Christian faith. No play of his is set in a more characteristically sixteenth-century Christian world than is *Richard III*. The articles and the formularies of sixteenth-century faith are assumed in its setting and are expressed or displayed in the scenes of it; and for the energising of its peripeteia and its conclusion, it relies on the current doctrines of Christian belief. The outer and the inner world presented by Shakespeare in this play are unmistakably the average Elizabethan picture of God's universe.

'The sacred name of God', 'the Almighty', the 'All-Seer', fall repeatedly and easily from the lips of all its characters, wicked and virtuous alike. The 'great King of Kings', 'the supreme King of Kings' has promulgated his edicts in the dreadful 'table of his law'. Sin is 'war on God', and 'God holds vengeance in his hands, to hurl upon their heads that break his law'. Whatever the offence, 'God will revenge it'. He visits his displeasure on those who repine at the sufferings which His will ordains for them: 'God is much displeased that you take with unthankfulness his doing', the afflicted Duchess is reminded. True Christian virtue is 'humility': 'I thank God for my humility'; 'I took him for the plainest harmless creature that breathed upon this earth a Christian'. Humility, devotion and 'right Christian zeal' are the inexorable demands of this stern God, who is still the Hebrew God of battles, putting into the hands of his captains his 'bruising irons of wrath'

> That they may crush down with a heavy fall
> The usurping helmets of their adversaries.

In a universe so conscious of God's vengeance, the 'precious image of our dear Redeemer' is barely seen, and the name of the Cross has lost its sanctity and has fallen into a mere conversational idiom, 'by the holy rood'. A penitent Edward and a despairing Richard may turn to Jesus with a prayer for mercy; but Christ is not otherwise nor at other times a part of their universe. The all-prevailing law is the law of God's vengeance: in his life, the sinner is afflicted by God's stern torturing engine, the remorse of conscience; he loses his life to fulfil the law that the wages of sin is death. Such a morality and such a theology could absorb as instruments of God's avenging power many of the articles of ancient pagan cults—presagings, forebodings, omens, dreams and ghostly vistants of terror: these a dramatist would find potent implements in his art. Dreams are a recurrent part of *Richard III*, heaven's 'dread fore-warnings' to men like Clarence and like Stanley, who are standing unwittingly on the brink of their fate. Hastings may mock at those 'so fond To trust the mockery of unquiet slumbers',[1] but the divine

---

[1] *Richard III* III. ii. 26.

authority of all such omens is vindicated by the dire result of Hastings' contempt for them. 'By a divine instinct men's minds mistrust Ensuing dangers':[1] Thomas More had given to Holinshed and Hall and Shakespeare this explanatory comment on incidents in Richard's story, as satisfied with its sufficient validity as were the prehistoric people of Seneca's *Thyestes*:

> mittit luctus signa futuri
> mens, ante sui praesaga mali;
> instat nautis fera tempestas,
> cum sine vento tranquilla tument.[2]

Most potent and most terrible are the unquiet slumbers which accompany consciousness of sin; their haunting shapes are the divine furies of a wrathful God, shapes assuming visible form as ghostly apparitions, as terrifying to Christians as for ages they had been for pagans. Even as ghosts may fittingly enter the supernatural regions of Richard's universe, so may this universe borrow from pagan cults (and pagan drama) the superstitious terror of the curse, vaguely investing it with the authority of divine anathema. Margaret utters her curses as spells magically charged with the double potency of Nemesis and God's law:

> If heaven have any grievous plague in store
> Exceeding those that I can wish upon thee,
> O, let them keep it till thy sins be ripe,[3]

and in the meanwhile she invokes the 'worm of conscience' to 'begnaw' Richard's soul.

All this, substance and furniture alike, of Richard's universe is part of common sixteenth-century opinion. In 1597, Shakespeare's contemporary, Thomas Beard, brought together in his *Theatre of Gods Judgements* a collection of 'Histories out of Sacred, Ecclesiasticall, and prophane Authours, concerning the admirable Judgements of God upon the transgressours of his

[1] *Ibid.* II. iii. 42. [2] *Thyestes*, 961–4.
[3] *Richard III* I. iii. 217.

commandements'. He had, of course, no doubt about the omnipotence of the Avenger:

Nothing in the world commeth to passe by chance or adventure, but onely and alwaies by the prescription of his wil; according to the which he ordereth and disposeth by a straight and direct motion, as well the generall as the particular, and that after a strange and admirable order.[1]

No less rigorously and certainly was 'God's justice manifested in the world upon sinners and reprobats'. The more worldly-minded Nashe utters the commonplace: 'how just God is evermore in punishing of murther'.[2] Richard III provided a signal illustration of this moral and theological dogma; and Beard himself cites him as such. As the enormity of Richard's evil-doing grew, his conscience duly afflicted him with dreams: the record of these dreams in the chronicles doubtless suggested the procession of ghosts in Shakespeare's play. When Shakespeare's Richard himself attributes these visions to his conscience which, with 'a thousand several tongues', condemns him for a villain, he is only saying what will be said by all the chroniclers from Polydore Vergil to Holinshed. Polydore recounts the Bosworth-eve dream and adds:

But (I beleve) yt was no dreame, but a conscyence guiltie of haynous offences, a conscyence...which thowght at none other time, yeat in the last day of our lyfe ys woont to represent to us the memory of our sinnes commytted.[3]

Hall repeats the details of this 'dreadful and terrible dreame' and its 'diverse ymages lyke terrible develles whiche pulled and haled hym', concluding his account with the approved comment, 'but I thynke this was no dreame, but a punccion and pricke of his synfull conscience'.[4] And Holinshed repeats word and doctrine verbatim even to the personal 'but I thynke'. It is then abundantly clear that to the sixteenth century, Richard

[1] L. B. Campbell, *Shakespeare's Tragic Heroes*, p. 11.
[2] *Ibid.* p. 32.   [3] Ed. Camden Soc. p. 222.
[4] Hall, p. 414.

was an outstanding and indubitable instance of the certain working of God's Vengeance and God's Justice.

Told as the chroniclers tell it, Richard's story must have been an acceptable piece of moralised history for the bulk of its Elizabethan readers, for Shakespeare, too, amongst them. It explained events satisfactorily in the accepted design of their philosophy of history. But drama is not history; the conditions of dramatic conviction are essentially different from those which give persuasion to historic narrative. Even for historic persuasion, the pattern of the philosophy of history adopted by the Elizabethan chroniclers would lack something in validity for to-day's mind; and drama is for all time; at least, for that long stretch of knowable time since Aeschylus put human tragedy into a form so independent of temporalities in its essence that it strikes conviction even yet in the mind and heart of man.

Shakespeare's dramatisation of Richard breaks down because he passively takes over from the chroniclers and from his contemporaries their universe, the universe in which literally the wages of sin is death. It is a universe which they accept and hold in the strength of their faith. Its dramatic insufficiency is in no sense bound up with questionings of its truth. Even the conforming Elizabethans knew that in day-to-day experience, murderers are not always brought to their due penalty; they knew, moreover, that Plutarch, fifteen hundred years before, had pondered, as they also pondered, 'how it commeth that the divine Justice differeth otherwhiles [i.e. defers on occasion] the punishment of wicked persons', the title under which Philemon Holland in 1603 translated Plutarch's essay περὶ τῶν ὑπὸ τοῦ θείου βραδέως τιμωρουμένων — *de sera numinis vindicta*. But these considerations were irrelevant to, or could be absorbed into, their religious acceptance of a universe in which the wages of sin is death. In tragic drama, however, the demands are of another order. Death, the end of mortal life, is absolute in tragedy: tragedy cannot, and Shakespeare's never attempts to, postpone payment of the wages to an eternal

post-mortem hell. Moreover, this absolute death is visibly displayed before mortals in whom the deepest secret instinct is their
'philanthropy'. To make the spectacle tolerable to them, the
death must proceed as the outcome of powers made to operate
by the play and in the play. Such forces may well be those commonly believed to operate in actual life. But the dramatist is
not a mere exemplifier of world-orders taken for granted:
each single play is a microcosm in itself and must actuate its
own cosmic powers. Tragedy does not merely exemplify
general views. It reveals their truth; it provides, not an illustration of what is generally held to be true, but a conviction that
this or that must be true. Richard must be killed by powers
which are as inherent a part of the energy of the play as he himself is. But his death is not so. To kill him, Shakespeare borrows
the weapon from the chroniclers and from his audience; he
destroys Richard with their belief in death as the certain wages
of sin.

The crucial break in the play occurs at the turning point of
Richard's career. What conviction is there that this turning is
an inevitable necessity? In rudimentary or local or medieval
or merely popular tragedy, a traditional invocation sufficed to
give validity to such decisive turns: the uncertainty of the
world was conventionally canonised and deified as the muta-
bility of Fortune, and the turning of her wheel gave sufficient
suggestion of regulated movement determined by the incalculable impulses of an unknowable will. At a later stage in the
development of tragedy, pagan Fortune was half-christianised
as the mode of God's providence, and theology was called on
to provide an instrument which would make the mystery of
doom seem more intelligible. It gave to one of man's deeper
instincts the name of conscience, and attributed to conscience
an acute susceptibility for discriminating between that which
prevalent Christian doctrine found to be good and that which
it forbad as evil. With this step forward, the art of tragedy was
moving into its natural terrain, morality, the search for abiding

values in the multitudinous acts of mankind. But at first, the search was no voyage of discovery; it was merely a scene exhibited in an already charted moral world. Tragedies were only formal *exempla*, pictures of a truth established without need of confirmation from the findings of the poet's imaginative insight. *Richard III* represents tragedy at this stage of its evolution; and as such, it stands in marked contrast to *Macbeth*, though both of them face the same human problem, the fate of the evil-doer. The way in *Richard III* is the theologian's; in *Macbeth*, the dramatic seer's.

When and why did conscience first begin to exert itself in rendering Richard incapable of achieving his evil purposes? The chroniclers, as was seen, have a ready answer to the 'why'—God's vengeance—and, accepting this answer, Shakespeare's dramatic imagination is untroubled by the question. The 'when' of the onslaught of conscience is also pat to the chroniclers' hands. It is the immediate result of the murder of the princes; and it inflicted permanent disablement on Richard's personality. Thomas More first told the story and passed it on to Hall and Holinshed, who repeated it in almost the same words, even, as was their habit, each one of them, reporting it as having come to him through personal information at only second hand from intimates of Richard himself. I quote Hall's version:

I have harde by credible reporte of suche as were secrete with his [Richard's] chamberers that after this abhominable deed done, he never was quiet in his mynde, he never thought him selfe sure where he went abroade, his body prively feinted, his eyen wherled aboute, his hande ever on his dagger, his countenaunce and maner lyke alwaies to stricke againe, he toke evill reste on nightes, laye long wakyng and musyng, forweried with care and watche, rather slombred then slept, troubled with fearefull dreames, sodeinly somtyme stert up, leapte out of his bed and loked about the chambre, so was his restlesse harte continually tossed and tombled with the tedious impression and stormy remembraunce of this abhominable murther and execrable tyrannye.[1]

[1] Hall, p. 379.

And a little later:

from thence forth not onely all his counsailles, doynges and pro-
cedynges, sodainlye decayed and sorted to none effecte: But also
fortune beganne to froune and turne her whele douneward from him,
in so much that he lost his onely begotten sonne called Edwarde…and
shortely after…he was unquieted by a conspiracye…. [1]

And so the tale goes on.

It is a record fully satisfying the contemporary canons of
'moralised' history. Retribution must overtake Richard, and
the way of its happening is authenticated by personal testimony
from an eyewitness' friend. How little the readers felt any
need of more substantial evidence is clearly seen, for they permitted Hall and then Holinshed to adopt More's 'I have heard'
as if they, who could not have done so, had themselves done
the actual hearing.

But while these whisperings of hearsay will serve as circumstantial corroboration in a tale of things gone by, they have no
entry into a play. For there the thing is present as alive, and the
scene itself must give direct authenticity to its people and their
doings. There is nothing in the play to compel the tide of
Richard's fortune to turn. It is not a tragedy of the same order
as the great four.

Of course, *Richard III* is a highly successful stage-play; it is
only its quality as tragedy which is defective. It can carry its
audience's attention from beginning to end even now as it did
in Shakespeare's day. Indeed, it is doubtful whether its peculiar
limitation in tragic quality would have been apparent to an
Elizabethan audience. That audience would itself accept the
particular articles of the cosmic penal code by which Richard is
punished, as if it had read them with its own eyes on the Mosaic
tablets. Even if belief in the precise formulation of any one
clause in the code should be a little less than absolute, groundlings
and gallery-spectators alike would eagerly accept the dramatist's
conclusion out of a natural desire to believe the providential

[1] Hall, p. 381.

scheme of it to be true. That, however, raises another of the considerations concerning the requirements of tragedy. *Richard III* fails to create the inevitability of its own organic structure. But one may also ask whether the frame of mind which it excites in the audience is fittingly to be called tragic emotion. For, whilst the witnessing of Richard's life might have induced in the audience the imaginative fears of exposure in real life to such devilish workers of cruelty, the sight of his death must have been balm and comfort, strengthening a firm joy in their fortune to exist in a universe whose police system is so palpably efficient in arrest of evil-doers and whose penal code adjusts the punishment so exquisitely to the crime. It seems a misuse of words to call this sentiment tragic. For some such reason Aristotle refused to admit the tragedy of mere villainy. 'Nor should the downfall of the utter villain be exhibited: a plot of this kind would doubtless satisfy the moral sense [I quote Butcher's version: Aristotle's word here rendered 'moral sense' is *to philanthropon*] but it would inspire neither pity nor fear.'[1] It would content the audience, as *Richard III* abundantly has done; but it would not be tragedy. If by tragedy we mean the ideal tragic form which Aristotle sought, or the particular forms in which Shakespeare embodied his greatest tragedies, then *Richard III* is not great tragedy.

3. *Richard II*

The chroniclers had given Shakespeare the first figure, Richard III, with whom to begin his imaginative adventure in search of the personality most apt to become a tragic hero. He found in him the gigantic dynamism of personality which for the Renaissance was the wonderful novelty they had discovered in the forces which were shaping human destiny. The most obvious sign by which colossal might is recognised is its capacity for conquest, and the strength of a conqueror is known by the weight of the opponent he overcomes. For his opportunity to

[1] *Poetics* XIII. 2.

display outstanding greatness, he must be set against stupendous odds. The superman hero is therefore almost inevitably a rebel, an antagonist of the established powers; to reach the utmost trial of his giantry, he will, in fact, be a terrific embodiment of evil. Such Richard III is. But being that, somehow he frustrates the realisation of a satisfying idea of tragedy. The more securely he establishes his autonomous energy, the more difficult it is to bring him to a tragic end; he has to be tricked into it by a theatrical sleight-of-hand, by one or other sort of *deus ex machina*.

So for his next tragedy, Shakespeare looked for a different kind of character in the traditional repositories of tragic heroes. The chroniclers offered him Richard II. Richard III had been rich in promise of tragic terror or fear; but he was lacking in capacity to excite the no less requisite pity or sympathy—the emotion comprised in the terminology of Aristotle's description of the tragic appeal, pity and fear, and the *to philanthropon* which is compassion, the instinctive sympathy with other men in distress. The Richard II of the chroniclers, however, seems as a person eminently fitted to supply this want. Indeed, in Holinshed's portraiture, he seems in all ways a striking contrast to Richard III; he proves his quality, in fact, by capturing Holinshed's own sympathy. 'He was of a gentle nature.' In him, 'if there were anie offense, it ought rather to be imputed to the frailtie of wanton youth, than to the malice of his hart'.[1] He lived in a time when 'there reigned abundantlie the filthie sinne of leacherie and fornication, with abhominable adulterie',[2] and though the King was by no means innocent of these, he was not more guilty of them than were many of his own prelacy. Even so, Holinshed, speaking apparently for himself, feels moved to speak his own approbation:

If I may boldlie saie what I thinke: he was a prince the most unthank-fullie used of his subjects, of any one of whom ye shall lightlie read.

---

[1] Holinshed, *Chronicles*, Oxford University Press (1923), p. 24.
[2] *Ibid.* p. 48.

For although (thorough the frailtie of youth) he demeaned himselfe more dissolutelie than seemed convenient for his roiall estate, and made choise of such councellors as were not favoured of the people, whereby he was the lesse favoured himselfe: yet in no kings daies were the commons in greater wealth, if they could have perceived their happie state: neither in any other time were the nobles and gentlemen more cherished, nor churchmen less wronged. But such was their ingratitude towards their bountifull and loving sovereigne, that those whom he had cheeflie advanced, were readiest to controll him.[1]

The figure of Richard II which Shakespeare took from Holinshed provided him with ampler opportunity than did Richard III for filling in the intimacies and the simpler subtleties of the finished portrait, for Richard II was so much more the ordinary normal human being, *l'homme moyen sensuel*, than was Richard III. He was a person who could be characterised as an individual rather than as a type, a creature stirred, as men are stirred, variously by various moods, and fluctuating at the impulses of his own mingled and wayward instincts. As portraiture progressing towards the psychological realism which is part of the great tragedies, Richard II is a great step beyond Richard III. But since our argument is primarily occupied with progress towards the realisation by Shakespeare of his own idea of tragedy, these many aspects of Richard II's characterisation which mark other features of Shakespeare's growth as a dramatic poet may be passed over. Our main concern is with the play of *Richard II* as an approach to Shakespeare's great tragedies; and our present interest in the character of Richard II himself is confined to those aspects of it which relate to its efficiency in the scheme of tragedy.

Though the characterisation is Shakespeare's, the character is in Holinshed, as also are occasional hints which Shakespeare developed in his more intimate realisation of the temperament, mind and sentiment of Richard as it expressed itself in the habitual circumstances of his life. Holinshed's Richard was not naturally an evil person; in the chronicler's phrase, he was

[1] *Ibid.* p. 49.

without 'malice in his hart', 'of nature good enough'. He was prodigal in a kingly way, and delighted in a luxurious display of the bounties which in royal bonhomie he dispensed to all within his circle, intimates and servitors alike.

> He was prodigall, ambitious, and much given to the pleasure of th . bodie. He kept the greatest port, and mainteined the most plentifull house that ever any king in England did either before his time or since. For there resorted dailie to his court above ten thousand persons that had meat and drinke there allowed them. In his kitchen there were three hundred servitors, and everie other office was furnished after the like rate. Of ladies, chamberers and landerers, there were above three hundred at the least. And in gorgious and costlie apparell they exceeded all measure, not one of them that kept within the bounds of his degree.[1]

By such vanity and prodigality he surrounded himself with the superficial friendliness of many and the real affection of the nameless and meaner few, 'the king's servants'. But it was, in these few, a genuine affection; when Richard was fallen on evil days it was these more lowly folk, 'diverse of the king's servants which by licence had accesse to his person', who sought to comfort him. Inevitably, however, these temperamental habits, 'though otherwise [he was] a right noble and woorthie prince',[2] exposed Richard to the guile of flatterers; 'he was given to follow evill counsell'. He never grew up to a sense of moral responsibility, to a settled judgement, a 'grounded wisdome and ripe discretion', qualities which the Archbishop in his 'breef collation' at Bolingbroke's coronation named as the new king's in express contrast with Richard's. The Archbishop's sermon took for its text *Vir dominabitur in populo*; it was 'recorded by Fabian in ample manner' and thence copied by Holinshed. Its main theme is the difference between man and boy, between Bolingbroke and Richard.

> Of his great mercie, he [God] hath visited us, I trust his peculiar people, and sent us a man to have the rule of us, and put by children that before

---

[1] Holinshed, *Chronicles*, Oxford University Press (1923), p. 48.
[2] *Ibid.* p. 47.

time ruled this land, after childish conditions, as by the woorkes of them it hath rightlie appeared, to the disturbance of all this realme; and for want and lacke of a man.

He goes on to describe these ways and conditions of children, and always with an eye on Richard,

in whome is no stedfastnesse or constancie: for a child will lightlie promise, and lightlie he will breake his promise, and doo all things that his appetite giveth him unto, and forgetteth lightlie what he hath doone.[1]

Holinshed's account of the deposing has also its hints for Shakespeare's portrait. He quotes the official text of the deposition document. Its articles record, with, of course, whatever degree of compromise between truth and policy the reader chooses to find in them, that Richard has abdicated 'of his owne meere voluntee and free will'. Cited as well is Richard's own declaration, official, too, and perhaps therefore phrased under duress; explicitly Richard renounces

the name, worship, and regalitie and kinglie highnesse, clearelie, freelie, singularlie and wholie, in the most best maner and forme that I may,[2]

and he confesses

for well I wote and knowledge, and deeme my selfe to be, and have beene insufficient and unable, and also unprofitable, and for my open deserts not unworthie to be put downe.

In the events leading to the deposition, Holinshed recounts that Richard sometimes said

that for the insufficiencie whiche he knew himselfe to be of, to occupie so great a charge, as to governe the realme of England he would gladlie leave of and renounce his right and title.

When the legal instrument of his dethronement was submitted to him, the King

familiarlie and with a glad countenance (as to them and us appeared) talked with the said archbishop and duke a good season.

---

[1] *Ibid.* p. 43.   [2] *Ibid.* pp. 35–8.

But Holinshed also inserts records of Richard in different moods from that of calm or even joyful resignation. At times, the King was utterly dejected, 'being with sorrow almost consumed, and in manner halfe dead'. The deposition formally concluded, as successive vassals of former days came to make formal renunciation of 'homage and fealtie', each occasion

> was a redoubling of his greefe, in so much as thereby it came to his mind, how in former times he was acknowledged and taken for their liege lord and sovereigne, who now (whether in contempt or in malice, God knoweth) to his face forsware him to be their king.[1]

And at that very point in the record, the prosaic Holinshed proffers some Latin verse from his contemporary Thomas Watson's *Amintas* which 'in his hevines Richard might verie well have said with a greeved plaintife':

> Heu quantae sortes miseris mortalibus instant!
> Ah chari quoties oblivia nominis opto!
> O qui me fluctus, quis me telluris hiatus
> Pertaesum tetricae vitae deglutiat ore
> Chasmatico?

In the chronicler's story there were hints sufficient to prompt Shakespeare to his portrait of the sensuous, sentimental, poetic king; inclined generally to goodness rather than to evil, but unstable, the sport of his own whims, moods, fancies, and 'rash fierce blazes of riot'; morally not so much wicked as frail; a man without backbone, a man who is really a child and suffers the nadir of desolation in the breaking of a doll.

But how could such a figure play effectively his appropriate part in a scheme of tragedy? He is essentially a weak, but not an evil man. Weakness, however, is fragility, and fragility is a liability to break. To be tragic, Richard must be broken; as a man whose prevailing characteristic is fragility, he has within himself the instrument of his own destruction. Ultimately his

---

[1] Holinshed, *Chronicles*, Oxford University Press (1923), p. 47.

tragic collapse is inevitable. As his end is thus inevitable, he provides that sense of inevitability which is the main source of tragic conviction. Richard II will not impose on Shakespeare, as did Richard III, an overt complicity in his hero's death; to that extent, he is more suited to the tragic hero's rôle. But his weakness has other dramatic implications. In some of its forms, weakness is a trait capable of stirring compassion, though a compassion which runs to pathos rather than to that pity which is a component of Aristotle's 'pity and fear'. As pathos, it is a potential spring of sympathy; but can it excite a sensation of momentousness, an impression of cosmic significance? This is a query which, on the whole, it is not unfair to submit to a box-office test. *Richard III* has been far more successful in the theatres of the last three hundred years than has *Richard II*. It has gripped the public; and the groundlings, the heterogeneous and representative crowd of average men, the *moltitudine rozza*, as an Italian Renaissance critic, Castelvetro, called it, are not only the cat-callers of theatrical success, they are, as Castelvetro claimed, the final arbiters, under available guidance, of permanent dramatic values. *Richard III* has proved a better play than *Richard II*. *Richard II* has failed to create a wide and deep sense of its significance for mankind. Though its hero is a king, as a man he is without distinction, too ordinary, of a kind commonly and frequently encountered in the familiar walks of life. Though his lot is formally of great moment, his fate is like that of a multitude of average human beings, men in their weakness overcome by circumstance. His fall, like that of many of Galsworthy's heroes, presents a general social problem rather than a moral tragic dilemma. Indeed, as mere man, shorn of his regal commitments, Richard might have dallied on with life much longer until at length his weakness should claim its final toll. It is in fact a real dramatic problem for Shakespeare in the latter part of the play to prevent the pathetic weakness of Richard from forfeiting the sympathetic interest of the audience: his hero is in danger of becoming too maudlinly insignificant to excite compassionate lookers-on to a deep concern in his fate. To prevent this, Shakespeare has to exploit many resources of his dramatic technique.

In *Richard II* the dramatist relies extensively on his own poetic as well as on his dramatic powers. Having given to Richard the distinctive moral weakness to which a highly sensuous and sentimental nature is liable, he can give him the exquisite luxuries of sentiment which he, Shakespeare, as a poet is peculiarly gifted to utter. He can lend to sentimentality the momentary might of passion; he can drain the well of pathos dry. But he has more strictly dramatic devices. For the second part of the play, he invents new people whose main function is to restore the fallen king's hold on the audience. There is the groom and the talk of roan Barbary, kindling at once a sense of Richard's gentleness, his power to arouse affection, and his human kindliness for his horse. There is also the queen, a mere child-wife in history, but in Shakespeare a woman grown to the full love of devoted wifeliness. The most audacious dramatic stroke, audacious because it breaks one dramatic law to achieve a larger dramatic purpose, is the arbitrary change of character forced on the Bolingbroke of the later scenes. In earlier stages of the play he has appeared an upright honest man suffering from a despot's injustice to him. But in later scenes, and without substantial warrant from Holinshed, he becomes the cunning political schemer who plots Richard's murder. The murder done, he turns the hired assassins off with a callous phrase, and in the same abrupt tone of mingled commodity and sanctimony, he makes summary plans for the funeral, and for his own journey to the Holy Land there to wash the blood from off his guilty hand. As Bolingbroke thus drops in our regard, his victim Richard inevitably rises. At length, as a final decisive stroke, restoring to Richard the full involuntary esteem of the audience, Shakespeare allows him the traditional heroism of a tragic hero's death. Assailed in his prison by Exton and the armed accomplices, Richard snatches an axe from one of them and kills him and another before he himself is overcome and murdered.

Though these devices are sufficient to counterbalance one shortcoming of Richard's weakness, namely, his danger of forfeiting the sympathy of the audience, they are of no avail to outweigh its major dramatic defect. They do not invest his weakness with the weight of momentousness. Nor does Shakespeare in this play make much use of other conventional ways of securing that effect. The queen's heavy heart has vague promptings of coming sorrow; there is an occasional and sporadic insinuation that the traditional omens and forebodings are lurking in the air:

> The bay-trees in our country are all wither'd
> And meteors fright the fixed stars of heaven;
> The pale-faced moon looks bloody on the earth
> And lean-look'd prophets whisper fearful change.[1]

Somewhat more frequently comes the familiar attribution of events to God's will and the plan of His just vengeance:

> Put we our quarrel to the will of heaven,
> Who, when they see the hours ripe on earth,
> Will rain hot vengeance on offenders' heads.[2]

But the story of Richard's fall needs no dramatic propulsion borrowed from a theological scheme. His weakness is sufficient in itself. Moreover, the assertion of divine participation is reserved for incidents in the political and public scenes rather than those in its personal and tragic ones. These political scenes are in a sense part of the tragic furniture of the play, for a kind of vicarious momentousness attaches to the tragedy of Richard because it happens to be the fall of a man who happens to be a king. But in so far as they do add a sense of larger issues, the result is a further blunting of the tragic efficacy of Richard the man. As king his faults are largely faults of policy and not of moral turpitude: the edict of deposition declared him to be (in

[1] *Richard II* II. iv. 8.   [2] *Ibid.* I. ii. 6.

Holinshed's words) 'unprofitable, unable, unsufficient and un-woorthie of the rule and governance' of the realm. Though these are marks of his inherent weakness, they are but signs of a professional or vocational misfit and not evidences of any fundamental blackness of the soul. Vicariously, too, the political setting pushes the personal story of Richard into a special orbit of God's providence as it was currently understood. England's destiny is in God's hands. Holinshed's archbishop pronounced the English 'God's peculiar people, I trust'. There was a special Providence to lend armies of angels for guarding the majesty of his anointed deputy, the temporal king. But somehow in the play itself neither the upholders nor the beneficiaries of this dispensation help either to make its ordinances intelligible or to illustrate their validity.

Summarily, then, *Richard II* does not carry Shakespeare appreciably nearer to his tragic pattern. He has hit on a means of securing a sense of inevitability in his tragic plot, and he has found a somewhat limited substitute for universality in its significance. But gaining these, he has sacrificed something which *Richard III* had, the indispensable impression of momentousness; and the generality of implication, which in *Richard II* is a kind of universality, is not the universality of significance which moves to a momentousness more imaginatively impressive than the momentousness produced merely by such gigantic massiveness as was *Richard III*'s.

CHAPTER III

EXPERIMENT AND INTERREGNUM

ROMEO AND JULIET, KING JOHN, JULIUS CAESAR

1. *Romeo and Juliet*

In their general structure and idea, the three tragedies so far reviewed were in the current dramatic tradition of their day. But *Romeo and Juliet* is a departure, a comprehensive experiment. It links the English stage to the Renaissance tragedy which by precept and by practice Cinthio [1] in the middle of the sixteenth century had established in Italy.

Cinthio's principles were in the main an adaptation of Seneca's, or rather of what he took to be Seneca's purposes, to the immediate needs of Cinthio's contemporary theatre. His own object he declared to be 'servire l'età, à gli spettatori'. Tragedy must grip its audience. It must therefore reflect a range of experience and base itself on a system of values which are felt by its audience to be real. Many of his proposals are the direct outcome of this general principle, and one or two of them are especially pertinent to our argument. For instance, tragedy must no longer rely mainly for its material on ancient mythology nor on accredited history; for these depict a world which may have lost urgent contact with a modern audience's sense of life. The best plots for modern tragedy will be found in modern fiction. For modern fiction is the mythology of to-day. It is the corpus of story through which the world

---

[1] See H. B. Charlton, *Senecan Tradition in Renaissance Tragedy*, first published in 1921 as an introduction to *The Poetical Works of Sir William Alexander* (Manchester University Press and Scottish Texts Society) and reissued separately by the Manchester University Press in 1946.

appears as it seems to be to living men; it mirrors accepted codes of conduct, displays the particular manner of contemporary consciousness, and adopts the current assumptions of human values. Let the dramatist, therefore, draw his plots from the novelists. An inevitable consequence followed from this. There is nothing in which the outlook on life adopted by the modern world is more different from that of the ancient classical world than in its apprehension of the human and spiritual significance of the love of man for woman. Love had become for the modern world its most engrossing interest and often its supreme experience. Modern fiction turns almost exclusively on love. So when dramatists took their tales from the novelists, they took love over as the main theme of their plays. Seven of Cinthio's nine plays borrow their plots from novels (most of them from his own series, the *Hecatommithi*); the other two are 'classical', but are two of the great classical love stories, *Dido* and *Cleopatra*. Jason de Nores, a much more conservatively Aristotelian expositor than his contemporary Cinthio, to exemplify the form which the most perfect tragedy could take, constructs the plot for it from one of Boccaccio's tales.

Whether by direct influence or by mere force of circumstance, Cinthio's practice prevailed. Sixteenth-century tragedy found rich material in the novels. But the traditionalists were perpetually reminding the innovators that tragedy always had had and always must have an historical hero. 'In tragoedia reges, principes, ex urbibus, arcibus, castris,' Scaliger, the Parnassian legislator, announced. No one would accept a hero as great unless his memory were preserved in the historian's pages. 'C'est l'histoire qui persuade avec empire', as Corneille put it. Shakespeare, an eager and humble apprentice, naturally followed traditional custom. *Titus Andronicus*, *Richard III* and *Richard II* belong in the main to the conventional pattern. They deal with historical material. Their heroes are of high rank and potent in determining the destiny of nations. The plot is never mainly a lovers' story, though a love-intrigue intrudes sporadically here and there within the major theme. But somehow the prescriptions had not produced the expected result. There was something unsatisfying in these plays as divinations of man's tragic lot. And so the conventions were jettisoned in *Romeo and Juliet.*

Shakespeare was casting in fresh directions to find the universality, the momentousness, and above all the inevitability of all-compelling tragedy. In particular, he was experimenting with a new propelling force, a new final sanction as the determinant energy, the *ultima ratio* of tragedy's inner world; and though *Romeo and Juliet* is set in a modern Christian country, with church and priest and full ecclesiastical institution, the whole universe of God's justice, vengeance and providence is discarded and rejected from the directing forces of the play's dramatic movement. In its place, there is a theatrical resuscitation of the half-barbarian, half-Roman deities of Fate and Fortune.

The plot of *Romeo and Juliet* is pure fiction. Shakespeare took it from Arthur Broke's poem, *The Tragicall Historie of Romeus and Juliet* (1562). Shakespeare knew from Broke's title-page that the tale was taken from an Italian novelist, 'written first in Italian by Bandell'. He knew, too, what sort of novels Bandello wrote, for Painter had retold them in his *Palace of Pleasure* (1567). They were clear fictions. Moreover the hero and the heroine, Romeo and Juliet, had none of the pomp of historic circumstance about them; they were socially of the minor aristocracy who were to stock Shakespeare's comedies, and their only political significance was an adventitious rôle in the civic disturbance of a small city-state. Romeo and Juliet were in effect just a boy and a girl in a novel; and as such they had no claim to the world's attention except through their passion and their fate.

To choose such folk as these for tragic heroes was aesthetically wellnigh an anarchist's gesture; and the dramatist provided a sort of programme-prologue to prompt the audience to see the play from the right point of view. In this play-bill the dramatist draws special attention to two features of his story. First, Verona was being torn by a terrible, bloodthirsty feud which no human endeavour had been able to settle; this was the direct cause of the death of the lovers, and but for those deaths it never would have been healed. Second, the course of the young lovers' lives is from the outset governed by a malignant destiny; fatal, star-crossed, death-marked, they are doomed to piteous destruction.

The intent of this emphasis is clear. The tale will end with the death of two ravishingly attractive young folk; and the dramatist must exonerate himself from all complicity in their murder, lest he be found guilty of pandering to a liking for a human shambles. He disowns responsibility and throws it on Destiny, Fate. The device is well warranted in the tragic tradition, and especially in its Senecan models. But whether, in fact, it succeeds is a matter for further consideration. The invocation of Fate is strengthened by the second feature scored heavily in the prologue, the feud. The feud is, so to speak, the means by which Fate acts. The feud is to provide the sense of immediate, and Fate that of ultimate, inevitability. For it may happen that, however the dramatist deploys his imaginative suggestions, he may fail to summon up a Fate sufficiently compelling to force itself upon the audience as unquestioned shaper of the tragic end. In such circumstance Romeo's and Juliet's death would be by mere chance, a gratuitous intervention by a dramatist exercising his homicidal proclivities for the joy of his audience. Hence the feud has a further function. It will be the dramatist's last plea for exculpation or for mercy; and it will allow his audience to absolve him or to forgive him without loss of its own 'philanthropy'; for through death came the healing of the feud, and with it, the removal of the threat to so many other lives.

It becomes, therefore, of critical importance to watch Shakespeare's handling of these two motives, Fate and Feud, to see how he fits them to fulfil their function, and to ask how far in fact they are adequate to the rôle they must perforce play. Both Fate and Feud, although absent as motives from the earliest European form of the Romeo and Juliet story, had grown variously in the successive tellings of the tale before it came to Broke.[1] The general trend had been to magnify the virulence of the feud, and, even more notably, to swell the sententious apostrophising of Fate's malignity. Broke, for instance, misses no opportunity for such sententiousness. Longer or shorter, there are at least fifteen passages in his poem where the malignity of Fate is his conventionally poetic theme. 'Froward fortune', 'fortune's cruel will', 'wavering fortune', 'tickel fortune', 'when fortune list to strike', 'false fortune cast for her, poore wretch, a myschiefe newe to brewe', 'dame fortune did assent', 'with piteous plaint, fierce fortune doth he blame', 'till Attropos shall cut my fatall thread of lyfe', 'though cruel fortune be so much my dedly foe', 'the blyndfyld goddesse that with frowning face doth fraye, and from theyr seate the mighty kinges throwes downe with hedlong sway', 'He cryed out, with open mouth, against the starres above, The fatall sisters three, he said, had done him wrong'— so, again and again, does Broke bring in

> The diversenes, and eke the accidents so straunge,
> Of frayle unconstant Fortune, that delyteth still in chaunge.[2]

Romeo cries aloud

> Against the restles starres, in rolling skyes that raunge,
> Against the fatall sisters three, and Fortune full of chaunge.[3]

---

[1] For differences between the many pre-Shakespearian versions, see H. B. Charlton, *Romeo and Juliet as an Experimental Tragedy* (British Academy Shakespeare Lecture, 1939) and 'France as Chaperone of Romeo and Juliet' in *Studies in French presented to M. K. Pope*, Manchester University Press (1939).

[2] Broke, *Romeus and Juliet* (Hazlitt's Shakespeare's Library, vol. I. 1875), p. 142.   [3] *Ibid.* p. 151.

There are more elaborate set speeches on the same theme:

> For Fortune chaungeth more, then fickel fantasie;
> In nothing Fortune constant is, save in unconstancie.
> Her hasty ronning wheele, is of a restles coorse,
> That turnes the clymers hedlong downe, from better to the woorse,
> And those that are beneth, she heaveth up agayne.[1]

So when Shakespeare took up the story, Broke had already sought to drench it in fatality. But since Shakespeare was a dramatist, he could not handle Fate and Feud as could a narrative poet. His feud will enter, not descriptively, but as action; and for fate he must depend on the sentiments of his characters and on an atmosphere generated by the sweep of the action. The feud may be deferred for a moment to watch Shakespeare's handling of Fate.

His most frequent device is to adapt what Broke's practice had been; instead of letting his persons declaim formally, as Broke's do, against the inconstancy of Fortune, he endows them with dramatic premonitions. Setting out for Capulet's ball, Romeo is suddenly sad:

> my mind misgives
> Some consequence, yet hanging in the stars,
> Shall bitterly begin his fearful date
> With this night's revels; and expire the term
> Of a despised life, clos'd in my breast,
> By some vile forfeit of untimely death:
> But he that hath the steerage of my course
> Direct my sail![2]

As the lovers first declare their passion, Juliet begs Romeo not to swear, as if an oath might be an evil omen:

> I have no joy of this contract to-night:
> It is too rash, too unadvised, too sudden;
> Too like the lightning, which doth cease to be
> Ere one can say 'It lightens'.[3]

---

[1] Broke, *Romeus and Juliet* (Hazlitt's Shakespeare's Library, vol. I. 1875), p. 147. See also pp. 97, 115.
[2] *Romeo and Juliet* I. iv. 106.   [3] *Ibid.* II. ii. 117.

Romeo, involved in the fatal fight, cries 'O, I am fortune's fool!'[1] Looking down from her window at Romeo as he goes into exile, Juliet murmurs

> O God, I have an ill-divining soul!
> Methinks I see thee, now thou art below,
> As one dead in the bottom of a tomb.[2]

With dramatic irony Juliet implores her parents to defer her marriage with Paris:

> Or, if you do not, make the bridal bed
> In that dim monument where Tybalt lies.[3]

Besides these promptings of impending doom there are premonitions of a less direct kind. The friar fears the violence of the lover's passion:

> These violent delights have violent ends
> And in their triumph die, like fire and powder,
> Which as they kiss consume.[4]

Another source of omen in the play is the presaging of dreams; for from the beginning of time, 'the world of sleep, the realm of wild reality' has brought dreams which look like heralds of eternity and speak like Sybils of the future. There is much dreaming in *Romeo and Juliet*. Mercutio may mock at dreams as children of an idle brain, begot of nothing but vain phantasy. But when Romeo says he 'dream'd a dream to-night', Mercutio's famous flight of fancy recalls the universal belief in dreams as foreshadowings of the future. Again Romeo dreams; this time, 'I dreamt my lady came and found me dead'.[5] As his man Balthasar waits outside Juliet's tomb, he dreams that his master and another are fighting and the audience knows how accurately the dream mirrors the true facts.

But Shakespeare not only hangs omens thickly round his play. He gives to the action itself a quality apt to conjure the

---

[1] *Ibid.* III. i. 141.
[2] *Ibid.* III. v. 54.
[3] *Ibid.* III. v. 202.
[4] *Ibid.* II. vi. 9.
[5] *Ibid.* v. i. 6.

sense of relentless doom. It springs mainly from his compression of the time over which the story stretches. In all earlier versions there is a much longer lapse. Romeo's wooing is prolonged over weeks before the secret wedding; then, after the wedding, there is an interval of three or four months before the slaying of Tybalt; and Romeo's exile lasts from Easter until a short time before mid-September when the marriage with Paris was at first planned to take place. But in Shakespeare all this is pressed into three or four days. The world seems for a moment to be caught up in the fierce play of furies revelling in some mad supernatural game.

But before asking whether the sense of an all-controlling Fate is made strong enough to fulfil its tragic purpose let us turn to the feud. Here Shakespeare's difficulties are even greater. Italian novelists of the quattro- or cinquecento, throwing their story back through two or three generations, might expect their readers easily to accept a fierce vendetta. But the Verona which Shakespeare depicts is a highly civilised world, with an intellectual and artistic culture and an implied social attainment altogether alien from the sort of society in which a feud is a more or less natural manifestation of enmity. The border country of civilisation is the home of feuds, a region where social organisation is still of the clan, where the head of the family-clan is a strong despot, and where law has not progressed beyond the sort of wild justice of which one instrument is the feud.

> For ere I cross the border fells,
> The tane of us shall die

It was wellnigh impossible for Shakespeare to fit the blood-lust of a border feud into the social setting of his Verona. The heads of the rival houses are not at all the fierce chieftains who rule with ruthless despotism. When old Capulet, in fire-side gown, bustles to the scene of the fray and calls for his sword, his wife tells him bluntly that it is a crutch which an old man such as he should want, and not a weapon. Montague, too, spits a little verbal fire, but his wife plucks him by the arm, and tells him to calm down: 'thou shalt not stir one foot to seek a foe'. Indeed, these old men are almost comic figures, and especially Capulet. His querulous fussiness, his casual bonhomie, his almost senile humour and his childish irascibility hardly make him the pattern of a clan chieftain. Even his domestics put him in his place:

> Go, you cot-quean, go,
> Get you to bed; faith, you'll be sick to-morrow
> For this night's watching,[1]

the Nurse tells him; and the picture is filled in by his wife's reminder that she has put a stop to his 'mouse-hunting'. There is of course the prince's word that

> Three civil brawls, bred of an airy word,
> By thee, old Capulet, and Montague,
> Have thrice disturb'd the quiet of our streets.[2]

But these brawls bred of an airy word are no manifestations of a really ungovernable feud. When Montague and Capulet are bound by the prince to keep the peace, old Capulet himself says

> 'tis not hard, I think,
> For men so old as we to keep the peace.[3]

and there is a general feeling that the old quarrel has run its course. Paris, suitor to Juliet, says it is a pity that the Capulets and the Montagues have lived at odds so long. And Benvolio, a relative of the Montagues, is a consistent peace-maker. He tries to suppress a brawl amongst the rival retainers, and invites Tybalt, a Capulet, to assist him in the work. Later he begs his friends to avoid trouble by keeping out of the way of the Capulets, for it is the season of hot blood:

> I pray thee, good Mercutio, let's retire:
> The day is hot, the Capulets abroad,
> And if we meet, we shall not scape a brawl;
> For now, these hot days, is the mad blood stirring.[4]

---

[1] *Romeo and Juliet* IV. iv. 7. [2] *Ibid.* I. i. 96.
[3] *Ibid.* I. ii. 2. [4] *Ibid.* III. i. 1.

When the hot-blooded Mercutio does incite Tybalt to a quarrel, it is again Benvolio who tries to preserve the peace:

> We talk here in the public haunt of men:
> Either withdraw unto some private place,
> And reason coldly of your grievances,
> Or else depart.[1]

Hence the jest of Mercutio's famous description of Benvolio as an inveterate quarreller, thirsting for the slightest excuse to draw sword.

Moreover, the rival houses have mutual friends. Mercutio, Montague Romeo's close acquaintance, is an invited guest at the Capulets' ball. Stranger still, so is Romeo's cruel lady, Rosaline, who in the invitation is addressed as Capulet's cousin. It is odd that Romeo's love for her, since she was a Capulet, had given him no qualms on the score of the feud. When Romeo is persuaded to go gate-crashing to the ball because Rosaline will be there, there is no talk at all of its being a hazardous undertaking. Safety will require, if even so much, no more than a mask.[2] On the way to the ball, as talk is running gaily, there is still no mention of danger involved. Indeed, the feud is almost a dead letter so far. The son of the Montague does not know what the Capulet daughter looks like, nor she what he is like. The traditional hatred survives only in one or two high-spirited, hot-blooded scions on either side, and in the kitchen-folk. Tybalt alone resents Romeo's presence at the ball, yet it is easy for all to recognise him; and because Tybalt feels Romeo's coming to be an insult, he seeks him out next day to challenge him,

---

[1] *Romeo and Juliet* III. i. 53.

[2] In the earlier versions the mask is not a precaution for safety. Shakespeare, taking it partly as such, has to realise how utterly ineffective it is. Romeo is soon known:

> This, by his voice, should be a Montague!
> Fetch me my rapier, boy. What dares the slave
> Come hither, cover'd with an antic face,
> To fleer and scorn at our solemnity?   (I. v. 56.)

so providing the immediate occasion of the new outburst. Naturally, once blood is roused again, and murder done, the ancient rancour springs up with new life. Even Lady Capulet has comically Machiavellian plans for having Romeo poisoned in Mantua. But prior to this the evidences of the feud are so unsubstantial that the forebodings of Romeo and Juliet, discovering each other's name, seem prompted more by fate than feud. There will, of course, be family difficulties; but the friar marries them without a hesitating qualm, feeling that such a union is bound to be accepted eventually by the parents, who will thus be brought to amity.

The most remarkable episode, however, is still to be named. When Tybalt discovers Romeo at the ball, infuriated he rushes to Capulet with the news. But Capulet, in his festive mood, is pleasantly interested, saying that Romeo is reputed to be good-looking and quite a pleasant boy. He tells Tybalt to calm himself, to remember his manners, and to treat Romeo properly:

> Content thee, gentle coz, let him alone;
> He bears him like a portly gentleman;
> And, to say truth, Verona brags of him
> To be a virtuous and well govern'd youth:
> I would not for the wealth of all the town
> Here in my house do him disparagement:
> Therefore be patient, take no note of him:
> It is my will, the which if thou respect,
> Show a fair presence and put off these frowns,
> An ill-beseeming semblance for a feast.[1]

When Tybalt is reluctant, old Capulet is annoyed and testily tells him to stop being a saucy youngster:

> He shall be endured:
> What, goodman boy ! I say, he shall: go to.
> Am I the master here or you? Go to.
> You'll not endure him ! God shall mend my soul !
> You'll make a mutiny among my guests !
> You will set cock-a-hoop ! You'll be the man !

[1] *Romeo and Juliet* I. v. 67.

59

...Go to, go to;
You are a saucy boy: is't so indeed?
This trick may chance to scathe you, I know what:
You must contrary me! marry, 'tis time.
Well said, my hearts! You are a princox; go.[1]

This is a scene which sticks in the memory; for here the
dramatist, unencumbered by a story, is interpolating a lively
scene in his own kind, a vignette of two very amusing people
in an amusing situation. But it is unfortunate for the feud that
this episode takes so well. For clearly old Capulet is unwilling
to let the feud interrupt a dance; and a quarrel which is of less
moment than a galliard is being appeased at an extravagant
price, if the price is the death of two such delightful creatures
as Romeo and Juliet;

their parents' rage,
Which, but their children's end, naught could remove,[2]

loses all its plausibility. A feud like this will not serve as the
bribe it was meant to be; it is no atonement for the death of the
lovers. Nor, indeed, is it coherent and impressive enough as
part of the plot to propel the sweep of necessity in the sequence
of events. If the tragedy is to march relentlessly to its end,
leaving no flaw in the sense of inevitability which it seeks to
prompt, it clearly must depend for that indispensable tragic
impression not on its feud, but on its scattered suggestions of
doom and of malignant fate. And, as has been seen, Shakespeare
harps frequently on this theme.

But how far can a Roman sense of Fate be made real for
a modern audience? It is no mere matter of exciting thought to
'wander through eternity' in the wake of the mystery which
surrounds the human lot. Mystery must take on positive shape,
and half-lose itself in dread figures controlling human life in
their malice. The forms and the phrases by which these powers
had been invoked were a traditional part in the inheritance of
the Senecan drama which came to sixteenth-century Europe.

[1] *Romeo and Juliet* I. v. 78. [2] *Ibid.* Prologue, l. 11.

Fortuna, Fatum, Fata, Parcae: all were firmly established in its *dramatis personae*. Moreover their rôle in Virgilian theocracy was familiar to all with but a little Latin:

> Qua visa est fortuna pati Parcaeque sinebant
> Cedere res Latio, Turnum et tua moenia texi;
> Nunc iuvenem imparibus video concurrere fatis,
> Parcarumque dies et vis inimica propinquat.[1]

For Romans here indeed were the shapers of destiny, the ultimate ἀνάγκη which compels human fate, whether as the μοῖρα of individual lot, or the εἱμαρμένη of a world-order. Horace himself linked Fortuna in closest companionship with Necessitas: 'te semper anteit serva Necessitas', he writes in his prayer to Fortuna.[2] It was a note which reverberated through Senecan stoicism.

But with what conviction could a sixteenth-century spectator take over these ancient figures? Even the human beings of an old mythology may lose their compelling power; 'what's Hecuba to him, or he to Hecuba?' But the gods are in a much worse case; pagan, they had faded before the God of the Christians: *Vicisti, Galilæe*! Fate was no longer a deity strong enough to carry the responsibility of a tragic universe; at most, it could intervene casually as pure luck, and bad luck as a motive turns tragedy to mere chance. It lacks entirely the ultimate tragic ἀνάγκη. It fails to provide the indispensable inevitability.

Is then Shakespeare's *Romeo and Juliet* an unsuccessful experiment? To say so may seem not only profane but foolish. In its own day, as the dog's-eared Bodley Folio shows, and ever since, it has been one of Shakespeare's most preferred plays. It is indeed rich in spells of its own. But as a pattern of the idea of tragedy, it is a failure. Even Shakespeare appears to have felt that, as an experiment, it had disappointed him. At all events, he abandoned tragedy for the next few years and gave himself to history and to comedy; and even afterwards, he fought shy of the simple theme of love, and of the love of anybody

---

[1] *Aeneid* XII. 147.   [2] *Odes* I. xxxv.

less than a great political figure as the main matter for his tragedies.

Nevertheless it is obvious that neither sadism nor masochism is remotely conscious in our appreciation of *Romeo and Juliet*, nor is our 'philanthropy' offended by it. But the achievement is due to the magic of Shakespeare's poetic genius and to the intermittent force of his dramatic power rather than to his grasp of the foundations of tragedy.

There is no need here to follow the meetings of Romeo and Juliet through the play, and to recall the spell of Shakespeare's poetry as it transports us along the rushing stream of the lovers' passion, from its sudden outbreak to its consummation in death. Romeo seals his 'dateless bargain to engrossing death', choosing shipwreck on the dashing rocks to secure peace for his 'sea-sick weary bark'. Juliet has but a word: 'I'll be brief. O happy dagger!' There is need for nothing beyond this. Shakespeare, divining their naked passion, lifts them above the world and out of life by the mere force of it. It is the sheer might of poetry. Dramatically, however, he has subsidiary resources. He has Mercutio and the Nurse.

Shakespeare's Mercutio has the gay poise and the rippling wit of the man of the world. By temperament he is irrepressible and merry; his charm is infectious. His speech runs freely between fancies of exquisite delicacy and the coarser fringe of worldly humour; and he has the sensitiveness of sympathetic fellowship. Such a man, if any at all, might have understood the depth of Romeo's love for Juliet. But the *cameraderie* and the worldly *savoir-faire of* Mercutio give him no inkling of the nature of Romeo's passion. The love of Romeo and Juliet is beyond the ken of their friends; it belongs to a world which is not their world; and so the passing of Romeo and Juliet is not as other deaths are in their impact on our sentiments.

Similarly, too, the Nurse. She is Shakespeare's greatest debt to Broke, in whose poem she plays a curiously unexpected and yet incongruously entertaining part. She is the one great addition which Broke made to the saga. She is garrulous, worldly, coarse, vulgar, and babblingly given to reminiscence stuffed with native animal humour and self-assurance. Shakespeare gladly borrowed her, and so gave his Juliet for her most intimate domestic companion a gross worldly creature who talks much of love and never means anything beyond sensuality. Like Romeo's, Juliet's love is completely unintelligible to the people in her familiar circle. To her nurse, love is animal lust. To her father, who has been a 'mouse-hunter' in his time, and to her mother, it is merely a social institution, a worldly arrangement in a very worldly world. This earth, it would seem, has no place for passion like Romeo's and Juliet's And so, stirred to sympathy by Shakespeare's poetic power, we tolerate, perhaps even approve, their death. At least for the moment.

But tragedy lives not only for its own moment, nor by long 'suspensions of disbelief'. There is the inevitable afterthought and all its 'obstinate questionings'. Our sentiments were but momentarily gratified. And finally our deeper consciousness protests. Shakespeare has but conquered us by a trick: the experiment carries him no nearer to the heart of tragedy.

2. *King John*

For a few years after *Romeo and Juliet*, Shakespeare found greater artistic satisfaction in exercising his genius for comedy. But about the time of *Romeo and Juliet*, there is another 'serious' play, a dramatising of the familiar 'life and death' kind of story, *The Life and Death of King John*. Its structural affinities are more with the tripartite *Henry VI* than with the English historical tragedies; but unlike all these it is not borrowed directly from Holinshed. It is as if even Holinshed was in disfavour on account of his dramatically or at least tragically sterile lures. For its events *King John* relies largely on a play published in 1591 by an anonymous author, *The Troublesome Raigne of John King of England*.[1] This is purely a theatre-piece, a staging

---

[1] References are to Hazlitt's reprint, Shakespeare's Library, vol. v, 1875.

of a string of scenes held loosely together by mere chrono-logical sequence. It is not dramatically organic; its shape lacks the control of an informing dramatic idea. Its events occur; they do not build themselves into that unity of organic plot which has a beginning, a middle and an end. Its author's pre-dominant purpose, indeed, is a political rather than an artistic objective. It is an expression of patriotism rather than of dramatic art; it seeks to arouse and gratify the prevailing nationalist sentiment, reminding Englishmen what fine fellows they were, and how, even when their kings were not too good, they could be trusted to triumph, especially if they remained alert to all the unscrupulous deceits of the papist hierarchy. This, however, is a political sentiment, not an aesthetic one. Yet, as the medium which the author is using is the theatre, some of his subsidiary instruments are conventionally theatrical ones. Within the formlessness of the whole play, there are little groups of scenes held together by one or another traditionally dramatic nexus. There are plotlets within the main plotless sequence: the Hubert-Arthur motive, the Constance-Eleanor antipathy, the rebel baron scenes with their conflicting loyalties to king and country, or to church and state, and so on. But the faint attempt to give dramatic substance to the central opposition of England to France, or of Protestantism to Catholicism is completely in-effectual. John himself is not the victim of a tragic conflict. He dies because history records that he died; he dies in the way in which history says he died, and his death is no artistic *dénouement*, it is just another example of the villainy of the papal regime.

Yet even in a crude piece of theatrical spectacle, there are sporadic appearances of the customary dramatic sanctions. The dying John is given a death-bed confession in which to declare his discovery that death is indeed the wages of sin, and that his own evil-doing has brought him to his ruin.

> Me thinkes I see a cattalogue of sinne,
> Wrote by a fiend in Marble characters,
> The least enough to loose my part in heaven.

> Me thinkes the Divill whispers in mine eares,
> And tels me, tis in vayne to hope for grace,
> I must be damned for Arthurs sodaine death,
> I see I see a thousand men
> Come to accuse me for my wrong on earth,
> And there is none so mercifull a God
> That will forgive the number of my sinnes.
> How have I liv'd, but by anothers losse?
> What have I lovd, but wracke of others weale?
> Where have I vowd, and not infring'd mine oath?
> Where have I done a deede deserving well?
> How, what, when, and where have I bestow'd a day
> That tended not to some notorious ill?
> My life repleat with rage and tyranie,
> Craves little pittie for so strange a death.[1]

In the end the poisoned drink treacherously given to him by a monk causes his death:

> Hath overcome in me weake Natures power,
> And in the faith of Jesu John doth dye.[2]

But this and the other dramatic motives work so arbitrarily and so much at haphazard in the play that in the prologue to his Second Part, the author tries to give them the added stiffening of more oracular utterance:

> The changeles purpose of determinde Fate
> Gives period to our care, or harts content
> When heavens fixt time for this or that hath end
> Nor can earths pomp or policie prevent
> The doome ordained in their secret will.[3]

Shakespeare took over this hotch-potch, and in the main left it in its pristine shapelessness, stringing together intermittently bits of comedy and bits of tragedy in a historical panorama which swerves away from the traditional forms of tragedy and moves vaguely towards the yet undiscovered artistic form of the Shakespearian history play. John himself is even less of a possible tragic hero than is the John of *The Troublesome Raigne*: his weakness is patent, but it is more of the

[1] Hazlitt, p. 315.   [2] *Ibid.* p. 316.   [3] *Ibid.* p. 282.

sinful wickedness of Richard III than of the temperamental and constitutional weakness of Richard II; and it has none of the dramatic magnificence of Richard III's evil. Indeed, John is dethroned from his central position amongst the *dramatis personae*. The hero of the play is England, and not its paltering king. Even in the old play, the person in it who was most apt to hold the audience's attention was Falconbridge the Bastard in the bluff and vulgar John Bullish moments of his otherwise respectable life. But hints of these private and unofficial proclivities helped Shakespeare to give some sort of dramatic coherence both to his figure of Falconbridge and to the play in which Falconbridge was an actor. To whatever extent the plot of Shakespeare's *King John* is the outcome of energies palpably working within it, its course as it runs is fashioned by Falconbridge. The plot is England's well-being; and as far as that well-being is ostensibly promoted in the play, it is the direct result of Falconbridge's presence. Moreover it is incontestably the visible result of Falconbridge's character, his personality, and his outlook on life.

Shakespeare's Falconbridge is not altogether, nor even essentially, the man of *The Troublesome Raigne*. In that play he has the vulgar ranting bonhomie and the rollicking self-assurance of braggadocio. These traits were sufficient to excite Shakespeare to a more consistent piece of characterisation. The old play's Falconbridge has all of a proper gentleman's scruples of conscience, and most of his sentiments about honour. In the old play, it is not Falconbridge, but his degenerate, though legitimate, brother Robert who for his own profit discloses their mother's infidelity; the Bastard himself is reluctant to unrip the shameful slander of his parents:

Please it your Majestie the wrong is mine: yet wil I abide all wrongs, before I once open my mouthe to unrippe the shamefull slaunder of my parents, the dishonour of my selfe, and the wicked dealing of my brother.[1]

[1] Hazlitt, p. 227.

He begs that the legal suit be dismissed lest it should tarnish the honour even of his reputed father. Shakespeare's Falconbridge is unhampered by such scruples. He exults that, whatever may be the reason, he has not the paternal traits of a Falconbridge. He rejoices in his mother's infidelity: 'your fault was not your folly...with all my heart I thank thee for my father':

> And they shall say, when Richard me begot,
> If thou hadst said him nay, it had been sin.[1]

The anonymous dramatist's Falconbridge has to be persuaded by visions and supernatural manifestations that he is Cœur-de-Lion's son:

> Me thinkes I heare a hollow Eccho sound,
> That Philip is the Sonne unto a King:
> The whistling leaves upon the trembling trees,
> Whistle in consort I am Richard's Sonne:
> The bubling murmur of the waters fall
> Records *Philippus Regius filius*:
> Birds in their flight make musicke with their wings,
> Filling the ayre with glorie of my birth:
> Birds, bubbles, leaves, and mountaines, Eccho, all
> Ring in mine eares that I am Richards Sonne.[2]

Even with these preternatural assurances, he is morally disquieted, and seeks escape from his perturbation by begging his mother's decisive affidavit:

> Then Madame thus, your Ladiship sees weil,
> How that my scandall growes by meanes of you,
> In that report hath rumord up and downe,
> I am a bastard, and no Fauconbridge.
> This grose attaint so tilteth on my thoughts,
> Maintaining combat to abridge mine ease,
> That field and towne, and company alone,
> What so I doo, or wheresoere I am,
> I cannot chase the slaunder from my thoughts.
> If it be true, resolve me of my Sire,
> For pardon Madam, if I thinke amisse.[3]

[1] *King John* I. i. 274.
[2] Hazlitt, p. 232.   [3] *Ibid.* p. 234.

When by his mother's confession he has no option but to accept the truth of the rumour, the circumstance redoubles the incentive to dedicate himself to serve a code of honour which the suspicion of royal lineage has imposed on him, but one whose articles are a little perplexing to us:

> Let land and living goe, tis Honors fire
> That makes me sweare King Richard was my Sire.
> Base to a King addes title of more State,
> Than knights begotten, though legittimate.[1]

But Shakespeare's Falconbridge must live his life with different moral compunctions. He will choose a code more immediately profitable to himself, taking his warrant from experience, and in the light of it discounting the authority of approved morality. He forswears conscience, and elects commodity, advantage, as the supreme guide to right living. But the old play's Falconbridge is entirely and even ostentatiously on the side of conscience as sole arbiter of good conduct, except when he is ransacking abbeys at the King's command and revelling in the expectation

> To make some sport among the smooth skin Nunnes.[2]

When the barons rebel, their delinquency is counted by Falconbridge as a sin against the Holy Ghost. He exhorts them in the name of righteousness:

> My Lord of Salsbury, I cannot couch
> My speeches with the needfull words of arte,
> As doth beseeme in such a waightie work,
> But what my conscience and my dutie will,
> I purpose to impart....
> I say tis shame, and worthy all reproofe,
> To wrest such pettie wrongs in tearmes of right,
> Against a King annoynted by the Lord.
> Why Salsburie, admit the wrongs are true,
> Yet subjects may not take in hand revenge,
> And rob the heavens of their proper power,
> Where sitteth he to whom revenge belongs.[3]

[1] Hazlitt, p. 232.   [2] *Ibid.* p. 260.   [3] *Ibid.* pp. 296–7.

But Shakespeare clearly could not fit these moral sentiments into the mind and the personality of his Falconbridge. For his was a man who owed his dramatic vitality to his instinctive intuitions, and the sense they furnished for him in making himself at home in the world. He knows that commodity is a smooth-faced bawd and broker, but it is the guide to mastery of circumstance. So Shakespeare's Falconbridge formally rejects the authority of conscience and dedicates himself to the service of commodity. Moreover, as the action of Shakespeare's *King John* proceeds, it is Falconbridge, prompted naturally by these instincts, and consciously constrained by no higher morality, who sways the course of events to England's advantage. He becomes an embodied pledge of England's greatness to be. In his personality there is, of course, an inarticulated something or other behind all these things: a jovial, secular and very nationalist 'philanthropia'. Yet only once, and then on discovery of Arthur's murder, does he consciously report the marks of conscience within him.

The Falconbridge of Shakespeare's *King John* is carrying Shakespeare towards the form of his distinctive history plays, *Henry IV* and *Henry V*; but it is clearly undermining the traditional sanctions on which dramatists had largely leaned for their tragic systems. It was an additional push to turn him for a while to comedy.

3. *Julius Caesar*

By the turn of the century, when in comedy after comedy Shakespeare's imagination had invigorated itself by creative experiences through the fashioning of man's capability for joy in this world of men, and when it had reached its beatitude in the human kindliness and the gay confidence of *Twelfth Night*, *As You Like It*, and *Much Ado*, Shakespeare's genius was ripe for the return to tragedy. This apparently sudden swerve from comedy to tragedy has excited the speculative fancies of those pseudo-psychological critics who explain the mystery of Shakespeare's art from supposititious entries in that spiritual laundry-book of his which they claim to have divined, and especially in its dirty-linen column. Much wiser people have also looked into the proved facts of Shakespeare's private life to find therein some external and adventitious cause of his return to tragedy, a son's death may be, rather than a vagary of *amour*. But is not the change an intelligible stage in the natural development of Shakespeare's artistic powers and of his poetic insight? There is really no necessity to assume a psychological gap between the mood for comedy and that for tragedy, and then proceed to discover transitional plays to bridge a hypothetical chasm. The so-called 'dark comedies',[1] *Troilus and Cressida, Measure for Measure* and *All's Well*, can most easily be read, not as cynical crypto-tragic comedies preluding the rejection of comedy for tragedy, but as troubled efforts to disperse the clouds temporarily and unexpectedly darkening the full brightness of the author's expanding comic vision, clouds to be completely dispelled when he revelled imaginatively in Illyria and in the forest of Arden. Nor is there sufficient reason for making *Julius Caesar* Shakespeare's way to tragedy.

As a play, of course, *Julius Caesar* has in it elements which might well be material for tragic handling. It deals with the assassination of a world ruler, and it also depicts the undoing of a noble-minded statesman broken by the practical exigencies of his political idealism. But Shakespeare's dramatic mood when he made this Roman matter into a play was not primarily the tragedian's. It was rather the point of view of the dramatist who had found a way of giving dramatic validity to the political material of chronicle-history without constraining it to the patterns of either tragedy or comedy. *Henry IV* and *Henry V* are dramatic inventions, discoveries of a new dramatic form.[2]

---

[1] See H. B. Charlton, *Shakespearian Comedy* (Methuen, 1938) *passim*.

[2] See H. B. Charlton, *Shakespeare Politics and Politicians* (English Association Pamphlets, No. 72).

The plot of them is not mainly planned to excite the dramatic suspense of watching the fate of an individual, as is the plot of comedy and of tragedy. The issues are different. What is primarily at stake is not a man, but a community. The hero is England; and its national well-being is the focal dramatic interest. To provide a true dramatic interest, however, the sequence of events which sustains it must have the compulsion of dramatic necessity. The end must come inevitably from what has gone before. When Shakespeare depicts the growth of England's well-being in his English plays, he must in a dramatist's way give sufficient conviction to the progress of events; he must explicitly or implicitly reveal why it is so and not otherwise. Hence his English history plays are an expression, not of his organised political philosophy (if he ever had one), but of his intuitive apprehension of the political forces which sway the destiny of nations. So far as English history is concerned, his Tudor patriotism led him to see England's greatness as mainly the personal achievement of her great kings. The plays are exhibitions of the qualities of successful kingship, and though his sense of the disparities between political goodness and moral goodness provided him with much suitable matter for drama, it must at the same time have disturbed his simple moral and patriotic nature, for 'your strong possession much more than your right' seems through all the plays to be the recipe for political success. Moreover, England's kings have not always been good at kingship: Shakespeare himself had made dramatic use of the political ravage attending on such bad kings as Richard III and Richard II. But when even a Tudor Englishman surveyed a vaster and much remoter tract of the past, his patriotism was less likely to bias his grasp of its historic and political significance. Rome and Greece were so far away that when their heroes sprang to imaginative life again from the pages of the historians, patriotic sentiments were hardly those which they aroused. They re-enacted a history which permitted a more dispassionate scrutiny and a calmer imaginative apprehension. *Julius Caesar* seems to have provided Shakespeare with some such extension of his political or historical awareness. He had hitherto accepted English history as, under God, a national growth determined largely by the political efficiency of its sovereign. But the wider range of ancient European record did not easily fit into such a system. It prompted the question, did men in fact make history, or did history make men? Renaissance minds were willing to attribute immense capacity to human personality; and the Renaissance stage had shown the mighty emperors of the past in all the impressive majesty of their achievements. Both by the massiveness of his achievements, and because the traits of greatness in his character were authentically recorded, Julius Caesar had been a favourite choice amongst theatrical heroes. But for centuries before Shakespeare, the very greatness of Caesar's success had prompted men to ask how far the very greatest strength of any one individual man could of itself have won for him the empire of the whole known world. In his *Parallel Lives*, Plutarch gives Caesar his full human stature; but in his *Morals*, he cites Caesar as a crucial instance in an argument which propounds that ultimately men owe more to fortune than to the power of their own personality. Plutarch's Elizabethan translator of the *Morals*, Philemon Holland, draws particular attention to Roman history as excellent material from which to deduce a philosophy of history. Thus, introducing Plutarch's essay *On the Romans Fortune* with a summary provided by himself, he writes:

If ever there were any State politike, in the rising, growth and declination whereof, we are to see and acknowledge the admirable providence of God, together with the strength and wisdome of man, certes the Romane empire ought to be set in the formost range.[1]

---

[1] Ph. Holland, *The Philosophie commonlie called The Morals of Plutarch*, 1603, p. 627.

He goes on at once to warn his readers not to expect the true
Christian philosophy of history, for Plutarch was a pagan sage:

The causes of the foundation and advancement of this great Monarchie,
are otherwise considered by those whom the heavenly trueth (revealed
in the holy Scripture) doth illuminate, than by the Pagans and Sages of
this world, guided only by the discourse of their reason, corrupted
with sinne and ignorance of the true God.

In the essay itself Plutarch, possibly slyly enjoying the thought
that his Roman readers would not entirely like and yet could
not resent his analysis of the causes of Rome's greatness, gives
his summary conclusion after a wide survey of Roman history:

The prosperous traine and happy course of their affaires, the violent
streame also, and current of their progresse into such puissance and
growth of greatnesse, sheweth evidently unto those who are able to
discourse with reason, and to judge aright, that this was a thing
conducted neither by the hands nor counsels, ne yet by the affections
of men, but by some heavenly guidance and divine direction, even by
a fore-winde and gale of Fortune blowing at the poupe and hastening
them forward.[1]

Within this rationale of Roman history, Plutarch specifically
includes Julius Caesar as a self-confessed instance:

As for that temple (upon the banke of the river *Tyber*) of Fortune
surnamed *Fortis*, that is to say, Strong, Martiall, Valiant, and Magna-
nimous, for that to her belonged generositie and the forcible power to
tame and overcome all things, they built a temple to the honour of her,
within the orchards and gardens that *Caesar* (by his last will and
testament) bequeathed unto the people of *Rome*; as being persuaded
that himselfe (by the gracious favour of Fortune) became the greatest
man of all the Romans, as himselfe doth testifie. As concerning *Julius
Caesar*, I would have been abashed and ashamed to say, that through
the favour of Fortune he was lifted up to that rare greatnesse, but that
his owne selfe beareth witnesse thereof.... So much perswaded was he,
and confidently assured, that Fortune sailed with him, accompanied
him in all his marches and voiages, assisted him in the campe, aided
him in battell, conducted and directed him in all his warres: whose
worke indeed it was, and could proceed from nothing els but her, to

---

[1] *Ibid.* p. 636. θείᾳ δὲ πομπῇ καὶ πνεύματι Τύχης is Plutarch's
phrase (*Moralia*, Loeb ed., vol. IV, p. 363).

command a calme at sea, to procure faire weather and a Summer season in Winter; to make them swift and nimble, who otherwise were most slow and heavie; to cause them to be couragious, who were greatest cowards and most heartelesse.[1]

Philemon Holland, as an orthodox Elizabethan, would not of course endorse the terminology of Plutarch's philosophy of history. 'Infidels and miscreants, who are not able to comprehend this secret [i.e. that there is nothing accidental in God's universe, all being His direct will] have imagined and set downe for governesses of mans life Fortune and Vertue' [i.e. personal character].[2] But both to Holland and to Plutarch the reading of Roman history suggests similar queries. How did Rome become so great? How much of its greatness was due to Caesar? To what did Caesar owe his own success? These seem, indeed, queries which would arise spontaneously in any reader's mind. Neither Holland nor Plutarch sees the Roman state, as Shakespeare hitherto had mainly seen the state of England, as the product of its ruler's personal genius, though of course both Plutarch and Holland would not deny qualities of immense greatness to Caesar. For both of them, Christian and pagan, the destiny of empire was ordained by something more than human will. As Shakespeare's own translator of Plutarch's *Lives*, Thomas North, has it in the *Life* of Brutus: 'Howbeit the state of Rome (in my opinion) being now brought to that pass, that it could no more abide to be governed by many lords, but required one only absolute governor, God, to prevent Brutus that it should not come to his government',[3] intervened in person in the direct disposal of events so as to secure Brutus' overthrow.

Certainly in Shakespeare's play, Caesar is not shown as the empire-builder controlling the world by the might of his own

---

[1] Holland, p. 631.

[2] *Ibid.* p. 627.

[3] *Plutarch's Lives of Coriolanus, Caesar, etc.* in North's translation (Clarendon Press), p. 157.

personality. On the contrary, for some dramatic reason or other, he is deliberately written down. With Plutarch's portrait before him as he wrote, Shakespeare made his Caesar very different, a Caesar who has been a consummate actor with the forum for his stage and the world for his theatre, but now a ranting shadow of his former self, senile, vainglorious, deaf, timid and superstition-ridden, a very parody of Plutarch's figure. This is no Shakespearian tragic-hero; nor is he even given the space which any hero requires in his own play.

To many, however, Brutus is the tragic centre of the play. Mr G. B. Shaw declared that Shakespeare wrote Caesar down for the technical purpose of writing Brutus up. But though Shakespeare's Brutus is not so degraded from his Plutarchian original as is his Caesar, he is nevertheless set much more on this side idolatry than is Plutarch's. For Brutus was a man after Plutarch's own heart. Brutus had

framed his manners of life by the rules of virtue and study of philosophy, and having employed his wit, which was gentle and constant, in attempting of great things: methinks he was rightly made and framed unto virtue....[1] Being moved with reason and discretion [he] did always incline to that which was good and honest....[2] Brutus...for his virtue and valiantness, was well-beloved of the people and his own, esteemed of noblemen, and hated of no man, not so much as of his enemies: because he was a marvellous lowly and gentle person, noble-minded, and would never be in any rage, nor carried away with pleasure and covetousness, but had ever an upright mind with him, and would never yield to any wrong or injustice, the which was the chiefest cause of his fame, of his rising, and of the good-will that every man bare him: for they were all persuaded that his intent was good.[3]

An Elizabethan, however, would not look with the same philosophic detachment on a man whose actions were those of a Brutus. Rebellion had a different set of implications; assassination, and especially the assassination of a ruler, appeared in a different order of ideas. Hence Shakespeare's Brutus has

---

[1] North, p. 112.
[2] *Ibid.* p. 116.   [3] *Ibid.* p. 138.

puzzled many wise critics. Coleridge was nonplussed by Brutus' speech, 'It must be by his death':

This is singular—at least I do not at present see into Shakespeare's motive, the *rationale*—or in what point he meant Brutus's character to appear. For surely (this I mean is what I say to myself, in my present quantum of insight, only modified by my experience in how many instances I have ripened into a perception of beauties where I had before descried faults), surely nothing can seem more discordant with our historical preconceptions of Brutus, or more *lowering* to the intellect of this Stoico–Platonic tyrannicide, than the tenets here attributed to him, to *him*, the stern Roman republican; viz, that he would have no objection to a king, or to Caesar, a monarch in Rome, would Caesar be as good a monarch as he now seems disposed to be. How too could Brutus say he finds no personal cause; *i.e.* none in Caesar's past conduct as a man? Had he not passed the Rubicon? Entered Rome as a conqueror? Placed his Gauls in the Senate? Shakespeare (it may be said) has not brought these things forward. True! and this is just the ground of my perplexity. What character does Shakespeare mean *his* Brutus to be?[1]

Hudson is similarly confounded:

Upon the supposal that Shakespeare meant Brutus for a wise and good man, the speech seems to me utterly unintelligible. But the Poet, I think, must have regarded him simply as a well-meaning, but conceited and shallow idealist; and such men are always cheating and puffing themselves with the thinnest of sophisms; feeding on air and conceiving themselves inspired; or as Gibbon puts it: mistaking the giddiness of the head for the illumination of the Spirit.[2]

It is indeed difficult to discount entirely the muddle-headedness of Brutus, in spite of our national proclivity to condone the intellectual fuddles of a man whose heart intends good. But even the generous humanity of Shakespeare must have recoiled from a Brutus who desires the proceeds of wrongdoing but upbraids the other man for soiling his hands in getting them for him, as Brutus pharisaically rounds on Cassius when, at the

---

[1] *Coleridge's Shakespearean Criticism*, ed. T. M. Raysor (Constable, 1930), vol. I, p. 16.

[2] H. N. Hudson, cited in Furness, Variorum, *Julius Caesar*, p. 74.

request of Brutus, Cassius has found pay for Brutus' army by an illegal capital levy. There is, too, a suspicion of the Pharisee's smirk in Brutus' ideal recoil from conspiracy at the moment .when he is about to welcome his fellow-conspirators. Neither is his conviction of assured intellectual superiority an engaging trait, when he puts aside the military dispositions of Cassius' more practical strategy. And these are broadly human obstacles to admiration. On the top of them, to Shakespeare, Brutus was politically a regicide in act, if not in name; and his own plea in claiming justifiable homicide was explicitly built on no more than a speculation about what the victim might possibly have aspired to. The victim, too, was one from whom he had himself enjoyed particular favour. Killing, surely, needs more excuse than this; and Brutus' murder of Caesar is a killing which excites faint or overt suspicions of murder, patricide and regicide linked in one dread deed. Even nearer to Shakespeare than are we with our readiness to forgive those who assassinate to bring about a vague sort of enfranchisement was Dante; and Dante on a political and theological rather than a personal and human issue, had no doubt whatever that the place of Brutus in eternity was in the icebound grip of Satan's mouth.

The Brutus of *Julius Caesar* is incapable of moulding the whole play to a tragic pattern. Yet, though he is a character whose organic function is dramatically part of another sort of play, he has traits which may suggest some of the lines along which a hero of tragedy may be built. He is indeed, in some ways, the prototype of Hamlet. But he plays his allotted part in a dramatic organism which is not as Hamlet's is, a universe forced on an imagination which is bent to discover the secret of human tragedy. The clash in Brutus between idealism and a national exigency may provide one example of the insoluble and tragic conflict between time and eternity, the finite and the infinite; and to that extent a Brutus may suggest a Hamlet. Perhap⁚, however, Shakespeare's triumphs in comedy brought him nearer to the apprehension of a tragic universe than did

Julius Caesar. With *As You Like It* and *Twelfth Night*, Shakespeare entered a world wherein the spiritual joys of living in time and space depended on, and were indeed produced by, the way of life of women whose impulses of human kindness or human kindliness were guided by an intuitive common sense which willingly consulted reason but resolutely refused to give it absolute authority. This they had power to do in virtue of that mysterious quality which is called their personality or character, the something or other mysteriously provided for them as the endowment with which they begin the process which humanity recognises as being alive. With Viola, Rosalind and Beatrice this dynamic impulse of personality appears to impel them to actions which are humanly explicable as the result of their having a character in which by some inscrutable and unexplored chance there is a happy harmony in the tripartite attributes of all mortals, an equipoise in the corporate demands of hand and head and heart. Living so, they achieve happiness for themselves and they radiate it amongst their neighbours in time and space. An immediate suggestion is that if the possession of this balance in character is a means of their own and this world's happiness, then the lack of such balance, the pull, for instance, of heart against head, or of hand against heart, would be likely to lead to failure; it would bring unhappiness, it would produce a tragic ending. But there is more than that in the imaginative operativeness of Shakespeare's comic heroines; there is something relating not only to the positive qualities of their character, but to the compelling condition of the world in which they have their being. It is a world in which they are themselves effective creative elements. They make the world to which they belong. It is not a world devoid of inscrutable mysteries; but the mystery is something mysterious within themselves, and not distinct from that outside them. It is the mystery of their own instinct and of its intuitive promptings towards human kindness. The speculative origin of this established phenomenon hardly excites intellectual interest in the watcher, who is enthralled by the spectacle of human beings making a world of human goodness and moulding a morality which enlarges life. Of course, it is an enlargement which may only seem so for a day or two. But Shakespeare's has seemed so for at least three hundred years, has seemed so, too, in that time-span, to many millions of normal human beings. The same millions, however, and at every stage in that time-span, have experienced the tragic possibilities of existence. Like Shakespeare, they have cast about for an ideal universe in which comedy and tragedy are existent side by side in the same intelligible cosmic system. Human nature and its moral substance are the same in Shakespeare's comedies as they are in his tragedies; they are the common material of both. In his comedies, the women are the shapers of their fate; in his tragedies the men are largely the smiths of their own misfortune. Both live in the same sort of world. It is maybe a limited world: it is the human world, the world in which human beings are exerting their conscious and unconscious personality in encounters with the near and the remote environment of circumstance. And their fellows on its nearer orbit are, with the main characters themselves, the more engrossing elements in the scene, especially when the deeds they do are the humanly intelligible outcome of their deliberate will, deliberate, though partly determined by a discourse of reason which accepts mysteries inscrutable yet not unintelligible. The universe of *Hamlet* is not essentially different from the universe of *As You Like It*: they are different continents on the same moral map; and the people in them are generically of the same human kind.

So, at length, whether through the comedies or through *Julius Caesar*, and much more probably and naturally, through both, Shakespeare came to that point in the growth of his genius of which *Hamlet* is the outcome. It is the first great embodiment of his tragic imagination, greater, that is, than such of his tragedies as by common consent are taken to have preceded it. By common consent too, it owes its greatness to the impression of finality with which it invests its hero's inescapable doom. His death is accepted as inevitable, accepted with complete conviction, without cavil or protest, and without subconscious antipathy, by all of us who see it, in spite of, or perhaps because of, our common heritage of *philanthropia* or human kindness. The means by which Shakespeare achieves this impression are, of course, the workings of his poetic genius. Why his genius should have this effect, and how it secures such effect, are closely related aspects of the aesthetic of poetic tragedy; and a speculative answer to each of these problems will gain in validity by the extent to which it is in part an answer to both questions, to the 'why' and to the 'how' Modern fashion is absorbed in exploring one problem, the 'how'. Its scope, in consequence, is almost entirely technical and almost exclusively within the range of verbal techniques. It deals mainly with rhythms, with 'objective correlatives' in diction, and such like; from these, it evolves a sort of symbolic logic of imaginative associations. One of the shortcomings of such a symbolic logic is that it lacks the control of mathematical axioms and of scientific referenda, and is deficient in any kind of syllogistic universality. One man's imaginative sequences are not another's: for each one, the *ultima ratio* is personal, individual and autonomous, and in practice, the findings of our modern critical exponents are markedly different from those of mankind at large. Another shortcoming of the modern critical mode is that it can find no adequate room for the kind of evidence by which the mass of Shakespeare readers has sought to justify its response to his tragic genius, its public and general answer to the 'why' of the problem. In the main, this is what the wide Shakespearian public's frame of mind would seem to be. A Shakespearian tragic ending excites in its onlooker's whole sentient nature an impression of inevitability. He accepts this total response as a fact of his nature. But he is equally conscious of other facts in his nature. He is as aware of his rational as of his aesthetic susceptibilities; aware, too, of an impulse to find the link which will unify these as elements of his own spiritual identity. He seeks corroboration, valid in reason, for events occurring in his aesthetic experience. Only partly can he satisfy his reason as to how Shakespeare's genius forces upon him the conviction of inevitability: under its spell, he does not even guess at the means by which Shakespeare shifts Hamlet from this situation or posture to that. But taking Hamlet intermittently at every moment of his progress, there is no one moment of the course which is incapable of corroborative justification from what survives of man's record as a moral being, that is, from those cumulative repositories in the archives or the arcana of spiritual history, from remembered experience, spontaneous common sense, the sense which man has in common with his fellows, the general lines of written history, the simple forms of vernacular adage and of folk-lore, and the sage observers' books of speculative wisdom. He finds Hamlet's end inevitable because it appears inevitable according to all that seems to have fixed itself through time and in public or general experience as a highest likelihood in the affairs of men. It is a universal inevitability; and the colloquial departure from strict philosophical terminology in phrasing it so, is really part of its higher philosophical validity. It carries a conviction such as that which justifies scientists in formulating what they call law. It has so much certitude that men are moved to follow it as the way in which to realise a larger goodness. It is a state of mind which recognises that within limits the irrational is reasonable. It is *to philanthropon* in action. It is human kindness.

This, it would seem, is the touch of nature which makes all Shakespeare's audience akin throughout the generations and the nations. They find *Hamlet* great, great as poetry, great as tragedy, great as poetic tragedy. The ground for their judgement is, broadly and colloquially, the effect it has on them of truth to life. They are most readily aware of this verisimilitude by recognising psychological truth in the behaviour of the characters of the play; but their awareness grows to include a willing acceptance of freshly apprehended truths which comprise, but go beyond, the established truisms of that which was their world before Shakespeare enlarged its horizons. For this reason, most enquirers into Shakespeare's tragic genius have occupied themselves with his instinct for characterisation, and expositions of his tragedies have been largely given to an analysis of the characters of his tragic heroes.

CHAPTER IV

HAMLET

Ostensibly the plot of *Hamlet* is simple. A son is called upon to kill his father's murderer. The son was wellnigh the perfect pattern of manhood, rich in the qualities which make for excellence in the full life of one who in himself is scholar, soldier and courtier. The murdered father, moreover, was dearly loved, one of so much worthiness that the earth seldom has produced his like. The murderer was not only wicked with the common wickedness of murderers; the man he murdered was his brother, and he took to himself not only the murdered man's crown but also his widow. The situation appears even extravagantly simple. The moment the son hears of the murder, he resolves that with 'wings as swift as meditation, or the thoughts of love' he will sweep to his revenge. There appears to be no reason on earth why he should not, and could not, do it in the next moment. Yet the whole stuff of the play is that he did not and could not do so. He fails until in the end by an unpremeditated stroke, he kills his uncle by his own last human act. Why then did he fail? What is the inevitability of his doom?

He fails because he is himself, Hamlet, and because the particular circumstance which he is called upon to encounter proves itself to be precisely of the sort which a man such as he cannot surmount. It is obvious that even in this statement of the situation there are elements belonging to the mysteries of life which the drama leaves in their own inscrutable darkness. Why, for instance, was Hamlet the sort of man he was, and why did he chance to be born with such an uncle and in times so very much out of joint? These are questions for all who seek a complete metaphysic; but they are neither raised nor answered in the play: they are *data*, even as in the *Iphigenia* of Euripides certain preliminary acceptances of given conditions are, in the view of Aristotle, to be fully approved: 'the fact that the oracle for some reason ordered him [her brother] to go there, is outside the general plan of the play; the purpose, again, of his coming is outside the action proper.'[1] Shakespeare takes it for granted as his starting-point that Hamlet is the sort of man he is, and that he was born to such circumstances as those in which we see him move. Round that smaller orb which engrosses Shakespeare's dramatic genius, his poetic imagination throws the sense of more ultimate mysteries, the speculative possibilities undreamed of by philosophy, and the vast dubieties of 'thoughts which wander through eternity'. But for his human purpose, the play is the thing: and the play is a revelation of how Hamlet, being the man he is, founders on the circumstances which he is called upon to face.

What, then, is there in Hamlet's nature to bring about this disaster? Why does he not kill his uncle forthwith? Teased by the problem, men have propounded many solutions, all of them abstractly possible, and many of them partly warranted by some trait or another in Hamlet's character. Let us look at some of these suggestions.

First of them: Hamlet is clearly a man of fine moral susceptibilities, so exquisite in his sense of right that questions such as that of chastity, and even of the purity of second marriage, touch him profoundly. He is disgusted wellnigh to frenzy by the thought of impurity. Hence, it is held, he was bound to find killing, though the killing of a villain, an immoral deed: still more, he was bound to find the act of killing a loathsome experience from which his sensitiveness would recoil. But though these are qualities commonly associated with to-day's men of fine moral fibre, they are not in themselves, not even now, a necessary adjunct of high morality; how, otherwise, would our war-heroes be fitted into a high moral system? Moreover, the association of these qualities with fineness of

[1] *Poetics* XVII. 3.

soul is of very recent growth: no human sentiment has spread so fruitfully as has the one we call humanitarianism, but its modern form is largely a product of the eighteenth century and after; witness the crusades for penal and social reforms in the last two centuries. In Shakespeare's day, however, a man could be hanged for pilfering, even for wandering without visible means of subsistence. And certainly Hamlet has no squeamishness at the sight of blood, and no abstract compunctions about the taking of life. 'Now could I drink hot blood', he says in one of his passions; and a skilled fencer is no more likely to swoon on seeing blood than is a surgeon. Or hear how he talks about the body of Polonius, a body which would still have been alive had not Hamlet just made it a corpse. 'I'll lug the guts into the neighbour room.' Here, at least, is no anti-vivisectionist's utterance. Nor is Hamlet's mind preoccupied with the sanctity of individual life. He has killed Polonius, not of intent, but by mistake; and Polonius was once to have been his father-in-law. Yet how easily, complacently, and even callously, he puts the incident aside:

> Thou wretched, rash, intruding fool, farewell!
> I took thee for thy better: take thy fortune;
> Thou find'st to be too busy is some danger.[1]

Further, when he plans the death of Rosencrantz and Guildenstern, there is positive gloating in his anticipation of the condign punishment—execution, in fact—which, by his contrivance, is in store for them:

> For 'tis the sport to have the enginer
> Hoist with his own petar: and 't shall go hard
> But I will delve one yard below their mines
> And blow them at the moon.[2]

Perhaps even more incompatible with Hamlet's alleged humanitarian recoil from bloodshed is his soliloquy, as, passing

---

[1] *Hamlet* III. iv. 31.   [2] *Ibid.* III. iv. 206.

by the king at prayer, he contemplates killing him, and then desists:

> Now might I do it pat, now he is praying;
> And now I'll do't. And so he goes to heaven;
> And so am I revenged. That would he scann'd.[1]

To kill the king in such circumstances, he decides, would be to do the king a favour, 'hire and salary', not revenge. And he is eager to defer the killing until its consequences will be fraught with the direst horrors:

> Am I then revenged,
> To take him in the purging of his soul,
> When he is fit and season'd for his passage?
> No!
> Up, sword; and know thou a more horrid hent;
> When he is drunk asleep, or in his rage,
> Or in the incestuous pleasure of his bed;
> At gaming, swearing, or about some act
> That has no relish of salvation in 't;
> Then trip him, that his heels may kick at heaven,
> And that his soul may be as damn'd and black
> As hell, whereto it goes.

In the face of these instances, it would seem wrong to detect modern sentiments and susceptibilities about bloodshed in the constraints which obstruct Hamlet's achievement of his object.

Perhaps the intrusion of a present-day point of view is also responsible for the notion that Hamlet is seriously withheld by a growing feeling of some insufficiency in the evidence on which he has pledged himself to avenge his father's murder. He begins really to distrust the testimony of the ghost, we are asked to believe; and, naturally, the suggestion is easily taken in an age like ours which is eminently sceptical about the supernatural. But does Hamlet ever seriously question the ghost's authenticity and the reliability of its intimations? Nominally he does, of course: but are these genuine doubts or are they

[1] *Hamlet* III. iii. 73.

excuses in the sense that they are his attempts to rationalise his delay after it has occurred?

One thing is certain. When Hamlet sees and listens to the ghost, there is not even the faintest hint of possible deception. He takes the spectre for what it really is, the spirit of his dead father. Moreover, the tale which the ghost tells him fits exactly into his instinctive sense of the wickedness of his uncle. 'O, my prophetic soul, my uncle!' is his immediate conviction of the truth of the ghost's evidence. He does not mean that he suspected his uncle of murder; he means that he has always felt that his uncle was a villain, and now the tale of the murder provides him with particular confirmation. Hamlet's acceptance of the ghost is instantaneous and absolute: and in the relative calm following the exacting encounter, he assures his friends, 'It is an honest ghost'. The first intimation from Hamlet that he is apparently wavering in this confidence comes only after the lapse of considerable time, and therefore when Hamlet must feel self-reproach at his tardiness. The time-lapse is made clear by the introduction of seemingly extraneous incidents. Laertes has gone back to Paris, and Polonius is sending his 'spy' there to see how Laertes is settling down. More striking, there is the dull drawn-out tale of the dispute between Denmark and Norway; a dramatically tedious scene is occupied by the instructions to the emissaries. These envoys have now fulfilled their mission and have returned to Denmark. Some time, therefore, some months, it would seem, have elapsed, and Hamlet's uncle still lives. Hamlet surely must needs justify his delay to his own soul. One can almost watch the plea of distrust in the ghost thrusting itself as an excuse into his mind. Chance has brought the players to the court. As Hamlet meets them, his former intellectual interests immediately reassert themselves: he becomes first-nighter and amateur dramatic critic again. There is green-room talk, and an actor or two is asked to go over a familiar speech. At the end, Hamlet asks the troupe to have ready for the morrow a murder play, into which he will insert some dozen or sixteen lines. Of course, the murder is in his mind, and a few lines easily added to a murder play will sharpen its application and will make the murderer writhe. But there is no hint yet that such writhing is being planned for anything more than to submit a murderer to some of the torments which he deserves. Indeed, the moment the players leave Hamlet, he reproaches himself bitterly for a rogue and peasant slave, since a merely fictitious grief can force a player to more passion than real grief seems able to arouse in Hamlet himself. What, thinks Hamlet, what would such a man do,

> Had he the motive and the cue for passion
> That I have?[1]

That is, he accepts entirely the ghost's tale of his uncle's villainy. Indeed he continues to reprove his inexplicable delay. 'Am I a coward?' and in bitter scorn of his own apparent inaction, he heaps contempt upon himself:

> 'Swounds, I should take it: for it cannot be
> But I am pigeon-liver'd and lack gall
> To make oppression bitter, or ere this
> I should have fatted all the region kites
> With this slave's offal.

In the heat of his searing self-analysis, he repeats the indictment of his uncle with complete conviction:

> bloody, bawdy villain!
> Remorseless, treacherous, lecherous, kindless villain!

It is at that very moment that he first invents a purpose for the play which he has already planned for the morrow. He knows of course, that instead of dabbling in theatricals, he should be sharpening his sword: and so he tells himself—and us—that the play is really a necessary part of his main plot:

> I have heard
> That guilty creatures sitting at a play
> Have by the very cunning of the scene

[1] *Hamlet* II. ii. 587.

Been struck so to the soul that presently
They have proclaimed their malefactions;
For murder, though it have no tongue, will speak
With most miraculous organ. I'll have these players
Play something like the murder of my father
Before mine uncle: I'll observe his looks;
I'll tent him to the quick: if he but blench,
I know my course. The spirit that I have seen
May be the devil: and the devil hath power
To assume a pleasing shape; yea, and perhaps
Out of my weakness and my melancholy,
As he is very potent with such spirits,
Abuses me to damn me: I'll have grounds
More relative than this: the play's the thing,
Wherein I'll catch the conscience of the king.[1]

But the plea is specious, too palpable; it is Hamlet excusing
himself for dissipating his energies and side-tracking his duty,
for the execution of which he had so passionately reiterated the
full and entire grounds a moment before. Moreover, how real
can the need for confirmation of the ghost's story be when,
though the plan to provide it is spectacularly successful, the
success is not followed by the slightest overt move to complete the alleged scheme? 'If he but blench, I know my
course.' But he knew it already; and the additional item of
credit now obtained, like his previous knowledge, leaves him
passive.

Further, if the play within the play was devised by Hamlet to
give him a really necessary confirmation of the ghost's evidence,
why is this the moment he chooses to utter his profoundest
expression of despair, 'To be, or not to be, that is the question'?
For, if his difficulty is what he says it is, this surely is the moment
when the strings are all in his own hands. He has by chance
found an occasion for an appropriate play, and, as the king's
ready acceptance of the invitation to attend shows, he can be
morally certain that the test will take place; and so, if one
supposes him to need confirmation, within a trice he will really

[1] *Ibid.* II. ii. 617.

know. Yet this very situation finds him in the depths of despair. Can he really have needed the play within the play? The point is of some importance, because in the 1603 Quarto of *Hamlet*, this 'To be, or not to be' speech occurs before Hamlet has devised the incriminating play. In the 1604 and later versions, the speech comes where we now read it. I know no more convincing argument that the 1604 Quarto is a master-dramatist's revision of his own first draft of a play.

Characteristic, too, is the nature of his alleged misgivings: they turn on the function and the nature of devils in general— 'the devil hath power to assume a pleasing shape'. But no stretch of words could describe Hamlet's encounter with the ghost as an appointment with 'a pleasing shape'. As we shall see, his account is as philosophically valid and as particularly inept as are so many of his generalisations. The fact is patent. He knew it was an honest ghost; he knew that its tale was true: and, not having fulfilled his promise to act on it, his moral nature could only be contented by plausible excuses.

Similarly one might go over other alleged explanations of Hamlet's inaction. There is the flat suggestion that he was restrained by material difficulties: he did not know how the Danes would look on his uncle's death, and he did not know how he could plan his *coup*. But these need not take up our time. Hamlet could rely on the people's approval of almost anything which he might choose to do; even Laertes had no trouble in rousing their suspicion of the new king. Moreover, no elaborate *coup* was needed; one stroke of the sword was all that was necessary; and, as we have seen, when Hamlet forgoes the opportunity, it is not for fear of the people's disapproval, it is because to kill the king at prayers would despatch him to heaven and not to the hell which he deserves. He never doubted that he had cause and will and strength and means to do it.

More difficult to set aside is the Freudian or the semi- or pseudo-Freudian explanation that a mother- or a sex-complex is the primary cause of Hamlet's delay. But the difficulty is one of terminology, not one of substance. The Elizabethans believed that a man could love his mother without being in love with her or without unconsciously lusting for her. Hamlet's filial love for his mother is certainly a main cause of his estrangement from the people who inhabit the world in which he lives, the world in which he must build his own soul. Certainly, too, her 'o'er hasty' re-marriage shatters the pillars of his moral universe. He has lived in an ideal world, that is, a world fashioned in his own idea, a world in which chastity is a main prop: and when he finds that, of all the women in his world, it is his own mother who seems unaware of this mainstay of the moral order, the structure topples over him. The only way to preserve purity is for womankind to seclude themselves from men: 'get thee to a nunnery'; and Ophelia becomes a potential source of contagion. 'Why wouldst thou be a breeder of sinners?' But sterility is a denial of life; as a moral injunction it is the tragic negation of morality. It is, however, only the young imaginative idealist's intellectual world which is fractured: but so far that is Hamlet's main, if not his only, world.

Consider, for instance, the difference in depth between his first soliloquy, 'O, that this too solid flesh' and the later one, 'To be, or not to be'. Both are contemplations of suicide. But what immeasurable difference between the constraining sanctions! When Hamlet speaks the first soliloquy, all that he knows to his own grief is that his father has died and that his mother has married again o'er-hastily. Neither he nor anybody else has any suspicion that murder, and murder most foul and most unnatural, has been done. His father has died from natural causes. But this death and, still more, his mother's re-marriage, have reduced Hamlet's ideal universe to chaos. His rich and exquisitely sensitive nature, the observed of all observers, has suffered a shock which starts it reeling. A father dead, and untimely dead, though in itself a common experience, may prompt some sceptical scrutiny of divine providence; but worse still, a mother so soon married again seems to reveal an even more immediate despair; for here, not the divine but the human will seems to be working without moral sensibility. Yet the seat of the sorrow is nothing near so deep in human experience as is that which Hamlet utters when later he knows that his father has been murdered by his uncle.

In the first soliloquy, 'O, that this too too solid flesh', Hamlet is not so much actively contemplating suicide as passively longing to be dead. And the respect which makes it unthinkable to resort to self-slaughter is that the Everlasting has set his canon against it. In a way there is something of a pose in Hamlet's gesture: as if a young poet peering into the waters of a pool should long for the eternal quiet of its depths, but should be kept to the bank for fear that the water might be too cold. How much deeper in human nature are the constraints which withhold the Hamlet of the 'To be, or not to be' soliloquy! No merely intellectual recognition of a theological injunction, but a primitive fear of the unknown after-world. 'What dreams may come when we have shuffled off this mortal coil.' The first speech is that of a sensitive soul in spiritual discomfort, the second is that of a man in profound despair. The discovery of the murder of his father by his uncle, of an act of uttermost human sacrilege, drives him to abysses of grief deeper than those occasioned by his mother's frailty. Something more human, more overt and intelligible than the Freudian hypothesis is the main stress of Hamlet's tragic incapacitation.

So far our explorations of the source of Hamlet's doom have been negative; mere statements of the inadequacy of suggested causes of it. But cannot something positive be propounded? Why cannot Hamlet perform the simple and righteous act of killing his uncle? The root of the trouble is generally agreed. He is too much 'sicklied o'er with the pale cast of thought'. That's the respect which makes calamity of life; he thinks too much, and conscience, that is (in the use of the word here), persistent rumination, makes cowards of us all:

> ...some craven scruple
> Of thinking too precisely on the event,
> A thought which, quarter'd, hath but one part wisdom
> And ever three parts coward.[1]

He is, we are told, a philosopher, and the habit of thinking unfits him for the practical needs of doing: and, of course, popular opinion will easily take it that a thinker is a dreamer, and a dreamer is incapable of ready and effective action. But, is this easy assumption sufficient to explain Hamlet's failure? Moreover, if it be true, is it not a proposition which must give us pause, especially those of us who as teachers are mainly bent on encouraging the younger world to think? If thought is but a snare, to what then shall we turn? Thinking, in itself, is surely what we all take to be the world's greatest need: if in itself it is an incapacitating and unpractical activity, then the sooner our schools and our universities are abolished the better.

Nor will it do to say that Hamlet fails, not because he thinks, but because he thinks too much. In one sense, if thought is what will save the world, there cannot be too much of it. In another, if all that is meant is that Hamlet thinks too often, then clearly this is no matter for tragedy: it is merely a question of a revised time-table, more time to be allocated for field sports and other non-intellectual forms of activity.

What is wrong is not that Hamlet thinks or thinks too much or too often, but that his way of thinking frustrates the object of thought. It is the kind of distortion to which cerebration is liable when it is fired by a temperamental emotionalism and guided by an easily excited imagination. The emotion thrusts one factor of the thinker's experience into especial prominence, and the imagination freely builds a speculative universe in which this prominence is a fundamental pillar. Hence, the business of thinking overreaches itself. The mind's function to

[1] *Hamlet* IV. iv. 40

construct an intellectual pattern of reality becomes merely a capacity to build abstract patterns, and the relation of these patterns to reality is misapprehended, if not discounted entirely. In the main, this way of thinking constructs a cosmic picture which only serves to give apparent validity to what the feeling of the person and of the moment makes most immediately significant. But examples will help to make the effect of it apparent. They will be better, because more certainly characteristic of the more normal working of Hamlet's mind, if they are taken from scenes before Hamlet is given the additional shock of discovery that his uncle is a murderer and has murdered his father. There are sufficient of them in his first soliloquy.

The scene of it is worth recalling to establish other qualities of Hamlet which are easily overlooked. He is the hero: and in our backward rumination when we have come to know him, unconsciously we idealise his earlier appearances. But in this first episode, he is not an altogether attractive person. The Court is in session: he is in the royal train, but not a part of it. In manner, in dress and in place, he is staging his contemptuous aloofness from it. He stands apart, taking no share in the social formalities of the occasion, and he draws attention to his aloofness by an extravagant garb of mourning and by excessive display of the conventional gestures of grief. He is swathed in elaborate black: his 'inky cloak', on top of his 'customary suits of solemn black' in full funereal fashion prescribed by the sixteenth-century mortician, his incessantly repeated sighs, his perpetual flow of tears, his fixed deflection of gaze: these are trappings and suits of conventional woe whose emphasis reflects suspicion of insincerity on their wearer, or at least, until a relative judgement is possible, mark him as liable to such suspicion. Nor is this possibility of a Pharisaic isolation weakened by memory of his only other words, his earlier sardonic interjections and his affectedly humorous comments on the king's greeting.

Hence, when he soliloquises, our willingness to sympathise with a son whose father has died and whose mother has hastily married again is suspended by our suspicion of the son's leaning to morbidity. His words appear to justify suspicion to the full:

> O, that this too too solid flesh would melt,
> Thaw and resolve itself into a dew!
> Or that the Everlasting had not fix'd
> His canon 'gainst self-slaughter![1]

We have seen that the utterance of a wish for death in such phrase lacks the convincing urgency of the constraints expressed in the incalculable fears of the 'To be, or not to be' speech. His imagination goes on to explore illimitable stretches of despair; 'weary' and 'stale' and 'flat' and 'unprofitable' are the suggestions by which it deprives the uses of the world of all their value. 'Things rank and gross in nature possess it merely.' Yet the absoluteness of this denunciation prompts our question. Hamlet has hitherto enjoyed a privileged life, and the good things of the world, material and spiritual, have been fully and freely at his disposal: but the passionate sorrow of the moment blots these out of his intellectual picture of the universe. His next remarks let us see how such obliviousness and its consequently distorted sense of reality are natural to Hamlet's mode of speculation. 'But two months dead.' Much will happen to these two months as Hamlet fits them into their place in his scheme of things; the fact that as a lapse of time they are in themselves a part of physical nature, unalterable and absolute, will be completely forgotten. 'That it should come to this': Hamlet's desperate anger heats his mind. 'But two months dead'—an incredibly short span wherein such things should have happened. 'Nay, not so much, not two.' The notion of a real measure of time, and of its unthinkable brevity for such occasion, is caught up by Hamlet's imagination, still further excited by intermitted recollection of the overwhelming difference between the dead husband and his successor, 'Hyperion

[1] *Hamlet* I. ii. 129.

to a satyr'. So the nearly two months is seized by the mind, not as a physical fact, but as a concept of brevity, just as thought habitually converts minutes into moments; and the concept is translated into imaginative symbols which will provide the framework of Hamlet's intellectual cosmology. 'A little month', little, that is, not objectively in relation to other months, but little in relation to the moral idea of propriety. As his imagination lashes his anger, other symbols still further hide the natural measure of a month:

> Or 'ere those shoes were old
> With which she follow'd my poor father's body;

the slip of the time-scheme here is perhaps not easily assessable, since we have no exact information as to how long a queen's shoes are held to be wearable. But the final symbolic expression for this 'little month',

> Ere yet the salt of most unrighteous tears
> Had left the flushing in her galled eyes,

can be estimated more readily, for the world knows how long it takes to remove signs of weeping from the complexion. A month, a real objective month, has been imaginatively caught up and is then imaginatively retranslated into objective reality as an hour. The sequence of ideas and the structure of the argument in the whole speech are symbolic of what Hamlet's mind perpetually does. With the philosopher's genius for intellectual creation, it fashions an image of the universe, but in the fashioning patently distorts fundamental elements of that universe. The world, as his mind builds it, ceases to be a representation of the world as it is.

This very soliloquy includes another striking instance of similar intellectual transformation. As he remembers his mother's lapse, his passion prompts the general condemnation, 'Frailty, thy name is woman'. As far as one knows, Hamlet, of all the women in the world, has known but two, his mother and Ophelia. His mother has unexpectedly proved 'frail', but, in the Elizabethan sense of the word, Ophelia is entirely free of such charge. Yet the generalisation: all women are frail. Again, the mind's picture of life is a distortion of real life, of even so much or so little of it as Hamlet really knew.

This does not mean, of course, that Hamlet's thinking is generally or regularly so prone to fallacious conclusions. His philosophic grasp of much of life's riddle is sure and permanent: and imagination has prompted his discoveries. But when the thought springs from a particular incident which moves his own feelings to new depths, imagination leads his speculations awry. Into the fate of man at large he has a deep and broad view: he holds the macrocosm more securely than the microcosm of his own personal experiences. Hence the magnificent appeal of the most famous of all the speeches in the play, 'To be, or not to be'. Here is a purely philosophical or speculative statement of the general tragedy of man. The problem is a universal, not a particular, one:

> Whether 'tis nobler in the mind to suffer
> The slings and arrows of outrageous fortune,
> Or to take arms against a sea of troubles,
> And by opposing end them?

That is, it is not really a question of whether Hamlet shall commit suicide, but whether all men ought not to do so. For Hamlet is a metaphysician, not a psychologist; he is speculative, but not essentially introspective. The ills of life are the 'heart-ache and the thousand natural shocks that flesh is heir to', all men's flesh, and not Hamlet's in particular. Indeed, when he recites his examples of man's outrageous fortune, there is scarcely one of them by which he himself has been especially afflicted: 'the oppressor's wrong, the proud man's contumely, the insolence of office and the spurns that patient merit of the unworthy take'—these are almost everybody's troubles more than they are Hamlet's: and the 'pangs of despised love' are no part at all of his relation to Ophelia. Naturally, although the whole problem is seen generally and impersonally, Hamlet's own personality affects his sense of relative values. The major ill—'what dreams may come when we have shuffled off this mortal coil'—is only major to such as Hamlet, though even this peculiar sentiment is only a particular form of the universal dread of something after death, something unpredictable in the limitless range of conjectural agonies. How completely Hamlet's mind is engrossed in the general philosophic problem is superbly revealed by the most familiar lines in the whole speech:

> The undiscover'd country from whose bourn
> No traveller returns.

The phrase has dwelt familiarly on the tongues of men as an indubitable miracle of poetic utterance, and such indeed it is. Hamlet is putting into words his sense of the after-world. He fastens on two of the aspects which belong to it in the minds and sentiments of mankind at large, namely, our complete isolation from it, 'from whose bourn no traveller returns', and our entire ignorance of its particular nature, 'the undiscover'd country'. But choosing these as the symbols by which to suggest the after-world he gathers to the general sense a host of other appropriate associations: our intuitive feeling about the after-world is made more conscious and intelligible. The phrase is, in fact, a statement of the after-world which at some, or at many, or at all moments is true for everybody. But the amazing thing is that what makes it impress all of us, its general truth, is a quality which it cannot have for Hamlet. For mankind at large the after-world is the undiscovered country from whose bourn no traveller returns: and the philosopher Hamlet is absorbed in this general truth so completely that he forgets that for him the general truth is a particular error. A traveller *has* returned to him from the after-world, a ghost, the ghost, moreover, of his dead father, to tell a tale setting his hair on end and completely changing the rest of his life. Yet, philosophising, he climbs to the world of ideas, of abstract truths; and forgets for the moment the most outstanding experience in his own life.

This flair of Hamlet's for abstract thinking is perpetually liable to make him momentarily indifferent to the concrete world about him. Another speech spoken before his mind is doubly strained by knowledge of the murder will show us how the natural functioning of his brain works. The situation is exciting. A ghost has been seen by Hamlet's friends. They have informed Hamlet that his father's spirit in arms has twice appeared at midnight. Hamlet is agog with excitement. The three of them plan to be in wait for the ghost: they are here on the battlements at midnight. 'The air bites shrewdly', 'very cold', 'a nipping and an eager air', 'it has struck twelve'—the whole atmosphere is one of strained excited nerves: suddenly, as they peer in hushed expectation, the silence is broken by the blast of cannon. It is a situation not likely, one would think, to soothe nerves on edge. Horatio, normally calmest of men, is rattled: 'What does this mean, my lord?' asking questions more from discomposure than from desire to have repeated what he surely knows. Yet at this very moment, of all moments the most inopportune, unexpected and inappropriate, Hamlet solemnly embarks on a regular professorial disquisition about the nature of habit and its influence on moral character: 'So, oft it chances in particular men': a characteristic academic text from the chair of philosophy. The discourse which ensues is typically philosophic in form. It glances round all the related contingencies, seeking to build them into a generalisation. As tentative propositions are put forward, the philosopher's mind turns momentarily aside to put their implications into line with the general argument. The very syntax of this speech, with its interrupted and broken structure, is Hamlet's brain in action under our eyes. And again he is so enthralled in its operations that when the ghost does appear, his attention to it has to be called, 'Look, my lord, it comes'.

But this abstraction is not in itself ominous. When he does see the ghost, he is fully capable of meeting the situation which is immediately presented, and, despite his friends' fear, he follows the ghost without hesitation. So he hears the terrible story. Murder had been suspected by nobody, not even by Hamlet. Now he finds villainy blacker than he had known, villainy infecting both his mother and his uncle. He dedicates himself passionately and immediately to obey the ghost's call to revenge. Nothing, he says, will ever cause him to forget:

> Remember thee!
> Ay, thou poor ghost, while memory holds a seat
> In this distracted globe.

Yet the words he continues to utter arouse our misgivings: they do not seem part of a promising project for sweeping to revenge with wings as swift as meditation:

> Yea, from the table of my memory
> I'll wipe away all trivial fond records,
> All saws of books, all forms, all pressures past,
> That youth and observation copied there.

He is, of course, talking metaphorically; the 'table of his memory' is the memorandum book, and whilst it is not inappropriate to symbolise memory by such figure, it is disturbing to connect the recollection of the task which Hamlet must perform with the need to jot it down against forgetfulness even in a metaphorical diary. Disturbance grows as the metaphor usurps reality. Hamlet in his excitement is driven by his imagination; its 'table', 'book and volume', have become palpable, and subconsciously Hamlet is impelled to take out his actual notebook:

> My tables,—meet it is I set it down.

The action is ominous, and would be even if Hamlet should set down his determination to kill his uncle within a week. But more ominous is what he does set down:

> That one may smile, and smile, and be a villain;

—a mere truism, given, too, the conventional philosophical safeguard by qualification,

> At least I'm sure it may be so in Denmark.

It is absolutely clear, then, that Hamlet's habit of mind will in some way or another complicate his procedure. His tendency to abstraction, his proneness to let imagination stimulate and direct his intellectual voyagings beyond the reaches of the soul, his liability to set the mind awork before the body takes its appropriate complementary posture: these may recurrently obstruct a ready response in action. But in themselves they will not induce a general paralysis: and, in fact, Hamlet is normally very ready to act. As soon as he has seen the ghost, he is planning a means to kill the king, though, characteristically, his mind is apter to long-term plans than to ready improvisations. He tells his friends that he may perchance find it convenient to put an antic disposition on. But there are other significant occasions when his deeds are those of the quick resolute actor rather than of the halting, undetermined hesitator. When pirates attack the vessel on which he is sailing to England, he is the first to jump aboard as they grapple. On an earlier occasion, when he sees a stirring behind the arras, he draws at once and kills Polonius: and it is no explanation to say that this was purely instinctive, for it is obvious that he has suspected eavesdropping and, presumably, has determined beforehand on the proper response. When, towards the end, he comes on Ophelia's funeral, he acts with almost a madman's precipitancy, and jumps into the grave; and though it is a frenzied display, it is not one of a man whose sinews have atrophied in general paralysis. It is, indeed, a very significant action. It has energy, deliberateness, and the application of force on circumstances in the world about him: and these qualities are what distinguish action from mere reflex activities. But its significance for the tragedy is this: it is the wrong action for the actual world in which Hamlet must live; it is proper only to the ideal world (that is, the picture of the world which he has built in his own mind) in which he now lives without knowing that it is a distorted image of reality. If his ideal world were a valid intellectual projection of the real world, his action would be apt and effective. A crucial illustration of this is provided by his treatment of Ophelia.

Nothing is more difficult to reconcile with our impulse to sympathise with Hamlet than are his dealings with Ophelia. However docile she may be to her father (and that has not always been regarded as a sign of weakness; moreover, she stands up triumphantly to her preachifying brother), she cannot hide her love for Hamlet from us. She is not forthcoming in the way of the modern girl, nor even as naturally wise as Shakespeare's comic heroines. But is this a moral defect? And can anybody suppose for a moment that it justifies Hamlet's abominable treatment of her? It is not so much that he determines to break with her. It is the manner of the breaking. He talks to her, at best, as a salvationist preacher would reprove a woman of the street, and then as a roué who is being cynical with an associate in looseness. His remarks are disgusting and even revolting; they offend because they are preposterously out of place, for Ophelia is in no wise deserving of such ineptitudes. But if frailty (that is, immorality) is woman's name, if Ophelia, because a woman, is therefore necessarily frail, then of course everything fits. The serious advice, 'get thee to a nunnery', is the only way to save the world; and the smut of the wise-cracks in the play-within-the-play scene is a proper garb. But, of course, these hypotheses are pure fiction. They are real only in Hamlet's 'ideal' world, and it is only in that world that his actions would be appropriate. The other and the real world, the one in which he must live and act and succeed or fail, is a different one; and we have seen how Hamlet came to create his ideal world and then to mistake it for a true intellectual projection of the real one.

This, it would appear, is the way of Hamlet's tragedy. His supreme gift for philosophic thought allows him to know the universe better than the little world of which he is bodily a part. But his acts must be in this physical world: and his mind has distorted for him the particular objects of his actual environment. So he cannot act properly within it: or rather, towards those parts of it which the stress of his feeling and the heat of his imagination have made especially liable to intellectual distortion, he cannot oppose the right response. He can kill a Rosencrantz, but not his villainous uncle. Yet though the paralysis is localised at first, it tends to be progressive. The world of action, or the world in which outward act is alone possible, becomes increasingly different from the world as his mind conceives it. Yet the mind increasingly imposes its own picture on him as absolute. The end is despair. The will to act in the one necessary direction is first frustrated and then gradually atrophied. Worst of all, the recognition of the will's impotence is accepted as spiritual resignation; and the resignation is not seen as the moral abnegation, the *gran rifiuto*, which it certainly is; on the contrary, it is phrased as if it were the calm attainment of a higher benignity, whereas it is nothing more than a fatalist's surrender of his personal responsibility. That is the nadir of Hamlet's fall. The temper of Hamlet's converse with Horatio in the graveyard, the placidity of his comments on disinterred bones, his reminiscent ruminations on Yorick's skull, and his assumed hilarity in tracking Alexander's progress till the loam whereto he is converted serves to stop a beer-barrel—these are traits of his final frame of mind and they indicate no ascent to the serenity of philosophic calm. They are only processes which reconcile him to his last stage of failure. His increasing nonchalance, he confesses to Horatio, is really part of his falling off. 'Thou wouldst not think how ill all's here about my heart.' And his gesture of noble defiance is no firm confession of trust in a benign Providence: it is merely the courage of despair:

We defy augury: there's a special providence in the fall of a sparrow.... If it be not now, yet it will come: the readiness is all: since no man has aught of what he leaves, what is't to leave betimes?[1]

[1] *Hamlet* v. ii. 230.

This is absolute abdication: if Hamlet's duty is to be done, Providence will occasion its doing, as indeed Providence does in the heat of the fencing match when chance discloses more villainy, and stings Hamlet into a reflex retaliation. But Hamlet has failed. That is the tragedy.

In his own world, Hamlet, this noble mind, has been o'erthrown. But as he has moved on to his undoing, his generous nature, instinctively averse from all contriving, has linked the whole audience with the general gender in great love and veneration for him. Yet when his doom overtakes him, there is neither from him nor from the audience any cry of resentment; no anger against the gods, no challenging of the providence that shapes our ends. The rest is silence. The play done, however, and the deep impression of it remaining, the mind of man remits this *Hamlet*-experience to the cumulative mass of spiritual data which is piling up within it through every channel and every mode of consciousness. *Hamlet* is added to the vast medley of other imprints which every act of our living stamps on our spiritual retina: and the mind strives to find some clue to a form in the enigma, some shape in an apparent confusion, a pattern which, giving full force to tragedy, will not compel despair.

For instance, under the seeming inevitability of Hamlet's tragic doom, is there not some crucial contributory item whose absoluteness is merely specious? Is Hamlet brought to his end by stresses in his environment which are accidental and factitious? What, in sum, is Hamlet's world? Is it the world known now to all of us, veritably our own world? And if it be his and our common world, are its tragic determinants inherent or are they merely fortuitous accessories?

The outlines of Hamlet's universe are fairly clear, and the dominant imaginative impression of them is the more striking because it is in such marked constrast to the backcloth in front of which Hamlet lives in the first record of his doings, the Hamlet of the twelfth-century Danish historian, Saxo Grammaticus. Shakespeare, of course, did not know Saxo, nor is it necessary to suppose that he knew Saxo's sixteenth-century translator, the French novelist Belleforest, who had started the Renaissance currency of the story. It is practically certain that the English prose version of Belleforest's French text, *The Hystorie of Hamblet* (1608) was written after Shakespeare had written his *Hamlet*.[1] There is the utmost likelihood that Shakespeare's sole source for his story was an Elizabethan play; and it is highly probable that many of the changes in the cultural setting of the story were made by the unknown contemporary of Shakespeare's, the man, perhaps Kyd, who wrote this first Elizabethan *Hamlet* tragedy. The points of scholarship raised by these circumstances, however, are not germane to our immediate argument, which is merely to note the different cultural background against which Saxo's and Shakespeare's Hamlet appear.

The world in which Saxo's Hamlet and Belleforest's lives (though in Belleforest there are very slight and very natural mitigations) is crude, coarse, primitive, uncivilised, fierce and pagan. It is, in fact, almost too crude for the taste of Belleforest's aristocratic clientèle. At least, he writes an apologetic introduction for using such barbarous stuff:

...revenant donc à nostre propos, et recueillans un peu de loing le sujet de nostre dire, faut sçavoir que longtemps au paravant que le Royaume de Dannemarch receut la foy de Jesus, et embrassast la doctrine et saint lavement des Chrestiens, comme le peuple fut assez Barbare et mal civilisé, aussi leurs Princes estoyent cruelz, sans foy ny loyauté, et qui ne jouyent qu'au boute hors, taschans à se getter de leurs sieges, ou de s'offencer, fust en leurs biens ou en l'honneur, et le plus souvent en la vie, n'ayans guere de coustume de mettre à rançon leurs prisonniers, ains les sacrifioyent à la cruelle vengeance, imprimee naturellement en leurs ame.[2]

---

[1] See text of Saxo, Belleforest and *The Hystorie* in Israel Gollancz, *The Sources of Hamlet* (Oxford University Press), 1926.

[2] *Ibid.* p. 178.

In Saxo's and Belleforest's story Hamlet is a far different man
and engages in far different exploits from Shakespeare's Hamlet.
Indeed the exaction of vengeance for a murdered father is
only a part of the original story. The son does, of course,
triumphantly and spectacularly exact vengeance. After doing
so, he goes on to other fierce exploits. He has already secured
a royal wife by inserting an additional demand in the
forged letter which he carries to the king of England as if
from his uncle: it orders, not only the slaughter of the two
messengers who are the prototypes of Rosencrantz and Guildenstern, but the hand of the king's daughter for Hamlet himself.
In due course, the wicked uncle successfully killed, Hamlet
conducts himself as such bold barbarians do. He marries an
additional wife, a queen, too, the queen of Scotland, who is
entranced by the barbaric vigour of his person. So the tale
continues, and in the end it is this second wife (to call her his
bigamous wife would be too modern a term, for bigamy
appears from the tale to be more a matter of taste than of law
or morals) who plays Dalilah and tricks Hamlet into death at
his enemies' hands. Clearly, very little of this world and its
people suggest Shakespeare's Hamlet and the world he lived in.
Even within that part of Saxo's story which covers the incidents
of Shakespeare's play, there are flagrant differences. When the
wicked uncle is seeking the true cause of his nephew's madness,
he devises a plan for using Hamlet's sexual passion to trap him
into disclosure. Saxo's Hamlet is snared by an alluring female;
but he is wise enough to carry her off into the woods so that
whatever he may babble in the excitement of his lust will not
be overheard:

igitur insidiarum suspitione conterritus, quo tutius voto potiretur
exceptam amplexibus foeminam: ad palustre procul invium pro-
trahit: quam etiam peracto concubitu: ne rem cuiquam proderet:
impensius obtestatus est. Pari igitur studio petitum ac promissum est
silentium.[1]

[1] Gollancz, *op. cit.* p. 108.

Belleforest is a little queasy about this incident. He must of course have a girl as the instrument of the uncle's scheme for discovering Hamlet's real sentiments. But he takes advantage of a hint in Saxo. When Saxo says that the woman 'promised silence', he adds 'maximam enim Amletho puellae familiaritem vetus educationis societas conciliabat: quod uterque eosdem infantiae procuratores habuerit'. Belleforest develops this. In his tale, the girl employed by the uncle to entrap Hamlet, though capable enough of 'mignardes caresses et mignotises', and perhaps because of this capability, excites tender sentiments in Hamlet, and becomes herself so much a victim of this amorous circumstance that she tells Hamlet why she has been placed in his way. She had loved him from infancy, and though her confession means sacrificing the love-making which she would have enjoyed, she has determined to confess. Clearly, it is not easy to fit this young girl into the part for which Saxo required a glamorous prostitute. Belleforest did his best, but not quite without incongruities: 'car elle l'aymoit des son enfance, et eust esté bien marie de son desastre et fortune'. So far, that is good enough for a respectable sixteenth-century girl who has to replace a mere *hetaira*, but Belleforest's attempts to increase the evidence of her love for Hamlet are awkward. She would be much distressed by any disaster which should befall him, but was more distressed that the immediate episode was suspended—'bien marie de son desastre et fortune, et plus de sortir de ses mains sans jouyr de celuy qu'elle aimoit plus que soymesme',[1] a trying situation which Belleforest's Elizabethan translator puts into cruder English—'much more to leave his companie without injoying the pleasure of his body, whome shee loved more than herselfe'.[2]

Not only is the Saxo story crude and primitive in its prevailing sexual animalism, but there are many other incidents which seem to belong with the crudities of primitive life. There is much of the clumsy supernaturalism of folk-tale. Sent to

[1] *Ibid.* p. 202.   [2] *Ibid.* p. 203.

England, Hamlet has tricks of wizardry and Mephistophelian diableries in his repertory. Belleforest again feels uneasy about these, and in a muddled sort of way seeks some aesthetic warrant by alleging historic or philosophic excuses:

veu qu'en ce temps là tous ces pays Septentrionaux, estans souz l'obeissance de Sathan, il y avoit une infinité d'enchanteurs....Et ainsi Amleth, vivant son pere, avoit esté endoctriné en celle science, avec laquelle le malin esprit abuse les hommes et advertissoit ce Prince (comme il peut) des choses ja passees. Je n'ay affaire icy de discourir des parties de divination en l'homme....[1]

Perhaps nothing more clearly symbolises the prevailing tone of primitive barbarism than the manner in which Hamlet kills his uncle. He returned unexpectedly from England and presented himself at court.

Hamlets arivall provoked them more to drinke and carouse, the prince himselfe at that time played the butler and a gentleman attending on the tables, not suffering the pots nor goblets to bee empty, whereby hee gave the noble men such store of liquor, that all of them being ful laden with wine and gorged with meate, were constrained to lay themselves downe in the same place where they had supt, so much their sences were dulled, and overcome with the fire of over great drinking (a vice common and familiar among the Almaines, and other nations inhabiting the north parts of the world) which when Hamlet perceiving, and finding so good opportunitie to effect his purpose and bee revenged of his enemies, and by the means to abandon the actions, gestures and apparel of a mad man, occasion so fitly finding his turn and as it were effecting it selfe, failed not to take hold thereof, and seeing those drunken bodies, filled with wine, lying like hogs upon the ground, some sleeping, others vomiting the over great abundance of wine which without measure they had swallowed up, made the hangings about the hall to fall downe and cover them all over; which he nailed to the ground, being boorded, and at the ends thereof he stuck the brands, whereof I spake before, by him sharpned, which served for prickes, binding and tying the hangings in such sort that what force soever they used to loose themselves, it was unpossible to get from under them: and presently he set fire to the foure corners of the hal, in such sort, that all that were as then therein not one escaped

[1] Gollancz, *op. cit.* p. 236.

away, but were forced to purge their sins by fire, and dry up the great aboundance of liquor by them received into their bodies, all of them dying in the inevitable and mercilesse flames of the whot and burning fire: which the prince perceiving, became wise, and knowing that his uncle, before the end of the banquet, had withdrawn himselfe into his chamber, which stood apart from the place where the fire burnt, went thither, and entring into the chamber, layd hand upon the sword of his fathers murtherer, leaving his own in the place, which while he was at the banket some of the courtiers had nailed fast into the scaberd, and going to Fengon [the uncle] said: I wonder, disloyal king, how thou canst sleep heer at thine ease, and al thy pallace is burnt, the fire thereof having burnt the greatest part of thy courtiers and ministers of thy cruelty, and detestable tirannies; and which is more, I cannot imagin how thou shouldst wel assure thy self and thy estate, as now to take thy ease, seeing Hamlet so neer thee armed with the shafts by him prepared long since, and at this present is redy to revenge the traiterous injury by thee done to his lord and father. Fengon, as then knowing the truth of his nephews subtile practise, and hering him speak with stayed mind, and which is more, perceived a sword naked in his hand, which he already lifted up to deprive him of his life, leaped quickly out of the bed, taking holde of Hamlets sworde, that was nayled into the scaberd, which as hee sought to pull out, Hamlet gave him such a blowe upon the chine of the necke, that hee cut his head cleane from his shoulders.[1]

Shakespeare's Hamlet is indeed a different man from Saxo's; he lives among different people, and in a different world. It is a world in which the external structures of society as well as the internal realms of thought and feeling exist on entirely different principles. Broadly speaking, the forms of public life in Shakespeare's *Hamlet* imply a highly developed stage of social organisation. There is a settled monarchical polity, dubious, may be, in the interpretation of its laws of primogeniture and dynastic succession, but nevertheless having its laws. It has, too, a well-evolved machinery of national government and of international diplomacy. Its Privy Council, though not so named, is as instrumental as was Elizabeth's own; it has its politic first minister, most immediate to the king's person,

[1] *Ibid.* pp. 253 *seq.*

and exercising both advisory capacities and the duties of a Lord Chamberlain. It has, too, a traditional machinery for the conduct of foreign affairs: ambassadors, both plenipotentiary and those acting under instructions, with their *aides-memoires* and rescripts in dilated articles of allowance, in fact the full panoply of a diplomatic service. In narrower fields of national custom, it has its established institutions for education, schools and universities which youth frequents in its adolescence. It has traditional practices for further education, either in foreign universities or in continental centres of culture. These social centres, too, are well equipped with the amenities of civilisation. The Paris of Laertes, both to his profit and his hazard, has all the facilities of the modern *quartier latin*, and all the resources of a man-of-the-world's paradise. It is a world of which the culture has so elaborated itself that its danger is the empty formalism of sophistication. The superb worldly wisdom of Polonius is a moral code in which manners and morals are equally significant articles in an ethic of material pragmatism. Speech itself has reached the stage of formal elaboration in which, besides displaying its usefulness in rhetorical dialectic and in politic sophistries, it has become an end in itself, an aesthetic pastime or an ornament of social prestige, like the silks, the three-piled velvets and the ruffs of the courtier. A society like this has inherited the means of corporate cultural entertainment; it has its theatres, public and private, and its elaborate organisation of green-room practice and theatrical economics. It is familiar with the ritual of the fencing school and the refinements of aristocratic horsemanship.

Such is the external world of Shakespeare's *Hamlet*, and the inhabitants of it exhibit its moral counterpart in their habits of thought and feeling. In form, at all events, it is an essentially Christian and Catholic world; it keeps religious festival when 'that season comes wherein our Saviour's birth is celebrated'. It is nominally conscious of a Christian providence dispensed by a divinity that shapes our ends. It has its established church

with full sacramental and liturgical formulary: burial, unless
its rites are maimed in accordance with ecclesiastical law, is
a committal to which no departed mortal should come
'unhousel'd, disappointed, unaneled'. Purgatory lies just beyond the grave, and, yawning ominously beyond that, are the
burning torments of the damned. Conventionally its inward
reminders of sin come from the prick of conscience, those
thorns that in the bosom lodge to prick and sting us. The
conscience-stricken, seeking consolation in prayer, is incapable
of formulating words, for the recognised theological reason
that penitence is hypocritical, if the sinner remains possessed of
his sinful gains. (How different is the king's formally justified
incapacity for praying from Macbeth's psychological inability
to say Amen!) As their religious, so the secular habits of
thought and feeling in Hamlet's world. Discourse of reason is
universally taken by them as the hall-mark which separates
man from beast: and by how much the larger is this discourse of the intellect which looks before and after, pushing
beyond the confines of finitude into infinity in its quest for
the things not yet heard of in philosophy, by so much the
higher is the exercise of man's intellectual faculties. It is
a world habituated to thinking, and its practitioners have
acquired the critical inquisitiveness and the accompanying part
sceptical, part agnostic forms of the modern mind. They are
Montaignes, each in his own small way, believers in general,
but, in detail, acknowledging and striving to answer their
doubts. They are men, like Horatio, who do in part believe
when they have the sensible and true avouch of their own
intellectual faculties. Morally, the trend of their conscious or
unconscious philosophic faith is towards a creed of more or
less humanised rationalism and a code of conduct which is
social rather than religious in its criteria. They are, in fact, men
such as we are. Hence, probably, modern man's choice of
Hamlet as the most humanly pertinent of all Shakespeare's
tragedies. It is the tragic fact seen in the form which it takes in

the whole complex of civilisation as we know it. It may be, however, that this very pertinence arises from features and phases of living which man now possesses by acquisition rather than by essential nature. Hamlet's tragedy may not be as inherently universal as tragedy seeks to be. At all events without Hamlet's highly evolved intellect, mankind would be spared such tragedy as befalls Hamlet himself.

CHAPTER V

OTHELLO

Under the spell of the play, of its people and of its poetry, the audience of *Hamlet* is impressed with the inevitability of Hamlet's end. As an imaginative apprehension, it incorporates itself within the whole stock of our cumulative awarenesses of life. It becomes a spiritual part of the hoarded body of our experience which impels the mind to seek some sign of shape and meaning in the mystery of mortality. The impressive and inescapable weight which imagination gives to the personal pain and to the world's loss in Hamlet's destruction increases the obstinacy of man's questionings of his fate. But perhaps the intellectual acquiescence which is part of our imaginative response to the play may not necessarily justify subsequent intellectual conviction. Or perhaps, if only to find consolation for our own lot, we must look for hints to mitigate the tragic sense of mortal existence. As the individual he is, and in his own particular phenomenal world, Hamlet is inevitably doomed. But is his doom demanded by the inevitable nature of things? May it not be the outcome of qualities and circumstances which are accidental and adventitious rather than of the essence of life itself? If it be not, is it yet essential to the human hope that man must push his moral imperatives till they reach out to the uttermost zenith of human ideals? From another point of view, is the pressure of external circumstance exerted on Hamlet by his external world a factitious or a controllable force, or has it the authority of necessity? We are thrown back on the primary problem. What indeed are the essential elements of human nature? Is man so fixed in spiritual form that he has always been and always must be exposed to the hazard of the tragic power within and without his own nature? Has such tragic liability an absolute universality? Or in the course of man's history, through the force of race, of tradition, of religion and of surrounding circumstance, has mankind assumed from time and place their needless accessory attributes? If he has, are they peculiar to time and place, or indispensable to his inherent nature? Does history warrant a hope that in some such way as this the absolute grip of tragedy may slacken its inevitable strangulation of human happiness? Is the tragic universe, indeed, an artificial structure of man's disordered dreams, an embodied and articulated fear, and not in fact a dispensation eternally invested with the compulsion of necessity? These are the thoughts which hurtle in the brain when *Hamlet* has become a living part of its content.

The next story which laid hold of Shakespeare's imagination, Othello's, brought questionings of this kind into the focus of his imaginative exploration. No doubt the story seized his attention at the outset by the vivid depth and breadth of its immediate human interest. But as his imagination warmed to the recreation of the figures who enacted its incidents, he found himself confronting an imaginative universe in which forces dormant or inactive in *Hamlet* are the operative agents of its tragedy.

Othello is the only one of the four great tragedies which is built on a contemporary novel, contemporary, that is, in the fullest sense, not only put into circulation contemporaneously in the way in which Belleforest gave the *Hamlet* story its currency, but a tale told by a contemporary of Shakespeare's and made up of incidents from their contemporary world. It was a tale which had been told in his *Hecatommithi*[1] by the

---

[1] No Elizabethan translation of Cinthio's story is known. The original Italian was published in 1565 as the seventh story of the third *deca* of *La prima Parte de gli Hecatommithi* di M. Giovanbattista Giraldi Cinthio (appresso Lionard Torrentino, pp. 571–586). A French translation, by Gabriel Chappuys, appeared in *Premier Volume des Cent Excellentes Nouvelles de M. Jean Baptiste Giraldy Cynthien*, Paris, 1584, pp. 323–333. This French version is very scarce. It follows the original

sixteenth-century Italian, Cinthio, novelist, critic and dramatist himself, whose doctrine and practice, as *Romeo and Juliet* led us to discover, inaugurated a determinative movement in the making of Renaissance tragedy. Cinthio urged his contemporaries to seek their dramatic material, not in ancient traditional myth, but in stories steeped in contemporary sentiment and orientated by contemporary outlook, such, for instance, as their modern love-stories were. Although Cinthio himself dramatised some of his own novels, he did not turn his Othello into a play. Yet as a story, it satisfied all the conditions he required in dramatic material. It was a love-story such as might have happened in his own day, and it told of such responsive passions and other motives for behaviour in its people as would strike its readers with the immediate effect of naturalness. It handled a particular problem of immediate contemporary interest, the situation created by the marriage of a man and a woman who are widely different in race, in tradition and in customary way of life. Though Shakespeare probably picked the story up because of the rich promise in it of passionate dramatic interest, his imaginative insight, once excited, pierced beneath the plot and its superficial circumstance to explore whatever essential dramatic substance might lie beneath. His genius sought to discover how far the composite stuff of the story shaped itself into a coherent human world. In the process, his imagination converts Cinthio's melodrama into tragedy.

The first impulse to the process is an instigation from Cinthio himself: for Cinthio made his Desdemona formulate a kind of

---

with a literal fidelity rare in such translations. Its closeness is such that it provides not the slightest clue as to whether Shakespeare had the tale from the Italian or the French. The effective words in the passage from Cinthio cited in our text (p. 116) occur as follows: 'i'ay grāde peur que ie ne donne exemple aux ieunes filles, de ne se marier, contre la volonté de leurs parens, & que les femmes Italiennes n'apprennent de moy, de ne s'accompagner d'homme, que la Nature, le Ciel, & la maniere de vivre rend differens de nous' (p. 329 obv.).

moral to the whole tale. Lamenting the sudden change in Othello's attitude towards her, she unburdens herself to Emilia, telling her that she fears that her example will be cited to posterity for a warning not to marry a man whose nature, race, upbringing, beliefs and mode of life are so different from one's own. Desdemona's words in Cinthio are not quite so amply explicit as that; but what he makes her say seems to require such amplification in a modern English context:

io non sò, che mi dica io del Moro, egli soleva essere verso me tutto amore, hora, da non sò che pochi giorni in quà, è divenuto un'altro; e temo molto di non essere io quella, che dia essempio alle giovani di non maritarsi contra il voler de suoi; e che da me le Donne Italiane imparino, di non si accompagnare con huomo, cui la Natura, e il Cielo, e il modo della vita disgiunge da noi.[1]

'Not to marry a man divided from us by Nature, Heaven and mode of life.'

This hint of Cinthio's is seized by Shakespeare and becomes a main motive in the thematic structure of *Othello*. Brabantio is completely mystified by his daughter's choice: 'for nature so preposterously to err'

> ...in spite of nature,
> Of years, of country, credit, every thing,
> To fall in love with what she fear'd to look on!
> It is a judgement maim'd and most imperfect
> That will confess perfection so could err
> Against all rules of nature.[2]

Iago has the sensualist's explanation of it, and the sensualist's sardonic expectation of the outcome of a union between two such complete opposites as are an erring barbarian and a super-subtle Venetian. Only one result is possible; it conforms so obviously to general truth that the putting of it as a truism will suffice to convince Othello that his wife must be false to him:

> ...as—to be bold with you—
> Not to affect many proposed matches
> Of her own clime, complexion, and degree,

[1] *Hecatommithi*, p. 580. [2] *Othello* I. iii. 96.

Whereto we see in all things nature tends—
Foh! one may smell in such a will most rank,
Foul disproportion, thoughts unnatural.[1]

Shakespeare continues throughout to give far greater prominence to this motive than did Cinthio. In Cinthio, indeed,
it is little more than a moral attached to his novel, and not
really an operative agent in it; it is a circumstance taken for
granted rather than a sequence exhibited as cause and effect.
He seldom recurs to it or to its incidental implications. On one
occasion only he mentions that Othello is black: he lets his
Iago explain to Othello that perhaps Desdemona is pleading
for Cassio's restoration because, finding now that her husband's
blackness is loathsome to her, she seeks consolation in Cassio.[2]
Only one further detail relevant to this racial motive is made
explicit in the Italian version: Desdemona tells her husband
that, like all Moors, he is of such hot nature that mere trifles
stir him to anger and to thoughts of vengeance: 'ma voi Mori
sete di natura tanto caldi, ch'ogni poco di cosa vi move ad ira &
à vendetta.'[3]

Such simple suggestions grew vastly in Shakespeare's imaginative recreation of the story, Othello is the heir of a race and
of a culture alien altogether from the society and the civilisation
of Venice. To the refined social habits and the civil institutions

---

[1] *Ibid.* III. iii. 228.

[2] 'per lo piacere, ch'ella si piglia con lui, qual'hora egli in casa vostra
viene, come colei, à cui già è venuta à noia questa vostra nerezza'
(p. 577). In the French version 'pour le plaisir qu'elle a avec luy,
quand il va en vostre maison, comme celle, qui est déia ennuyée de
vostre taint noir' (p. 327). Whenever in the text above the people of
Cinthio's story are referred to, they are given the names which Shakespeare gave to them. Cinthio gives only Disdemona a personal name.
Othello is simply 'il Moro' and the others have merely occupational
labels, e.g. Iago is 'l'alfiero', Cassio 'il capo di squadra' etc.

[3] p. 576. In the French version (p. 326 obv.): 'mais vous autres
Mores estes naturellement tant chauds, que la moindre chose du
monde vous incite a courroux & vengeance.'

of the Italian world he is a complete alien, an extravagant and wheeling stranger of here and everywhere. Its curled darlings, its manners of obsequious and ceremonial bondage, the elaborate graces of its social discourse, those soft parts of conversation which chamberers have, all these are foreign and unfamiliar to Othello. Its simpler amenities and its customary household comforts are luxuries which he has only come to know in the last nine moons since his military occupation brought him to Venice. Before that, and he is now somewhat declined into the vale of years, the young effects being now in him defunct, his boyhood and his adult life had been lived in the unhoused free condition of the soldier, in the tented field, a flinty and steel couch for his softest bed, inured to all circumstance else that pertains to feats of broil and battle. In his own distant homeland, he had fetched his life and being from men of royal siege, but his royal inheritance was the simple valour of those who have won leadership of men in an altogether more primitive cultural society, men of a race whose country has always been much nearer to the sun and on whose characters the heat of the sun has exercised its influence, distilling and sublimating their fluid humours, and marking them off from other men distinctively by the outward signs of their countenance. For Othello is incontestably black, black with the blackness of a negro, not merely tinted with the sun-tan of the Hollywood sheik. 'Black as mine own face', he says himself; 'for that I am black', he repeats; and Brabantio refers in disgust to his 'sooty bosom'. Neither Coleridge nor Lamb could bring themselves to accept a negroid Othello. Coleridge would grant him a sort of indeterminate blackness, but nothing more negroid. Lamb would not even retain the colour, dissolving its momentary pictorial appearance into the poetic hues of Othello's moral brightness. But Othello is in fact negroid—'thick-lips' he is called. Another of Shakespeare's Moors, Aaron, in *Titus Andronicus*, is called by the Roman Titus 'a coal-black Moor';[1]

[1] *Titus Andronicus* III. iii. 78.

and Aaron himself described a fellow-Moor as a 'thick-lipp'd slave'[1].

Distinctive as his countenance is the soul of the man Othello. Feeling life as a thing to be lived rather than as a succession of experiences to be measured philosophically, his sense of values is built on the worth of those moral qualities which inspire fitting and effective action, and hardly at all on the abstract compatibility of articles comprised in a metaphysical or a religious creed. He has adopted the Christian faith and holds it with unaffected sincerity. To describe the strength of Desdemona's power over him, Iago says that she, and she alone, might even move him to give up his most precious hopes:

> were 't to renounce his baptism,
> All seals and symbols of redeemed sin.[2]

Implicitly he has accepted its essential dogmas. They are links to bind him in longed-for domestic happiness with the entirely Christian Desdemona. He adopts all Christianity's major articles of belief; for instance, belief in the immortality of the soul. It is the worth of man's eternal soul which makes him different from a dog.[3] In the dread solemnity of his putting Desdemona to death, he will destroy her body but not her soul:

> I would not kill thy unprepared spirit;
> No, heaven forfend ! I would not kill thy soul.[4]

But these pronouncements of accepted Christian doctrine spring vitally to his mind only in the stress of agitated feeling, and most often in immediate connection with some crucial action. He holds the threat of everlasting damnation over Iago to compel him to undistorted honesty:

> If thou dost slander her and torture me,
> Never pray more...
> For nothing canst thou to damnation add
> Greater than that.[5]

[1] *Ibid.* IV. ii. 175.　　　　[2] *Othello* II. iii. 348.
[3] *Ibid.* III. iii. 362.　　　　[4] *Ibid.* V. ii. 31.
[5] *Ibid.* III. iii. 368.

What he chiefly finds in Christian practice is an ethical satisfaction, a pattern and an impulse to moral goodness:

> Are we turn'd Turks, and to ourselves do that
> Which heaven hath forbid the Ottomites?
> For Christian shame, put by this barbarous brawl.[1]

But in Othello's simple sincerity, his Christianity is mainly
a gracious demeanour and a habit of noble conduct. When his
innermost being is stirred to its depths, he breaks out into
utterances of a remoter and more mystically articulated religion.
First fully resolved on Desdemona's guilt, he pledges himself
by sacred vow to the terrible act of condign vengeance: but he
does so with gestures and phrases which are dues of the reverence
which belongs better to dim pagan cults than to any form of
Christian worship:

> Even so my bloody thoughts, with violent pace,
> Shall ne'er look back, ne'er ebb to humble love,
> Till that a capable and wide revenge
> Swallow them up. Now, by yond marble heaven,
> In the due reverence of a sacred vow
> I here engage my words.[2]

Iago falls easily into the paganism of the ritual:

> Do not rise yet.
> Witness, you ever-burning lights above,
> You elements that clip us round about,...

committing himself, as they kneel together, to obey Othello,
'What bloody business ever'. Even the culminating scene of
the tragedy, the deed of Desdemona's death, is wrapped about
with a holy atmosphere of solemn sacrifice: but its solemnity
is that of some universal rite, in reverence to the chaste stars,
and belonging to a religion whose sacraments are not those of
a Christian origin. So, too, at the end of the play, in the last
moments of Othello's life, in full realisation of the deception
which has been so destructively practised on him, and in full
consciousness of the enormity of his wrong in slaying his

---

[1] *Othello* ii. iii. 170.   [2] *Ibid.* iii. iii. 457.

innocent wife, he is agonised by piercing anticipations of his fate in an afterworld wherein the Christian elements are confusedly mixed with cruder old-world dreads; and even so, the deepest torment which is filling his mind is the feeling that from now and for ever he is irrevocably cut off from Desdemona's spiritual presence:

> Where should Othello go?
> Now, how dost thou look now? O ill-starr'd wench!
> Pale as thy smock! when we shall meet at compt,
> This look of thine will hurl my soul from heaven,
> And fiends will snatch at it. Cold, cold, my girl!
> Even like thy chastity. O cursed slave!
> Whip me, ye devils,
> From the possession of this heavenly sight!
> Blow me about in winds! roast me in sulphur!
> Wash me in steep-down gulfs of liquid fire!
> O Desdemona! Desdemona! dead!
> Oh! Oh! Oh![1]

Othello's religion is of a parcel with his whole nature. The elements of moral manhood are simple and unadulterated in him, and they exhibit themselves in their primitive purity and strength. He is 'of a constant, loving, noble nature'.[2] His response to life is simpler far than that of more civilised man: living has been for him a continuity of passionate experience and not a series of intellectual states. A spontaneous surge of feeling is the vitalising form of his being. As his instinct rouses feeling, he is compelled to express it in deed. But his nature has prompted him equally powerfully to seek self-mastery in the control of his passionate impulses. He has built for himself a simple moral ideal, and has schooled himself to realise its constraints in habitual practice. He has trained himself in settled habits of control which will act as his safer guides by impeding the onset of his blood as it rushes in to rule. For encounters with most of the incidents of life, this hard-won discipline serves him faithfully. At the very outset, a day of

[1] *Ibid.* v. ii. 271.   [2] *Ibid.* II. i. 298.

unique excitement unexpectedly culminates in distractions of another kind: on his wedding day, summoned at night to an urgent session of the Council, Othello meets in the street the clamour of Brabantio and his armed followers, angrily seeking to lay hold of the black scoundrel who has ruined Brabantio's dutiful daughter. Othello meets him with superbly calm poise and quiet dignity:

> Keep up your bright swords, for the dew will rust them.
> Good signior, you shall more command with years
> Than with your weapons,[1]

an assured calm which he maintains because he knows that he has acquired mastery of his impulses:

> Were it my cue to fight, I should have known it
> Without a prompter.

He has fashioned his moral standard by the same conditions of discipline as those which his military life has taught him to be obligatory:

> Good Michael, look you to the guard to-night:
> Let's teach ourselves that honourable stop,
> Not to outsport discretion.[2]

He has framed himself so that now the fullest happiness is no longer an intense pulsating sensation of vivid feeling, but an all-satisfying supreme emotional contentment:

> O my soul's joy!
> If after every tempest come such calms,
> May the winds blow till they have waken'd death!
> And let the labouring bark climb hills of seas
> Olympus-high and duck again as low
> As hell's from heaven! If it were now to die,
> 'Twere now to be most happy; for I fear,
> My soul hath her content so absolute
> That not another comfort like to this
> Succeeds in unknown fate.[3]

---

[1] *Othello* I. ii. 59.　　[2] *Ibid.* II. iii. 1.　　[3] *Ibid.* II. i. 186.

The spiritual resource of which this moral demeanour is the outward expression is the impulse of his native nobility. He has through life relied hardly at all on the tutelage of intellect. Indeed, whereas his instinct and his nature strengthen themselves in the conflicts of a moral situation, an intellectual dilemma confounds his mind. He has neither faculty nor skill to resolve it. His reason is inadequate for dialectic, and his power of thought is not sufficiently acute to sift the likelihoods of problematic circumstance. He is inexpert in simple intellectual judgement; and the intellectual confusion which such effort induces in him gives further opportunity for his passion to break through its disciplined courses and submerge his whole apprehension. His mind is unequal to his soul. Hence his inevitable predicament:

> No! to be once in doubt
> Is once to be resolved.[1]

But resolutions taken in such manner are neither guided by reason nor directed by moral nobility; they are determined and propelled by the sheer might of passion. Iago knows this and builds his evil schemes on it: he knows Othello's nature, and with consummately audacious artistry, dares to rely on a plot so simple that Othello alone of all mankind is the one man certain to be caught by it.

The downfall of Othello as the tragic hero is the core of Shakespeare's tragedy. But he is a tragic figure in a tragic world, a world which is the disastrous meeting point of two cultural and spiritual traditions. The story of the plot is the story of a marriage; it becomes the tale of a frustrate human effort to link the two worlds together. In the setting divined by Shakespeare's genius as the one most suitable for the dramatic fulfilment of such scenes, the dramatist has at hand a means by which his hero may grow to full tragic stature. To

[1] *Ibid.* III. iii. 179.

those of his readers and audience who are trying to understand his artistic vision, and are therefore seeking to trace the artistic methods which it devises, the particular problem would seem technically to be this. His tragic hero is Othello, a man formed by nature so simply, and in some things (and those the things of the mind) so much behind the men of Shakespeare's day, so obviously gullible in his guilelessness, that he is a perfect woodcock for any sort of simple springe. Such a person promises easy satisfaction of the author's and the audience's demand that his death shall be inevitable. But such a dissolution might easily evoke no greater response than, 'Oh! the pity of it!' Like Richard II's fate, it might well seem lacking in momentousness. It might achieve no more than the logical universality inherent in the pathos of all weakness; and it might fail to engender the imaginative universality of that tragedy of human nobility which is inherent in the best life that man can contemplate as morally ideal. Moreover, in a human as distinct from a technical sense, Othello's tragedy might create no greater perturbation than a mildly pathetic regret at the rigorous law of nature which condemns to extinction the last relics of an outworn world, the inevitable fate of one who is an alien not only to our customs, our habits and our shores, but to the very spirit of our times, another lamentable but familiar example of the evolutionary might which destroys the unadapted survivors of the past. The risk of this becomes greater as Shakespeare is seen plainly emphasising those traits in Othello which alienate him from our culture and from our epoch. But the marriage theme gave to Shakespeare's Othello his opportunity to grow to full tragic significance.

Though in the finished play, Othello's undoing is still mechanically compelled by the flat logic of measured cause and effect, and though it is still apparent to cold reason that so much blind gullibility as was his must destroy its victim, the quality of Othello's love for Desdemona, and of hers for him, is Shakespeare's occasion for exalting the mechanics of mundane causality into the wider and the more mysterious dispensation of human fate at large. The figure of Othello is exalted as the theme is raised to higher imaginative planes. His gullibility recedes as a positive lack which must perforce make him less significant as a man; it takes on the appearance of an obverse reflection of those qualities which are the native nobility of the soul. So the story which was originally an example of lurid domestic melodrama is made anew to become part of sheer poetic tragedy. The sublimation is largely done by Shakespeare's handling of the emotional and spiritual relationship which draws the lovers to each other.

Although to a cursory reader, there is little difference in the early part of Cinthio's story and Shakespeare's version of it, the modifications made by the dramatist even in this preliminary part are vital. One of them is especially important. There is no account of a wooing scene in Cinthio. In a few lines,[1] he tells how a Moor of great merit and courage happened to meet a marvellously beautiful Venetian girl. They fell in love with each other, she drawn to it not by sensual impulse but by the Moor's virtue, and he by the lady's beauty and by the nobility of her mind. They married forthwith, in spite of her parents' opposition. That is all Cinthio tells us about the preliminaries to the marriage. But, both realistically and poetically, Shakespeare felt the need of more substantial information: for the quality of the bond between them was vital to his imaginative

---

[1] 'Fù già in Venetia un Moro, molto valoroso, il quale, per essere prò della persona, & per havere dato segno, nelle cose della guerra di gran prudenza, & di vivace ingegno, era molto caro à que signori, i quali nel dar premio à gli atti vertuosi avanzano quante Republiche fur mai. Avenne, che una virtuosa Donna, di maravigliosa bellezza, Disdemona chiamata, tratta non da appetito donnesco, ma dalla virtù del Moro, s'innamorò di lui. & egli, vinto dalla bellezza, & dal nobile pensiero della Donna similmente di lei si accese, & hebbero tanto favorevole amore, che si congiunsero insieme per matrimonio, anchora che i parenti della Donna facessero ciò che poterono, perche ella altro marito si prendesse, che lui' (p. 572).

apprehension of the facts. Shakespeare's own account of their wooing is given in the play as a statement offered in formal evidence, and as such it is confirmed by both parties to the compact which came out of it. First of all, Othello, in Desdemona's absence, tells his tale to the court of enquiry. It fills out the hint of Cinthio that their mutual magnetism was spiritual and not corporeal in its origin. But before it is recited, Shakespeare has presented forcibly the explanation which the wide experience of men well versed in worldly wisdom would inevitably offer of such a union, whether they spoke as men of approved moral habit or as those who cynically were prone to see the beast emerge in most of the actions of men. One must be fair to Brabantio, and must see his fury as fully righteous wrath. If the modern earl of Westshire's daughter announced her intention to marry the negro general whom she had met at a Red Cross party, his perturbation would be easily understood: as would his frenzied wrath, if she had cut out the intimation and straightway eloped with the man. It is the situation of Desdemona. A daughter has made a gross revolt; she has abandoned duty, beauty, wit and fortune to fly to the gross clasp of a lascivious Moor: and even now, now, this very now, as the news of her flight is brought to him an old black ram is performing the act of his kind with Brabantio's white ewe. Brabantio's astonishment, his incredulity and his wrath are natural responses. It is incredible that his own daughter, 'a maid so tender, fair and happy, so opposite to marriage'[1] that she modestly shunned the company of eligible young men, should have done what will inevitably expose her to general mock by flying to the sooty bosom of a middle-aged and loathsome-seeming negro. To fall in love so is to act in spite of nature, against all rules of nature. Even when, in the light of all the evidence accepted by the Duke, Othello's tale of his courtship is approved as legitimate love-making, the Duke

[1] *Othello* I. ii. 66.

condones the lovers without commending their action. The affair is, in fact, to him a misfortune:

> When remedies are past, the griefs are ended
> By seeing the worst, which late on hopes depended.
> To mourn a mischief that is past and gone
> Is the next way to draw new mischief on.[1]

But this indeed is cold comfort for Brabantio, who is still incapable of squaring the incident with any kind of fitness in the nature of things. For him, there is but one reasonable explanation of Desdemona's infatuation. Othello must have practised on her with foul charms by which the property of youth and maidhood are abused. He has enchanted her delicate youth with drugs and minerals, corrupted her by spells and medicines bought of mountebanks and bound her thus in chains of magic. He has wrought upon her with mixtures potent to induce such vile corruption in the blood. It is plain practice of arts inhibited and out of warrant, rank witchcraft, and sans witchcraft, it could never have occurred. Brabantio is, of course, speaking in perplexity and bitter sorrow. But, let the world calmly review the facts of the case, and his suggested explanation is very probable and palpable to common-sense thinking. And in fact the spell which struck Othello and Desdemona and bound them together was an enchantment. But it was not an operation of black magic with drugs and minerals. These two people, utterly different in race, in age, in appearance, in upbringing, in tradition and in experience, were mysteriously moved to mutual attraction. It is magic: but it is natural magic, the magic of the heart of human beings, the mysterious impulse which is mankind's behaviour in the love of man for woman.

Othello's story of his wooing recreates the scene in which were forged the first links of this spiritual affinity. It reveals the texture of them, and shows how tensile and how penetrating

---

[1] *Ibid.* I. iii. 202.

are the hooks they cast, and how unbreakably tight is their bodiless grip. Their substance is the stuff which has been growing gradually in the hitherto unrealised ideals of two human beings who for the first time are discovering a unique world common to both of them, a world realised in their imagination, and in it they recognise their spiritual likeness to each other. It is a revelation of community in things entirely of the spirit. As Desdemona weaves her entranced sympathy into this imaginative world which the vivid recital of Othello's history has made their mutual meeting-place, a spiritual partnership is struck. They fall in love with each other. The whole thing can be seen in the making in the manner of Othello's retelling of his wooing.

He is cited to give the story as evidence in a formal judicial enquiry. His evidence is an account of what had occurred in the domestic calm of Brabantio's drawing-room. What had happened there was that Othello, admitted to a normal Venetian milieu of social converse, had been led by outer and inner impulse to recall the course of his adventures; having no skill in the usual commonplaces of social talk, his own experiences were all on which he could fall back. As he tells the tale to the court, the feelings of the moment, and the recollection of what he remembered feeling as he had told his story to Desdemona and to Brabantio, and the resurgence of the excitement which the episodes of which he then told once more move within him, all crowd on each other in natural casualness and recover the creative vitality of the wooing-scene. His narrative reproduces a situation and an atmosphere in which, by imaginative sympathy, unguessed and unlikely spiritual affinities are discovered.

He starts in completely assured calm. 'Her father loved me; oft invited me.' The father himself had first felt the spell:

> Still questioned me the story of my life
> From year to year.[1]

[1] *Othello* I. iii. 129.

But as Othello runs over the memory of battles, sieges, fortunes, which have filled his life since his boyhood days, the power of recollected feeling distributes its emphasis over the order and the choice of the things which memory recalls, this or that disastrous chance or moving accident, that hair-breadth escape from just that deadly breach. And the succession of crowded detail remembered suffers an additional diversification from its accompanying associations which had sprung from the inter-mittent presence of Desdemona at its first recital, as she had flitted eagerly from her domestic duties to resume her place in the magic circle: 'Such was the process'; in that way, their love revealed itself:

> My story being done,
> She gave me for my pains a world of sighs:
> She swore, in faith, 'twas strange, 'twas passing strange,
> 'Twas pitiful, 'twas wondrous pitiful,

the timid, innocent Desdemona trying to find the words which in part conceal and in part give way to her agitation as she clutches at phrases permissible both by social propriety and by moral sincerity. Then the half-recoiling and half-welcoming consciousness of the insistent sentiment: 'She wish'd she had not heard it', followed at once by her acceptance of its real import:

> Yet she wish'd
> That heaven had made her such a man,

and then the innocent gaucherie with which in accents between the affected shyness of a husband-hunter and the naïve sincerity of a love-stricken girl, she stammers her sincerity in ambiguous terms:

> She thank'd me,
> And bade me, if I had a friend that loved her,
> I should but teach him how to tell my story,
> And that would woo her.

Even Othello's diffident simplicity caught the meaning:

> Upon this hint I spake;
> She loved me for the dangers I had passed,
> And I loved her that she did pity them.

Desdemona adds her own testimony. To obey the irresistible inner call she adopted every resource, and willingly defied all the conventions which impeded her way to happiness: she loved the Moor, and she loved him to live with him.

That is how Shakespeare's representation of their wooing runs. He makes a dynamic scene out of a situation which Cinthio had recorded inertly in a line or two. The scene was indispensable to Shakespeare's sense of the tragedy inherent in the ensuing situation. The love of his Othello and of his Desdemona was to become a spiritual union of two noble souls. It was the sort of love which might well become an ever-fixed mark to look on tempests and be never shaken. But its worth at the outset is unknown; its potential height is unlimited, but like all other human states, it is subject to the circumstance of time. Thus, time becomes a crucial element in Shakespeare's story of Othello; for it is a story which enacts itself in a world like ours, a world within which temporal circumstance may stifle the fulfilment of spiritual impulse. Our world, the factual world, is subject to time's folly and to its incalculable whimsey; it may refuse the temporal circumstance within which an ideal love such as that of Desdemona and Othello could find fulfilment.

So the element of time is the crucial factor in Shakespeare's transformation of Cinthio's melodrama into his Othello's tragedy. With unobtrusive thoroughness, he completely re-plans Cinthio's calendar, and imposes his own time-scheme on the episodes of the story. In Cinthio's novel, after their marriage Othello and Desdemona lived for some measurable period in settled matrimonial happiness at Venice: 'vissero insieme di sì concorde volere & in tanta tranquillità, mentre furono in Venetia, che mai tra loro non fù non dirò cosa, ma parola men, che amorevole'.[1] In due course, and not by reason of sudden military emergency, Othello was drafted to command the Venetian forces in Cyprus. This distressed him

[1] *Hecatommithi*, p. 572.

because it looked as if the happy domesticity which he was
sharing so delightfully with his wife would be interrupted.
But his fear was overcome, for Desdemona lovingly declared
that she would eagerly risk the hazards of the voyage to accompany him to his new post. They travelled with each other
on the same ship to Cyprus, the whole battalion, commander,
lieutenant, ensign and other ranks embarking together in
orderly transport. In this sizeable interval since the marriage,
Iago had had opportunity to fall lustfully in love with Desdemona, and to hope that in the oncoming months he might
find occasion to gratify his lust; by now, he had begun to
watch for suitable time and circumstance for such occasion:
'per la qual cosa si mise ad aspettare, che il tempo, & il luogo
gli apprisse la via da entrare à così scelerata impresa'.[1] It was
essential to await a propitious opportunity. He knew that,
after settling in Cyprus, Desdemona had grown into the habit
of visiting his wife Emilia at their own house, and of taking
affectionate interest in their three-year-old daughter. It suggested to him the stealing of her handkerchief. Some days
after the theft—'indi ad alquanti giorni'[2]—Desdemona realised
that she had lost her handkerchief. In the meantime Iago was
elaborating his plot. After waiting for an opportune occasion,
he planted the handkerchief in Cassio's room. In his turn,
Cassio, having now fallen into disgrace, was watching for
a suitable time at which to see Desdemona in her house and
to plead for her assistance. Unfortunately his visit coincided
with the unexpected return of Othello, whose suspicions were
increased. Othello determined to wait until he should see Iago,
and to ask Iago to approach Cassio in order to sound him for
information. To make the enquiry look as if it were prompted
by a chance encounter, Iago put off asking it until 'one day'
he ran into Cassio: 'et al Capo di squadra parlò un giorno
costui'.[3] In due course, Iago's report to Othello led to the next
move. One day, after dinner, 'un giorno dopo desinare',

[1] *Hecatommithi*, p. 575.   [2] *Ibid*. p. 578.   [3] *Ibid*. p. 579.

Othello asked Desdemona for the handkerchief. Her reply seemed to confirm his suspicions, whereafter he ruminated night and day to hit on a fitting revenge, 'pensando giorno & notte sopra ciò'.[1] Nursing such thoughts, Othello had to find all sorts of excuses to explain to Desdemona the new demeanour which he was displaying towards her; for his change had distressed her for some days, 'da non sò che pochi giorni in quà'.[1] She took counsel with Emilia, who advised her to adopt a studied habit of affection and sedulously to avoid all cause of suspicion. Whilst she was practising this carefulness, 'in questo mezzo tempo',[2] Othello was still looking for more conclusive proofs of her guilt. He sought out Iago and asked him to find such evidences. Iago had noticed that Cassio had handed the handkerchief to a needlewoman with whom he was familiar so that she could copy its pattern before he returned it. She did her stitching in the daylight which she secured by sitting up to her window, where, of course, she was in view of passers-by. Hence, and again in due course, Othello could pass the window of the house and see the apparently incriminating piece of muslin. He was entirely convinced by the ocular demonstration. He proceeded forthwith to plot with Iago a scheme of vengeance; together they thought out a plan which required a certain amount of preliminary preparation, and, of course, a further stretch of time between the planning and the execution.

That is how the time-scheme of Cinthio's novel ambles on. As a time-element, it is in no way a prominent feature of the story. The narrative proceeds with no particular demand on the calendar, and certainly with no deliberate compression of the tale into incidents which flare up all together in the events of a day or two. Cinthio's telling tacitly assumes that the things of which it tells happened in normal circumstance over an appropriate stretch of time. There were, for instance, the first months of unclouded happiness in wedlock, and then such

[1] *Hecatommithi*, p. 580. [2] *Ibid.* p. 581.

lapse of time—days, weeks, months—as might suggest itself as
a natural span for the incidents which made the plot.

Time is handled far differently in Shakespeare's *Othello*.
There, the time-span is not tied to any measurement of the
Greenwich mean calendar. But sufficiently positive data of
clock-time are put into the play to indicate the scope within
which imagination is imposing its own dramatic chronology.
The fingers on the dial spin furiously, and sequences of action
are geared to fantastic rapidity of motion. The pace is set at
once. The voyage to Cyprus occurs on the very day of the
wedding, and before its consummation. The tragedy follows
in what seems to be but the second day after Cyprus is reached;
and in the interval required for the sea-voyage from Venice to
Cyprus, Othello and Desdemona, unlike Cinthio's, had been
sailing in different ships. The night and day of the Cyprus scene
is an astronomical phenomenon existing only in a stellar universe of the dramatic imagination, the 'double-time' of the
Shakespearian commentators.[1] But the persistent strokes by
which Shakespeare's genius transmutes natural time into the
ideal compass of dramatic moments reveal the circumstances
which Shakespeare's insight had grasped as the compelling
features of Othello's tragedy.

The cumulative effect of this imaginative handling of the
time-lapse is palmary. It gives the sense of inevitability to
a story which otherwise, as in Cinthio, must run on only as
a striking succession of barely credible and but remotely
possible events. It makes the episodes intelligible deeds of
intelligible human beings. In making the characters intelligible,
it discovers in them a nobility of soul which Cinthio never
looked for in Desdemona and of which he luridly deprived
Othello. In thus exalting the moral qualities of his hero and
his heroine, Shakespeare transmuted melodramatic accident
into a universal idea of tragedy. He revealed the tragic fact

---

[1] See especially H. Granville Barker's superb handling of this in his
Prefaces to Shakespeare (Oxford University Press), vol. IV 'Othello'.

within the finer spiritual substance of his imaginative world. Its roots lay neither in extraneous chance, nor even in the terrible malevolence of evil. The handkerchief became but a convenient mode, not an essential instrument. Even Iago serves as no more than a means, not as an indispensable cause of the calamity.

The varied features of this complete sublimation can be more distinctly realised if Cinthio's novel is put in detail side by side with Shakespeare's play, the differences of factual incident noted, and the trend of these differences used as a clue for exploring the unconscious artistic purposes of Shakespeare's genius as it imposed the changes on his material data. Take, for instance, the remaking of the time-scheme. The wooing scene has disclosed the nature and the quality of the links which first bound the lovers together in imaginative and emotional sympathy. They are direct and immediate bonds of the spirit, purely ideal in their nature. Each of the lovers is held by the impassioned idea of what the other is intuitively seen to be: it is the conviction of a bodiless affinity of two souls. But souls on earth dwell only within their bodies: and on earth intuitive revelations seek the sustaining corroboration of slower and more mediate cognition. Love of such ideal kind as that of Desdemona and Othello needs time and occasion to habituate itself to temporal and corporeal domesticity. Their love promises full power to irradiate a lifetime of human wedlock: but it must have opportunity to learn its way amongst the household furniture and the social institutions in the midst of which all human life has its being. The lovers knew each other's soul in its pure essence; but they were ignorant of the temporal and habitual forms in which the other's soul responded characteristically to the particular circumstances of its material environment. They needed to learn to live together in what they must perforce make their actual world. But time forbade. They never lived together, as Cinthio's had done, in the settled mundanities of a domestic household. They were linked by a spiritual chain immensely strong in essence, but frail in work-a-day substance. The exigencies of the world denied them the home in which the spiritual power of their love could have pervasively informed the whole body of its material appurtenances. Their ideal union was not permitted to domesticate itself into wedlock. And thus, remaining an ideal creation in an ideal realm, being entirely a thing of the mind, it was exposed to the onslaught of intangible suggestion; even the slightest hint of taint, and far more, the plausible suspicion of infidelity would blast it entirely. The Desdemona who drew forth the passionate love of Othello was the Desdemona in his mind; it was in his mind that she was to become an angelic-seeming ogre of putrescent flesh. The cause, the cause itself, on which all human goodness depends, demanded her sacrificial murder. Die she must, and at Othello's hands.

Within such an imaginative universe, clearly the inhabitants have become different beings from those of the same name who lived in the physical and mechanical world of Cinthio's novel. His Othello and Shakespeare's belong to entirely different human kinds. The differentiation need not be pursued in continuous detail, since it comes sufficiently into light in all that pertains to the ultimate situation which Shakespeare makes a scene of solemn sacrifice. Contrast the manner in which it is prepared for and enacted in Cinthio. At the very moment when Cinthio's Othello declares his final conviction of Desdemona's infidelity, he resolves to murder her; but, in the very same breath, adds that the way of it must be such that no suspicion of his complicity will arise, 'sì che à lui non fosse data colpa della sua morte'.[1] Othello pondered night and day on

---

[1] *Hecatommithi*, p. 580. In the first edition, there is a possible misprint. It reads 'sì che à lor non fosse', etc. Of course Othello may automatically have thought of himself and the associated conspirators he would need—'lor', therefore. But his French translator took the 'lor' as a misprint for *lui* and translated 'maniere qu'on ne le taxast de leur mort' (p. 329): he may however have been using a later Italian edition, where the word is *lui* and not *lor*.

the most effective contrivance. He decides to kill both his wife and Cassio. He plots with Iago to achieve this, in the first place assigning to Iago the slaughter of Cassio. Iago needs a substantial bribe, 'buona quantità di danari',[1] for he is afraid of the deed and of Cassio's bravery. In the end Iago consents. But he bungles the job and only wounds Cassio. Desdemona, however, is the main object of Othello's vengeance. He confers with Iago, whether her murder shall be by dagger or by poison, 'se di veleno, ò di coltello si devea far morir la Donna'.[2] Iago advises against both schemes; they must find one which will not direct suspicion towards them, 'non se ne haurà sospetto alcuno'. He has a plan to suggest. Othello's house is an old structure whose roof-beams are faulty. Let Desdemona be battered to death by a stocking filled with sand, then displace a beam and let it seem to have fallen on her head and so have killed her. The plot pleased the Moor; 'piacque al Moro il crudel consiglio'.[2]

The whole situation is utterly incongruous with the character of Shakespeare's Othello. The plan is bestial enough, but the manner of its execution drags its perpetrator even deeper into human contempt. Othello watched for a ripe moment for the murder. He secreted Iago one night in a dressing-closet opening on the bridal chamber. When Othello and Desdemona were in bed, Iago made some pre-arranged noise in his hiding place. Othello turned to his wife and asked her if she had heard anything. She replied that she had, and Othello commanded her at once to get out of bed and see what was afoot. 'Hollo sentito, disse ella: levati, soggiunse il Moro, & vedi che cosa è'—a curious code of conjugal chivalry. As she went to the closet door, Iago rushed out and struck her with the sandbag. Almost unable to speak, she managed to call to her husband for help; he then arose from bed, only to tell Desdemona gloatingly that this was proper treatment for a faithless wife. As she lay

[1] *Hecatommithi*, p. 582.
[2] *Ibid.* p. 583.

stunned and prayed mazedly to God, she was struck a second
and a third blow until she was dead. At this, the Moor and Iago
lifted her corpse onto the bed, smashed its skull, and, dislodging
a beam, lowered it down on to the skull. All this carefully
accomplished, Othello rushed into the street and called passers-
by, informing them of the terrible accident which had just
occurred and had deprived him of a dear wife. There is nothing
in this whole episode which could have been done or said by
the Othello who sacrificed his wife with the solemn invocation,
'It is the cause, it is the cause, my soul!',[1] and who performed
the sacrifice with all the dignity of a religious ceremony. The
nearest hint that Cinthio's Othello gets to an expression of
a sentiment more moral than that of naked vengeance is put in
phraseology which belongs rather to the streets than to a temple:
'così si trattano quelle che fingendo di amare i loro Mariti,
pongono loro le corna in capo'.[2]

On such different planes do Shakespeare's Othello and
Cinthio's Moor live: and so, appropriately, they come to their
equally different manner of death. For Shakespeare's Othello,
''tis happiness to die'. He can be nobly spoken of as he nobly
was, 'one that loved not wisely but too well', one who, in
perplexity,

> Like the base Indian, threw a pearl away
> Richer than all his tribe; of one whose subdued eyes
> Albeit unused to the melting mood
> Drop tears as fast as the Arabian trees
> Their medicinal gum.[3]

---

[1] *Othello* v. ii. 1.

[2] *Hecatommithi*, p. 583. There is another phrase in Cinthio which
may remotely have suggested some sort of vague principle behind the
Moor's thirst for revenge. Even so, however, if a principle at all, it is
no more than that of primitive intuition. When Iago has told him
that Cassio is life and soul to her—'essendo colui l'anima sua', Othello
replies, 'Anima sua, eh? Io le trarrò ben'io l'anima del corpo che mi
terrei non essere huomo, senon togliessi dal mondo questa malvagia'
(p. 582).

[3] *Othello* v. ii. 347.

The medicine has purged the soul of its contracted impurity; he dies of his own will no way but this, raining kisses on Desdemona who through his folly can no longer know them his:

> Killing myself, to die upon a kiss.

He was of great heart: and as he passes, all that's spoke by us is marr'd.

But Cinthio's Moor has rightfully another destiny. Though the crime of murdering his wife is so far undisclosed, he sinks into madness through the lack of her presence. He grows to hate Iago, but is afraid to have him put to death, so strict in its enquiry would be the impartial justice of Venice. But he deprives him of his military commission. Iago thereupon discloses something of the crime to Cassio, and in the upshot, Othello is cited before Venetian judges on a capital charge. He is put to torture, but escapes death by the strength of mind which sustains him against proffering a confession of guilt. He was, however, sentenced to long imprisonment and then to perpetual exile. In the course of it, he was slain vendetta-wise by relatives of Desdemona.

Iago is thus in the Italian account the primary and the effective cause of all Othello's trouble. He is first heard of as a member of Othello's regiment when it embarked for Cyprus. Othello had in his company an ensign of charming appearance and manner, but in character the wickedest man who ever lived. He was however very dear to the Moor, for the latter had failed to see every trace of his wickedness; in fact, although the ensign had a most craven spirit, he had managed to cover his badness with such proud bearing and confident speech that he seemed noble as a Hector or an Achilles. Though he was himself married, he forgot all ties both to his wife and to Othello and fell violently in love with Desdemona and gave all his energies to devising a plan whereby he might enjoy her: 'voltò tutto il suo pensiero à vedere, se gli poteva venir fatto di godersi di lei'.[1] But he had to be extremely cautious, lest, discovering his purpose, the Moor should kill him. He tried in every indirect way to make Desdemona understand his passion. But her whole thought was on her husband: the ensign could not excite her interest at all, still less inflame her with desire. Hence he concluded that she must be in love with the lieutenant, and his passion changed from love of Desdemona to the most intense hatred of her. He thought of nothing henceforward except to kill the lieutenant, and, if he could not enjoy Desdemona himself, to prevent Othello from happiness with her. Hence the whole plot: to insinuate against her a charge of adultery.

Shakespeare's conception of Iago is more complex: he is not entirely, even not mainly, actuated by the simple motive of sexual desire. There is his resentment at Cassio's preferment, a motive which does not occur in Cinthio. There is also another feature with which Cinthio's novelistic or anecdotal art had no need to be concerned. In a drama, Iago has to enter the community of the human race. To be an embodied self-consciousness, he has to have his own personality; his separate identity must assert its own autonomy. He can no longer be a merely satanical agent of evil; he must be an artist in his own evil creations. He must enjoy the human emotions which accompany their making. He must have his own aesthetic gratification in their structure and in their form. When Coleridge spoke of Iago's motiveless malignity, he meant that Iago's evil-doing lacked intelligible causality in any rational response to the circumstantial occasion. But Iago's malignity is propelled from within. He acts as he does to satisfy the cravings of his own person and of his own personality. He tries to fashion circumstance to the form in which it will most completely satisfy his own aesthetic and amoral nature. His motive is artistic and not moral. In one crucial episode, however, Shakespeare appears to be deliberately denying to

[1] *Hecatommithi*, p. 574.

Iago opportunity for a piece of craftsmanship which Cinthio had allowed to him. It is the handling of the handkerchief. In Shakespeare, Iago's possession of it is in the first instance an outcome of mere chance. Desdemona happens to drop it unwittingly. In the Italian novel, and traces of this original version survive in Shakespeare's *ex-post-facto* assertions that Iago had urged his wife to steal it for him, Iago foresees a purpose for using the handkerchief, and schemes a plan whereby he may acquire it. Desdemona regularly visits his house and caresses his three-year-old daughter. As one day she is doing so, the baby being pressed to her bosom, he filches the handkerchief from the sash in which she carries it. His later use of it follows a similarly deliberate planning, a planning, too, ever ready to improvise on a chance occurrence, as when he finds that Cassio has loaned it for copying to a needleworker who does her stitching in the full view of passers-by, and can therefore be seen in possession of it by Othello. But the part the handkerchief plays in Shakespeare is different. It falls into Iago's hands by mere chance; Desdemona inadvertently drops it. It just happens to be the particular fact which most effectively serves a purpose which many another casual occurrence might have served in its own way. It is not in itself a first cause. Shakespeare is more concerned with the design of the moral universe than with the material instruments of Iago's technical craftsmanship. His Iago is a consummate master of villainy: but he shows it not so much by subtlety of intrigue as by astuteness in diagnosing the situation and in daring then to put his whole trust in a device appropriate to that occasion, but to that occasion alone, knowing full well that what will infallibly trap Othello would be ineffective against any other man.

Othello's tragedy is Othello's and not the outcome of a chance which made him contemporary with Iago.

CHAPTER VI

MACBETH

With *Macbeth*, the place of evil in the tragic universe thrusts itself once more into the forefront, from which for a time Shakespeare had precluded it. Neither Romeo, nor Brutus (if Brutus is to be seen tragically), nor Hamlet, nor Othello had been primarily impelled towards his tragic lot by plain wickedness within himself. There was, of course, vast and ponderable evil in the world of each one of them. But even as a power outside their own person, it had not ostensibly compelled their tragedy. If, at moments on their way to destruction, these tragic victims commit acts which in themselves seem sinful, the killing of Polonius, for instance, or the sacrifice of Desdemona, such deeds are preserved by the dramatist from all stigma of turpitude. But Macbeth has sin in his soul: his own evil brings about his own doom. On the surface, the situation is exactly similar to that in *Richard III*: it is superficially merely another illustration of the moral truism that the wages of sin is death.

But there is a huge difference. In *Richard III* the ultimate principle is dogmatically assumed: in *Macbeth* its necessity is demonstrated, and the roots of it are revealed in the bare rudiments of human nature. As an all-prevailing moral law, the system appears in *Richard III* with the cosmic appurtenances appropriate to its universal acceptance; it has its heaven and its hell, its God and its Satan. In its temporal world it comprises all the institutions which have emerged through succeeding moments of historic time as man was gradually coming to see and to accept this world of his as a realm swayed by that moral law. It is a society enfolded within a Christian and Catholic church. Its religion has evolved its proper sacerdotal institutions, its rites, its liturgy, its ceremonies and its dogma as an integral part of its spiritual existence. Moreover, within it man himself has achieved the inner faculties requisite to incorporate himself in this spiritual communion. Above all, he knows that within the privacy of his own consciousness some arresting signal is perpetually reminding him of his obligations to the spiritual power of his universe. He is, in fact, consciously possessed of a conscience, and he implicitly accepts the absoluteness of its moral authority. From time to time there are men who will dare to defy its injunctions, as Richard did. The consequence, however, is sure. Richard is broken. But can drama translate that certainty through its own media into the conviction of imaginative inevitability? Moreover, what is this strength in Richard to which drama can demonstrably give vital energy? How can such power be frustrated by an energy tacitly taken to be stronger, but an energy which somehow in *Richard III* drama is unable to vitalise by its own ways? The formal answer is, of course, that Richard's was the strength of original sin. But original sin presupposes that the universe outside the play is the Christian universe which has emerged out of nature's cosmos; it presumes also an after-world for final reckonings: but the final judgement in drama is and must be a judgement to be given here and now. Is there something behind this historic articulation, something in nature itself, the nature of which human nature is a part, which compels man, with an imperativeness of its own, to forms of conduct which are manifestly promoting the well-being or are even sustaining the existence of the human kind? What, in fact, is this arbiter, this guide, this 'conscience', as its name is now reverentially inscribed on the solemn roll of moral statutes? *Macbeth* explores imaginatively and dramatically the operations of the human conscience as it worked in a spiritual epoch before it had been precisely named and before it had been provided with letters-patent variously formulated according to the authority of sectarian synods.

Macbeth the man is different from Hamlet and from Othello

in one prominent respect. He has something of the mind of one, and something of the emotional energy of the other. But he differs from both in this: his moral sense is weaker. The sanctions which it makes him consciously recognise in his own personal world are less ideal and more temporary in their nature: they lack the absoluteness of those which Othello accepts as by direct intuition, and they lack the universality of those towards which Hamlet is for ever reaching. The moral sentiment by which Macbeth is moved is no more than that of a goodness which is slowly emerging through human experience. The inward power by which it operates is not as yet a purely spiritual authority; it is much more actively a corporeal and nervous sensation. Macbeth's conscience is mainly a feeling of fear, and his criteria of goodness are those of a simpler and more primitive morality. By his own acts, his destruction is wrought within the world of man; its necessity springs from roots which grow here, 'but here, upon this bank and shoal of time'; its evil is unnaturalness rather than unrighteousness; it jumps the life to come.

To set the stage for an action like this, Shakespeare provides Macbeth with appropriate environing circumstance. He inhabits a world which strikes us with the effect of an elder age, yet not with the impression of a remotely distant past. It appears like a ruder, simpler epoch preceding but at times surviving into contemporary time. Its trading fleet to Aleppo is only faintly incongruous, and though the good ship Tiger looms up with slightly disturbing modernity, its shipman's cards steer it safely into backward time: even the intrusive jest about new-fangled French hose does not dissipate the predominating imaginative impression. Indeed, the material furnishings of social and domestic life are sparsely represented in the dramatic architecture of the world which Shakespeare makes for Macbeth. In effect, he gives it its appointed place in time by shrouding it in its own peculiar atmosphere, rather than by stuffing it with appropriate archaeological impedimenta.

Its persisting backcloth is the massive masonry of ancient fortress strongholds, surrounded by wind-swept, storm-wracked heaths and vast expanses of wild moorland where rival armies clash in the barbaric fury of hand-to-hand encounter, and brandished steel smokes with bloody execution as it unseams an enemy from the nave unto the chaps. Over it all for the most part is spread the gloom of twilight or the thick blackness of night. Even when momentarily light breaks in, it is but a second's ironically false dawn, or a flash of lightning, or the lurid glow of a witch's cauldron, or the red gleam from the hearth whereat Lady Macbeth spins her evil hopes, or the imagined phosphorescence of a ghost, or the faint flare of a candle moving down dark corridors in a sleepwalker's hand; or still more luridly, the purely imaginative candle which briefly flickers to light humanity on its way to dusty death. But the abiding impression of Macbeth's universe is that of night's predominance. As light thickens, night's black agents to their preys do rouse. Owls shriek, ravens croak, wolves howl and the villainies of nature keep their festival. In the dunnest hell-smoke of black night, murdering ministers throng in their sightless substances to wait on nature's mischiefs. Behind the clamour of the obscure bird, lamentings pierce the air; there are strange screams of death and terrible accents of prophecy. Almost as macabre, and even more terrifying, are other apparitions which hurtle through the upper skies:

> pity, like a naked new-born babe,
> Striding the blast, or heaven's cherubim, horsed
> Upon the sightless couriers of the air.[1]

The winds are drowned with tears; the very earth seems feverish, and its inhabitants are ridden incessantly by their haunting apprehensions.

But the presentation of this scene of earth is in no wise for its independent pictorial quality. It is an integral part of the drama;

[1] *Macbeth* I. vii. 21.

it is a source of its dynamic energy, the dramatic means for giving compulsion to the movement of the action in the play. It resuscitates the forces of nature which are exerting themselves in the men inside the play. It gives their world an imaginative reality for us. It exists for the same purpose as the witches exist. The witches indeed are the quintessence of it. They are the embodied malevolence which bubbles up from nature's earth, roaming the darkness, in thunder, rain and lightning, secret, black, and midnight hags, who hover in the borderland between the natural and the supernatural and fuse the two in the dark mystery of man's universe. It is a mystery into which faint gleams of light are breaking. There is a vague and general sense of a religious dispensation. Behind the play is the shadow of a divinity who is the one God, but a God who is as yet but dimly realised. He is remotely the All-mighty, and men may find in his favour a power to sustain them in their strife against evil:

> In the great hand of God I stand; and thence
> Against the undivulged pretence I fight
> Of treasonous malice.[1]

Human happiness may be secured on earth by virtuous deeds, 'with Him above to ratify the work'. His mercy is supplicated in phrase and form which vaguely foreshadow the Christian way. Men say their prayers, and, in their need, cry out 'God bless us'; and 'Amen' is the antiphonal accompaniment. But all active consciousness of the Christian after-life is kept in even dimmer remoteness. A chance phrase here or there intimates the accepted existence of a heaven and a hell: but neither heaven nor hell is permitted to lay hard hold of men's convictions and thus participate visibly as a motive in their actions. The after-world remains mistily beyond the edges of the known, and exerts no pressure on the minds and the feelings of living men.

> Banquo, thy soul's flight,
> If it find heaven, must find it out to-night.[2]

[1] *Ibid.* II. iii. 137.   [2] *Ibid.* III. i. 141.

The flippancy of the remark is Macbeth's, but the casualness of its suggestion is in keeping with the whole trend of the play. Even when there occur phrases which seem to connote a more deeply penetrating body of Christian sentiment, Shakespeare appears to throw around them a more general and a more indefinite atmosphere. The language in which he wrote was one which had grown in and had built itself into the minds of a Christian community. Its everyday idiom was rich in words whose source or whose associations were with particular features of current faith. But Shakespeare seems frequently to dissolve them into a less tangible sense of poetic generality. He relies at his need on any of the shades of meaning in such a word as 'conscience'. 'Remorse', too, in his text has wide and sometimes strange implications. Most striking is his adaptation of religious phraseology to a purely secular significance or relationship. In the Sonnets, human beauty is 'sacred'; [1] stretches of earthly time are 'holy, antique hours'; [2] his 'dear religious love' of a mortal has stolen 'holy tears' [3] from his eyes; and in *Lucrece*, he invokes 'holy human law'. [4] There is a similarly extended generality in Lady Macbeth's use of 'holily':

> what thou wouldst highly,
> That wouldst thou holily. [5]

In the same way, a memorable phrase of Macbeth's releases itself from the precise limits of direct statement:

> and mine eternal jewel
> Given to the common enemy of man. [6]

This does not put a simple meaning into poetic diction: it uses the poetic suggestiveness of words to intimate a vaster, more general and more intangible range of sentiment. 'Mine eternal jewel' is usually glossed as 'my immortal soul'; but it is nowise

---

[1] *Sonnet* CXV.
[2] *Sonnet* LXVIII.
[3] *Sonnet* XXXI.
[4] *The Rape of Lucrece*, l. 571.
[5] *Macbeth* I. v. 21.
[6] *Ibid.* III. i. 68.

so explicit and precise. One recalls that Cassio called his 'reputation' the 'immortal part' of him, and Iago described 'good name' as the 'immediate jewel of the soul'. By 'mine eternal jewel' and 'the common enemy of man' Macbeth's sense of the corruption of his spiritual nature comprehends all such evil in general, and is not restricted to the diagnostic terminology of any particular school of spiritual pathology.

Encircled by this physical and metaphysical climate, the people of *Macbeth* live according to a simple, rude and primitive moral code. Its sanctions seem to grow directly out of nature and of rudimentary human society. The exigencies of existence compel man to recognise the necessity of goodness; and his criteria of moral values are scaled in an order which corresponds intelligibly to the degrees of urgency with which the elements of his universe impinge on him. The general temper of the prevailing moral consciousness is indicated by the shape which it takes in the peripheral characters of the play, the outlying figures who come in only as agents of the minor mechanisms of the plot and who yet supply the play's universe with its surrounding moral atmosphere. The most noteworthy of these accessory people in *Macbeth* is old Siward. His outlook exemplifies what the world to which he belonged placed first amongst man's moral qualities. After a battle has been fought, he is informed that his son has been killed:

> Your son, my lord, has paid a soldier's debt:
> He only lived but till he was a man;
> The which no sooner had his prowess confirm'd
> In the unshrinking station where he fought,
> But like a man he died.

The old man asks, 'Then he is dead?' and hears the answer:

> Ay, and brought off the field; your cause of sorrow
> Must not be measured by his worth, for then
> It hath no end.

The real test of this appears in Siward's immediate question, 'Had he his hurts before?'. Getting the answer, 'Ay, on the front', he finds joy in his sorrow:

> Why then, God's soldier be he!
> Had I as many sons as I have hairs,
> I would not wish them to a fairer death:
> And so, his knell is knoll'd.[1]

Siward's son has displayed supreme valour—'worthiness', as worth was assessed when valour was the name given to it. To have valour was to have attained high moral excellence; to be acclaimed 'valour's minion', and, of her minions, to be Bellona's very bridegroom, was the highest mark of moral excellence. In such a scale, courage, and unswerving courage against greatest odds, was the measure of man's real worth. Undaunted and undauntable mettle is the stuff which proves the man. In crucial tests the true quality of his manhood is revealed. The Romans called such manhood *virtus*, 'man-ness'. All the western nations have borrowed the label from them, 'virtue', and it stands as the symbol for whatever is regarded as the character of supreme moral worth, the name for that 'which best becomes a man'. When England takes over from foreigners their variant spellings, and writes *virtù* or *vertu*, it is preserving in the labels a verbal reminder of the shifting ideals of human excellence, at one time the sheer personal force of an amoral Renaissance *virtù*, at another the cultured connoisseurship which surrounded itself with art and articles of *vertu* in the seventeenth- and eighteenth-century salons of the *haut monde*. Valour, undaunted bravery, is the virtue of primitive ages, the era of the Homeric epic or of the age of *Beowulf*; it is moving slowly to the discipline out of which in good time *prouesse* appeared to be the better label for it. But it remained the foundation of the virtue which, as valour or prowess or by some other heroic term, continued to be regarded as primary

[1] *Macbeth* v. viii. 39.

in those qualities which best became mankind. In its simpler or in more developed forms, it is demonstrably a quality of highest communal worth at the most crucial times, the times, for instance, when the community's mere existence is exposed to the most dangerous threat, the frequently recurrent times, that is, when massed enemies in arms challenge it in warfare.

Old Siward's measure of human worth, however, is in the play and it is not merely personal to himself. It is a standard of which all its inhabitants are conscious, and which they all adopt as fundamental. Macbeth himself acclaims its supremacy when, suddenly realising that Macduff was no man of woman born, he declares that this has 'cow'd my better part of man'.[1] With the general adoption of such a scale of moral assessment, the least manly characteristics are obviously those of the coward, the craven, the fearful, the man whose shame it is to wear a heart so white. Though only the heroes among men are perpetually immune from fear, those whose very fears have made them traitors may still recover sufficient measure of moral esteem if their last trial finds them capable of courage. The traitor Cawdor confessed his treason and went valiantly to his execution:

> Nothing in his life
> Became him like the leaving it; he died
> As one that had been studied in his death
> To throw away the dearest thing he owed
> As 'twere a careless trifle.[2]

Lady Macbeth knows how searching for this test of human worth is the suggestion of cowardice. The sharpest instrument of reproach which she uses to spur the sides of Macbeth's weakening intent is to accuse him of lack of courage, of fear and cowardice:

> Art thou afeard
> To be the same in thine own act and valour
> As thou art in desire? Wouldst thou have that
> Which thou esteem'st the ornament of life,

---

[1] *Ibid.* v. viii. 18.   [2] *Ibid.* I. iv. 7.

> And live a coward in thine own esteem,
> Letting 'I dare not' wait upon 'I would',
> Like the poor cat i' the adage?[1]

Macbeth's defence of himself accepts the criterion as valid, 'I dare do all that may become a man': for him, too, dauntless courage is supreme virtue. But in his own spiritual sensitiveness he is vaguely aware that other conditions which are comprised amongst those that become a man may properly limit the scope within which bravery can act as an independent determinant. Simple daring must perhaps submit to be overridden by higher moral restraints. He is moving uncertainly from the moral plane of Lady Macbeth to the next higher level of moral perception. In his heart, he half-recognises the superior spiritual sense of Banquo, the intuitive moral insight, the moral wisdom which makes Banquo's a royalty of nature:

> to that dauntless temper of his mind,
> He hath a wisdom that doth guide his valour
> To act in safety.[2]

Macbeth is fully aware, of course, that he is deliberately committing himself to what he knows to be evil. His personal ambition is prompting him for his own selfish ends to acts which are contrary to all accepted codes of right conduct. As he broods over the inward impulses which force themselves into his consciousness and strive to divert him from his purpose, he considers the approved moral values whose sanctions he proposes to defy. In considering them, he reveals what in his innermost nature he regards as the worthiest and most desirable objectives of human life.

These revelations are forced from him especially when his agitation is most strongly strained. They emerge when he is under the stress of resolving on Duncan's murder, and then later when he bitterly discovers what the deed has cost him. In the earlier state of mind, there are certain explicitly moral

---

[1] *Macbeth* I. vii. 39.   [2] *Ibid.* III. i. 52.

considerations which are paralysing his resolution. Duncan is 'here in double-trust': Duncan can properly assume that Macbeth will accept the obligations involved in the relationship of kinsman to kinsman, and of subject to king. Moreover, there is the additional obligation comprised in the duties of hostship. The deed proposed is murder. For the moment Macbeth is not consciously moved by the thought that murder as such is evil, though, as will later appear, he shares with all his contemporaries the sense that murder in itself is, of all things, most 'unnatural', an offence against nature, a 'death to nature'. Apparently, at this moment he will readily defy this particular edict of nature. But there are other and more overt moral principles which he must defy, and it is these which press most insistently on his consciousness. Such, for instance, are the duties of kinship, of loyalty and of hostship. These are rules of conduct which were the compelling obligations of codes which obtained in earlier epochs in the awakening of man's moral sense. Their injunctions have lost their absoluteness in later days, or at least, they are no longer primary and fundamental in later moral systems. The murder of a brother is more revolting than the murder of a stranger, but morally the sin is the same. Obedience to the authority of secular government has also lost almost all trace of absolute sanctity. The duties of hostship even more significantly reveal the level of moral perception which prevails in the people of the play. In earlier civilisations, the bonds of host and guest involved the most stringent moral sanctions; they were amongst the strongest moral compunctions, even the most sacred in their authority. One thinks of the code of hospitality in the Homeric age. One remembers the turpitude with which Euripides invests his Orestes by varying the manner in which Orestes performs that particular act, the slaying of his mother's paramour, which, as Aeschylus had envisaged it, had proceeded with the dignity of a solemn religious deed. One even recalls the tales of travellers in our own days who describe the ceremonial welcome offered to them by modern Arab chieftains. Such reverential hospitality is wellnigh a necessary protecting guardianship in lands where civilisation has not organised extensive systems of communication and of wayside requisites for travellers, or in regions whose political organisation is in countless minor groups of autonomous and hostile lordships. Hospitality is indeed the recognition of one of the earlier injunctions in that body of codified obligation which in *Macbeth* is comprehensively described as the 'humane statutes'[1] which have purged the gentle weal. Another moral regard which weighs heavily with Macbeth is that Duncan

> hath honour'd me of late: and I have bought
> Golden opinions from all sorts of people
> Which would be worn now in their newest gloss,
> Not cast aside so soon.[2]

As a motive, the hope to stand well in the esteem of one's fellows, to be worthy of fame amongst them, is an old-ingrained moral impulse. The desire which had urged men of the ancient world to be worthy of this tribute of fame struck Petrarch as a still mighty instrument to inspire moral excellence. For the ancients, indeed, it had been the 'immortal part' of them, their hope of immortality. One has no need to recall the argument of Browning's *Saul* and of his *Cleon* to realise that the moral incentives which measure their highest object in terms like these are vitally different from the absolute good of Christian morality. Theirs is a goodness which mankind at large is shaping for itself. At various stages or on various levels in his moral enlightenment, man recognises and accepts 'honour', and 'renoun and grace' (where 'grace' is what Duncan's attribute was, the quality which caused men to call him 'gracious', the 'grace' which still formally entitles a monarch to the title of 'gracious majesty'). A closely related moral sense may be seen as the springhead of other codes of 'what becomes a man', from the 'cricket' or 'sport' in a school-

---

[1] *Macbeth* III. iv. 76. [2] *Ibid.* I. vii. 32.

boy's vocabulary of honour, to the 'good form' and 'decency' of polite society. Macbeth, so his wife tells us, would not play false, but yet would wrongly win.

But it is not the power of any or of all these moral prohibitions which weighs as the heaviest deterrent in Macbeth's mind. It is something more immediate and direct: it is the even-handedness of human justice, the thought of the temporal consequences of the projected deed. 'We still have judgement here.'[1] His crime will but teach bloody instructions which, being taught, return to plague the inventor. The murder is not certain to bring after it the earthly success which it seeks. On the contrary, it may call on to Macbeth the dread punishment which mankind visits on such malefactors. In men's esteem, Duncan worthily stands high: his murder will inflame public antagonism against Macbeth as a vile outrager of their common sense of right. It is especially this last regard which stirs Macbeth to the deepest awareness of what his fearful lot may be, and heats his imagination to forecast the most lurid terrors which may immediately await him:

> this Duncan
> Hath borne his faculties so meek, hath been
> So clear in his great office, that his virtues
> Will plead like angels, trumpet-tongued, against
> The deep damnation of his taking-off;
> And pity, like a naked new-born babe,
> Striding the blast, or heaven's cherubim, horsed
> Upon the sightless couriers of the air,
> Shall blow the horrid deed in every eye,
> That tears shall drown the wind.[2]

These are the terrors which fill his apprehension; but they are fears of what may happen to him here and now, upon this bank and shoal of time. They are not, as their phrases, torn from their context, might seem to betoken, the penalties reserved for future suffering in the depths of Hell. Shakespeare has commandeered the theological engines of divine wrath to

[1] *Ibid.* I. vii. 8.　　　　[2] *Ibid.* I. vii. 16.

participate with other sources of imaginative energy in realising the torment of Macbeth's mind. For Macbeth's Hell, like that of Marlowe's Mephistopheles, and even at times that of Milton's Satan, is here and now in his own mind and in earth's own time.

In spite of all his premonitions of agony, however, Macbeth's ambition overcomes all his moral scruples. He murders Duncan. The deed done, retribution starts. Throughout the later stretches of the play, he endures its toll: and at moments he tells us his sense of the price he is paying. He has lost all that makes living worth-while, all the real ornaments of life:

> And that which should accompany old age,
> As honour, love, obedience, troops of friends,
> I must not look to have.[1]

In these words, he is expressing his inmost conviction of the nature of moral value, and it accords with the ideals which he had recognised and put aside at the bidding of his ambition. The measure of this moral excellence is worthiness to earn the esteem and the veneration of one's fellows. But by his acts he has forefeited these, and finds   in their stead,

> Curses, not loud but deep, mouth-honour, breath,
> Which the poor heart would fain deny, and dare not.

That is the bitterest penalty of wickedness, its direct and immediate torment. Its pangs empty life of all that is worth having:

> There's nothing serious in mortality:
> All is but toys: renown and grace is dead;
> The wine of life is drawn, and the mere lees
> Is left this vault to brag of.[2]

This is how Macbeth speaks to Ross and Lennox when the murder of Duncan is discovered; and of course, there is a certain degree of hypocrisy in Macbeth's attitude. He is attempting to deceive them and to prevent suspicion from

---

[1] *Macbeth* v. iii. 24.   [2] *Ibid.* ii. iii. 98.

falling upon himself. But though the gesture of desolation he assumes is a piece of dissimulation, the words in which he puts it are an indication of what he takes the values of life to be.

So much for the general moral structure of Macbeth's world Shakespeare's dramatisation resuscitates the vital processes of it, revivifies its men and women as creative human beings, whose deeds and whose destiny are being shaped again under our very eyes. He liberates as dynamic energies the peculiar force of each of its people and watches the inevitable outcome as these powers hurtle amongst the countless other elements which together make the life of humanity an organic universe. Shakespeare is pre-eminently concerned with Macbeth as a personality expressing itself in action, and he is mainly occupied in realising the springs of these acts.

The bare record which he takes as his raw material he found once more in Holinshed. But once more Holinshed is interested chiefly in the telling of the deeds with merely superficial remarks about the motives which produced them; and also, of course, with the traditional explanation of them as further illustrations of the dispensation of providence. Holinshed gives to Shakespeare the main traits of Macbeth's personality and the main sequence of the incidents of Macbeth's life. But in one significant episode, particularly significant for his purpose, Shakespeare supplements Holinshed's record of Macbeth by bringing into it details of a similar episode in which another of Holinshed's Scottish kings had been involved. The chronicler records that Macbeth coveted the crown, and how

the woords of the three weird sisters also (of whom before ye have heard) greatlie incouraged him hereunto, but speciallie his wife lay sore upon him to attempt the thing, as she that was verie ambitious, burning in unquenchable desire to beare the name of a queene. At length therefore [as the record forthwith and summarily puts it], communicating his purposed intent with his trustie friends, amongst whome Banquho was the chiefest, upon confidence of their promised aid, he slue the king at Enverns [Inverness].[1]

[1] Boswell Stone, *Shakspere's Holinshed* (1896), p. 25.

That is all that is told of the murder. But Shakespeare wanted to see more of the inward stirrings within the murderer, the promptings which preceded the murder and the reactions as the deed itself was being performed. He found material which he could employ in another chapter of the chronicle, where Holinshed tells of another Scottish regicide, Donwald, who slew King Duff, and, like Macbeth, had been goaded to the murder 'through setting on of his wife'.[1] This Donwald felt that the king had slighted his family, and so

conceived such an inward malice towards the king (though he shewed it not outwardlie at the first) that the same continued still boiling in his stomach, and ceased not, till through setting on of his wife, and in revenge of such unthankfulnesse, hee found meanes to murther the king within the foresaid castell of Fores where he used to soiourne. [King Duff] oftentimes used to lodge in his house [Donwald's castle at Forres] without anie gard about him, other than the garrison of the castell which was wholie at his [Donwald's] commandement.

So Donwald's wife 'ceassed not to travell with him', and counselled him to make Duff away, showing him 'the meanes wherby he might soonest accomplish it'.

Donwald thus being the more kindled in wrath by the words of his wife, determined to follow hir advise in the execution of so heinous an act. Wherupon devising with himselfe for a while, which way hee might best accomplish his cursed intent, at length gat opportunitie.

On the last day of the king's stay with them, when he had retired 'into his privie chamber, onelie with two of his chamberlains, who having brought him to bed, came foorth againe', Donwald and his wife 'had prepared diverse delicate dishes and sundrie sorts of drinks for their reare supper or collation'; they invited the chamberlains to the 'banketting',

whereat they sate up so long, till they had charged their stomachs with such full gorges that their heads were no sooner got to the pillow, but

---

[1] Boswell Stone, *Shakspere's Holinshed* (1896), p. 27. The rest of the citations of Holinshed in this chapter are from Boswell Stone.

asleepe they were so fast, that a man might have remooved the chamber over them, sooner than to have awaked them out of their droonken sleepe.

This was Donwald's opportunity, though he had not cast himself to be the actual murderer.

Then Donwald, though he abhorred the act greatlie in heart, yet through instigation of his wife hee called foure of his servants whom he had made privie to his wicked intent before... [and they] speedilie going about the murther...secretlie cut his [the king's] throte as he lay sleeping, without anie buskling at all.

They disposed of the corpse according to an arranged plan. Meanwhile

Donwald, about the time that the murther was in dooing, got him amongst them that kept the watch, and so continued in companie with them all the residue of the night. But in the morning when the noise was raised in the king's chamber how the king was slaine... he with the watch ran thither as though he had knowne nothing of the matter, and breaking into the chamber...he foorthwith slue the chamberleins, as guiltie of that heinous murther.

Here, clearly, is an account of an act of regicide which Shakespeare could easily fit into his *Macbeth*: its facts fill out the detail of incident which Holinshed had not attached to his Macbeth story, and, still more, it suggests lines of enquiry into the murderer's motive. Donwald had some grounds for resentment; his wife fostered and nourished them; he himself 'abhorred the act greatlie in heart', and he planned for the deed itself to be done by suborned assassins. The whole situation is charged with promptings to stir Shakespeare's imagination to those psychological explorations which reproduced his own Macbeth.

Holinshed's Macbeth is hardly harassed at all by inner perturbations and doubts. He is a natural leader 'of such valiant and hardie men of warre as the Scots were': 'he was a valiant gentleman and one that if he had not beene somewhat cruell of nature, might have beene thought most worthie the

government of a realme'. He complained bitterly against
Duncan's 'softnes and overmuch slacknesse in punishing
offendors'. When, at the king's request, he took charge of
a punitive expedition against rebels who also regarded Duncan
as 'a faint-hearted milkesop, more meet to governe a sort of
idle monks in some cloister' than to rule a kingdom, he was
utterly ruthless, 'remitting no peece of his cruel nature' in the
barbarous measures he employed. Returning with Banquo
from a later expedition in which he had 'made such slaughter
on all sides without anie resistance that it was a woonderfull
matter to behold', he met 'three women in strange and wild
apparell, resembling creatures of elder world', and heard their
prophecies. In reply to Banquo's questioning after their
prophesying, the first of the witches answered Banquo:

Yes, we promise greater benefits unto thee than unto him, for he shall
reigne in deed, but with an unluckie end, neither shall he leave anie
issue behind him to succeed in his place, where contrarilie thou in deed
shalt not reigne at all, but of thee those shall be borne which shall
governe the Scotish kingdome by long order of continuall descent.

When two of these prophecies had come true,

Mackbeth revolving the thing in his mind, began even then to devise
how he might atteine to the kingdome: but yet he thought with
himself that he must tarie a time, which should advance him thereto
(by the divine providence) as it had come to passe in his former
preferment.

There is a complacent resignation to the Almighty's rule in
this, which is utterly different from the self-cowed inertia of
Macbeth's:

If chance will have me king, why, chance may crown me
Without my stir.[1]

But shortly afterwards, Duncan promoted his elder son
Malcolm prince of Cumberland 'as it were thereby to appoint
him his successor in the kingdome'. Macbeth was sore troubled

---

[1] *Macbeth* I. iii. 143.

by this—and apparently it would seem to have been an attempt to forestall the old laws of the realm, which barred succession to a minor. So regarding this as a 'just quarell', and encouraged by the words of the witches, and still more pushed on by his wife's ambition, he murdered Duncan. He was confirmed in the kingship, and for some years ruled diligently and well, suppressing evil-doers, causing 'young men to exercise themselves in vertuous maners, and men of the church to attend their divine service according to their vocations', so that, in sum, the country enjoyed 'the blisseful benefit of good peace and tranquilitie'.

To be briefe such were the woorthie dooings and princelie acts of this Mackbeth in the administration of the realme, that if he had atteined thereunto by rightfull means, and continued in uprightnesse of justice as he began, till the end of his reigne, he might well have beene numbred amongest the most noble princes that anie where had reigned....But this was but a counterfet zeale of equitie shewed by him, partlie against his naturall inclination, to purchase thereby the favour of the people. Shortlie after, he began to shew what he was, in stead of equitie practising crueltie....The pricke of conscience (as it chanceth ever in tyrants, and such as atteine to anie estate by unrighteous means) caused him ever to feare, least he should be served of the same cup, as he had ministered to his predecessor.

So he plotted to murder Banquo and Fleance. 'By the helpe of almightie God reserving him to better fortune', Fleance escaped.

After the contrived slaughter of Banquho nothing prospered with the foresaid Makbeth: for in maner everie man began to doubt his owne life, and durst unneth appeare in the kings presence; and even as there were manie that stood in feare of him, so likewise stood he in feare of manie, in such sort that he began to make those awaie by one surmized cavillation or other, whom he thought most able to worke him anie displeasure. At length he found such sweetnesse by putting his nobles thus to death, that his earnest thirst after bloud in this behalfe might in no wise be satisfied.

The whole story thus told, Holinshed has no difficulty in recognising its fitness with the eternal scheme of things.

In the beginning of his reigne he accomplished manie woorthie acts, verie profitable to the common-wealth (as ye have heard) but afterward, by the illusion of the divell, he defamed the same with most terrible crueltie.

But when Shakespeare took the story into drama, he made Macbeth an intelligible embodiment of the human spirit, and Macbeth's world a universe whose operative principles could be seen in action as an inevitable and a necessary order.

Macbeth is a piece of human nature. Stirred by impulses familiar to human beings, he embarks on certain actions. How does his human nature react to the doing of them? What is the consequent effect on him as a piece of human nature? The person and the personality of Macbeth is the whole reticulation of corporeal and spiritual agencies which his consciousness reveals to him as himself. His limbs, his senses, his nerves, his instincts, his impulses, his passions, his emotions, his imagination, his mind, these are all corporate members of *his* state of man. The state of man loses its capacity to function effectively in response to life's exigencies unless it is a 'single state of man', that is, unless the component agents of all its capabilities respond harmoniously and collectively in a common effort. If head and heart and hand are out of unison, the state of man is disrupted and the 'self' suffers anarchic dissolution. The nerves must steadily communicate the will to limbs which must infallibly adopt the appropriate activity. The senses must accurately transmit their impressions to the mind, and the receiving mind must hold proportion between its imaginative and its rational interpretation of them. Unless feeling is in league with will and purpose, it is liable to frustrate the desired objective. The immediate experience of Macbeth is that his project has involved him in an endless succession of strains on his 'singleness' of man. The hand is incapable of performing the willed movement; the eye distorts the image it perceives; the very hair erects itself unseasonably; the blood flushes or leaves pale the face, unsubjected to a controlling will. The anarchic discomfiture induces perturbed sensations, which settle into a growing feeling of fear. Imagination intensifies the fear inordinately until function is smothered in enervating surmise; the fear-haunted mind is incapable of the repose which mind and body require in sleep. Through such incessant turbulence, the state of man is fractured, and life becomes a fitful fever which is manifestly fatal. The conscious experience of Macbeth displays all these symptoms; and they are consistently presented by Shakespeare in this way of simple psychopathological observation. They are records of physical and physiological conditions. No diagnosis is formulated; but the case is laid bare.

Though before his entry we have heard of Macbeth's brave deeds, we first see him on the heath with Banquo, returning from a bloody victory. Macbeth speaks a casual line: 'so foul and fair a day I have not seen', merely meaning that the weather is terrible, but the day is otherwise highly auspicious for them. (Critics of symbolist and imagist proclivities force much of their esoteric doctrine into these words, and, for once, they may even plead Bradley's connivance.) Suddenly they encounter the witches. Banquo first sees them and for a moment is intelligibly nonplussed:

> What are these
> So wither'd and so wild in their attire,
> That look not like the inhabitants o' the earth,
> And yet are on't?[1]

Macbeth has a second's time to grasp the situation; and is ready with peremptory demand:

> Speak, if you can: what are you?

The witches pronounce their prophecies. They concern Macbeth nearly; but only from Banquo's observation do we

---

[1] *Ibid.* I. iii. 39.

know his reception of them. He says not one word: he 'starts', and starts as in fear:

> Good sir, why do you start; and seem to fear
> Things that do sound so fair?

Macbeth appears for the moment to be possessed by the prophecy, lost in a mood of abstraction. He 'seems rapt withal'. Recovering immediate awareness of circumstance, he knows that by his father's recent death he is now thane of Glamis. But forecasts of further advancement to higher thane-ship and to the very promise of the crown are for the moment purely speculative. Yet his long-cherished ambition makes him see them already as within 'the prospect of belief' and not merely as possibilities of conjecture. Hence his immediate concern is for corroborative authentication:

> Say from whence
> You owe this strange intelligence? or why
> Upon this blasted heath you stop our way
> With such prophetic greeting? Speak, I charge you.[1]

But without reply to the urgent question, the witches vanish into the air to the palpable disappointment of Macbeth's eagerness: 'Would they had stay'd!' For Banquo the episode has been one of the casual mysteries which life so frequently, if not generally so startlingly, presents.

> Were such things here as we do speak about?
> Or have we eaten on the insane root
> That takes the reason prisoner?

Macbeth, however, has already accepted the witches as no hallucination but as authentic prophets: for their knowledge of what is to be fits in so easily with Macbeth's repeated ima-ginative experience of what he hoped might be. 'Your children shall be kings', he remarks to Banquo—a phrase in more determinate form than a remark that if strange things should

[1] *Macbeth* I. iii. 75.

happen Banquo might be the father of kings. The phrase, however, sets a line of conversation into which Banquo naturally and casually falls. 'You shall be king', and, jumping eagerly at any corroboration for the sort of future which his ambition has in the past repeatedly held before his mind, Macbeth spontaneously bursts out:

> And thane of Cawdor too: went it not so?

At that moment they are interrupted by the entry of Ross and Angus, who come to convey the king's thanks for Macbeth's services to his country in the recent victory, and to bring him the first fruits of royal gratitude. By the king's command, Macbeth is granted the thaneship of Cawdor. The intimation, so directly corroborating the witches' prophecy, stupefies Banquo: 'What, can the devil speak true?' But, even in such brief second of time, and, one must perforce believe, because of dreams through the long past which have now fixed themselves as immediate hopes in Macbeth's mind, Macbeth is neither startled nor obviously surprised. Calmly, he asks the messengers to explain how circumstance has made such promotion feasible:

> The thane of Cawdor lives: why do you dress me
> In borrow'd robes?

As he hears that it is just such an occurrence as is familiar in the world he knows which has rendered the thaneship vacant and has thus put it at the king's disposal, his frame of mind, already strongly tending by subconscious cumulative impulse to take the witches' intimations for veracious foreknowledge, leads him to add greater strength to the lure of his hope:

> Glamis, and thane of Cawdor!
> The greatest is behind.

And so two truths are told as happy prologues to what ambition and imagination and circumstance seem to assure for him in the swelling act of the imperial throne. So fully convinced does he feel that he sees no need for closer examination of the credentials of supernatural fortune-telling:

> This supernatural soliciting
> Cannot be ill, cannot be good.

The metaphysical question is irrelevant. He is preoccupied with the sense that the kingship is very near to his grasp. His mind at once involuntarily recalls what hitherto, before fate had so palpably prepared the way to his future greatness, he had frequently pondered over as the means to the crown. Murder had then seemed the only way: and he had so often shudderingly recoiled from the prospect of it. But these earlier memories are now again stirred up in his consciousness, the debris of his ambitious dreams. They flood back into direct awareness, and the very factor which had just lent corroborative force to the prophecy, the succession to Cawdor without contrivance of his own, is blotted from his mind. The horror of murder, though no murder might need be, suffuses his sensation. His hair stands on end, his pulse throbs furiously, his heart beats wildly:

> Why do I yield to that suggestion
> Whose horrid image doth unfix my hair
> And make my seated heart knock at my ribs
> Against the use of nature? [1]

His perturbation is increased by the vividness with which his imagination recalls the accumulated details of all the previous rackings which he has suffered in earlier premeditations at those times when the act of murder seemed the only way to reach his goal. He is torn in agonies of fear: but

> Present fears
> Are less than horrible imaginings:
> My thought, whose murder yet is but fantastical,
> Shakes so my single state of man that function
> Is smother'd in surmise, and nothing is
> But what is not.

[1] *Macbeth* I. iii. 134.

He is unequal to the circumstance. He cannot face the facts.
He renounces the project, and finds temporary easement in the
hope that kingship may come as the thaneship has just come:

> If chance will have me king, why, chance may crown me
> Without my stir.

But the easement is only temporary; for mere waiting will not
satisfy ambition, and there is no renunciation of his ambition
to attain the throne. The momentary composure rests merely
on a fleeting hope that he may reach the throne without the
necessity of horrifying contrivance on his own part, a hope
which in itself still further intensifies his imperial desire. The
very idea that all the horrors of a dreadful act which in imagination he has so frequently and so gruesomely felt, may not
be needed makes the crown seem more easily accessible. Yet
speculatively, some drastic action may still be necessary, and
hence there is urgent occasion for further conference with
Banquo, a potential ally, though for the moment no particular
agendum for such conference can be prescribed:

>   at more time,
> The interim having weigh'd it, let us speak
> Our free hearts each to other.

But very soon afterwards, the easier way is barred. Malcolm,
now named as hereafter to bear the title Prince of Cumberland,
stands in the road by which, should Duncan by course of
nature prematurely die, Macbeth might have hoped to climb
into the royal inheritance. This unexpected turn of events is
decisive:

>   that is a step
> On which I must fall down, or else o'erleap.[1]

To o'erleap it, murder is the way. So, in a frame of mind under
the more or less quiescent surface of which there are embedded
these three nerve-centres of turbulence—ardent desire for the

---

[1] *Ibid.* I. iv. 48.

crown, conviction that only by murder can it be achieved, and cumulative memory of the horrors attending imaginative rehearsals in preparation for such murder—Macbeth joins his wife.

In the meantime, however, his letter, informing his partner of greatness of the still larger greatness promised to them by the witches who are now clearly accepted as authentic fore-tellers of the future, has made Lady Macbeth ponder on the obstacles which may still dash their mutual hopes. These hopes are surely mutual; the quality of ambitious desire in each of them is so deep-seated and so much akin that it must often have thrust itself forward as a conjugal link in their fire-side fancies. In the intimacy of her knowledge of him, and the privacy of her own sense of what the occasion requires, she has a realistic appreciation of the immediate hazards.

Like Macbeth, she has no doubt whatever that the crown will be theirs: '(thou) shalt be what thou art promised'. But there are difficulties to overcome; and most of them lie in the personality of the person who must be the 'corporal agent' of the appointed scheme. She knows and justifiably fears that Macbeth's nature may break in the act of attainment. It is the attempt, the actual contrivance of the doing and the doing itself, which may be fatal, and not a merely abstract con-sideration of the deed in respect of ideal moral principle: 'The attempt, and not the deed, confounds us.'[1]

Though fate and metaphysical aid are conspiring to give Macbeth the crown, he himself will be the main impediment. The obstruction will not lie mainly in his conscious moral scruples; it will be in his mere human nature. Fear will surge up in him and paralyse his practical energies. He will be over-come by what he fears to do, and not by any wish that such a deed may be undone. He is 'too full of the milk of human kindness'. It is not as ironic as might at first appear that Shake-speare should allow Lady Macbeth to invent this phrase,

[1] *Macbeth* II. ii. 11.

a phrase which as it has rolled down the generations from hers to our own, has gathered on its way an associative content which has made it the symbol of what is quintessential in the spirit of human nature. But, of course, it had not that meaning for Lady Macbeth; and neither the Macbeth whom Shakespeare took from Holinshed, nor the man into whom he transformed him, displayed much, if any, of this quality of compassionate kindliness, not even in those earlier years before murder had become habitual to him. It is clear that for Lady Macbeth, and perhaps for most of Shakespeare's audience, the interwoven associations which unwrapped themselves in their consciousness when the verbal stimuli of 'milk' and 'kindness' struck their apprehension, did not arouse the same reverberations as they stir in the modern mind.

'Milk', for instance, amongst its other links, had associated itself with the unmanliness of 'milksops': Richard III, in his battle-speech, knows the common contempt his troops will have for a 'milksop',

> one that never in his life
> Felt so much cold as over shoes in snow,[1]

and Holinshed had recorded that Duncan was taken to be a milksop by those who judged his government to be lacking in firmness. There were biblical memories to authorise this implied sense of human values. 'I have fed you with milk and not with meat', St Paul tells the Corinthians, 'for hitherto ye were not able to bear it, neither yet are ye able';[2] '[ye] are become such as have need of milk and not of strong meat: for everyone that useth milk [or as the Greek has it, hath no experience] is unskilful in the word of righteousness; for he is a babe.'[3] 'Milke for Babes and Meat for Men' is the title of a Puritan tract of 1641. 'To wash the milk off one's liver' is glossed by Cotgrave 'to purge oneself of cowardice'. Milk

---

[1] *Richard III* v. iii. 324.   [2] I Corinthians iii. 2.
[3] Hebrews v. 12–13. The inserted gloss is in the margin of the Geneva Bible.

stood widely, then, as a symbol for the opposite of manliness. Of course, there were also biblical associations of milk and honey, of milk as a sustenance and a source of pure nourishment. But even here, its links are usually with the weakness which needs sustaining.

Long before Shakespeare wrote, 'kindness' had taken on its sense of benevolence. Even so, it retained sufficient suggestion of the un-moral connotation with which it had started. For 'kindness' is the quality of 'kind', the specific attribute pertaining to the nature of the distinctive natural kind. 'The waters brought forth abundantly after their kind and every winged fowl after his kind',[1] as Genesis records in its account of the birth of creation. God made the beasts of the earth each after his own kind. 'Kind' in this original and persisting sense has no implications of peculiarly moral properties. But in the long course of his history, mankind was finding generic distinctions between the natures of the animate species, and in particular between the human kind and the rest of the animal kingdom. As St Paul put it: 'all flesh is not the same flesh: but there is one kind of flesh of men, another flesh of beasts, another of fishes, and another of birds.'[2] There was a distinctive human kindness; and almost at once, since language is solely used by humans, the plain unqualified quality of kindness took on the sense of charitable disposition. Kindness meant the moral kindness specific to the human kind. 'Kindly', an epithet specifying at first a merely genetic relationship, began at once to stand for a moral quality of sympathetic benevolence; and 'kindliness' in its turn became the label of the human quality, of that *philanthropia* which mere experience demonstrated to be the characteristic attribute of the human kind. All through the sixteenth century, however, the moral and the amoral senses of 'kind' and 'kindness' are in common use, and often their ambiguity provides opportunity for stylistic tricks. 'Kindly', for instance, has its completely unmoral meaning in a phrase of Holinshed's

[1] Genesis i. 21.   [2] I Corinthians xv. 39.

in which he tells why Richard III had the young princes put to death:

Forasmuch as his mind gave him, that, his nephues living, men would not reckon that he could have right to the realme, he thought therefore without delaie to rid them, as though the killynge of his kinsmen could amend his cause, and make him a kindlie kyng.[1]

Almost invariably Shakespeare uses the adjective 'kind' and the substantive 'kindness' in their moral sense, and the substantive 'kind' for 'natural species', or, more frequently, for a 'class' or 'sort' in general. But occasionally he plays with the older and the newer senses. There is Hamlet's 'kin' and 'kind'; and in *Richard III*, Clarence tells the murderer that his brother Richard is 'kind', to which the murderer retorts by a *double-entendre* in which 'kind', is taken to mean, not benevolent, but of a quality as unmorally natural as is the natural force which sometimes brings snow at harvest time.

To Lady Macbeth, the milk of human kindness in her husband is a defect in his nature, an obstacle to the full exercise of his 'man-ness' or valour. But even within herself, this instinctive sense of her accepted values of life is vaguely perturbed by other intimations. Advertently or inadvertently, she describes the quality which he lacks, the quality which would assure to Macbeth the full realisation of his valour, as something or other which is an 'illness', a thing in itself evil:

> thou wouldst be great;
> Art not without ambition but without
> The illness should attend it.[2]

But Lady Macbeth is not given to speculative rumination about ethics. Life, for her, is the expression, through action, of the impulses which are strongest within her; they are set towards a realisation of those objects which the world about her seems to hold as things of highest worth in life, the rewards of undaunted valour. She stands within a moral world which is

---

[1] Boswell Stone, p. 388.   [2] *Macbeth* I. v. 19.

giving way, far more than she realises, to a higher order; but the need for the newer dispensation, and the cause for it in the shortcomings of the current one, have no effective impact on her mind. She finds no cognitive difficulty in determining to defy the constraints which are establishing themselves in the new and gentler world. But the decision taken, she is at once aware of perturbing sensations. Perhaps the very nipples of her woman's breasts will stimulate prickings which will agitate her milk and arouse the stream of human nature in her blood. She must resolutely safeguard herself against all such 'compunctious visitings of nature'; she will deny the right of nature within her; by her own will, she will transform her milk to gall, and offer it as sustenance to the sightless substances that wait on nature's mischief:

> Come to my woman's breasts
> And take my milk for gall, you murdering ministers,
> Wherever in your sightless substances
> You wait on nature's mischief![1]

She will nerve herself to such a state of being that her knife will be blind to the wound it makes, and her ears deaf to every mysterious signal which might deflect her from her purpose:

> Come, thick night,
> And pall thee in the dunnest smoke of hell,
> That my keen knife see not the wound it makes,
> Nor heaven peep through the blanket of the dark,
> To cry 'Hold, hold!'

Her mind is irrevocably fixed. Duncan shall never leave their house alive: and she herself will take command of all the necessary steps:

> you shall put
> This night's great business into my dispatch.

It is exactly the right proposal to ensure Macbeth's concurrence. At once his mood, to leave to chance the bringing of him to

---

[1] *Macbeth* I. v. 48.

the throne, is unsettled: 'we will speak further'. The situation is in Lady Macbeth's hands.

But Macbeth, his agitated ambitions thus renewed, cannot yet frame himself to the collected attitude demanded by immediate circumstance. He cannot at once bring himself to greet the king in person. Duncan arrives and is welcomed by Lady Macbeth alone. Macbeth pulls himself together and meets the king at dinner. But it would appear that he could not see the whole ordeal through; he leaves the chamber and wrestles with all the insurgent impulses which are distracting him. Yet his agitation is not overtly prompted by pressure of an absolute moral law:

> if the assassination
> Could trammel up the consequence, and catch
> With his surcease success; that but this blow
> Might be the be-all and the end-all here,
> But here, upon this bank and shoal of time,
> We'ld jump the life to come.[1]

As far as he reveals it directly, his consciousness is occupied by very relative considerations—judgement here, probability of retaliation from his fellows, and the grounds which would seem to justify their retaliation, such as his breach of social bonds and his slaughter of one who has earned their high esteem. He is overwhelmed with the trepidations which these mighty threats excite: and, as promptings to him to risk them, there is nothing but his ambition:

> I have no spur
> To prick the sides of my intent, but only
> Vaulting ambition.

The whole scheme is not worth it: it o'erleaps itself and falls on the other side to certain destruction. Hence his announcement to Lady Macbeth, who has come in to pour her spirits into his ear:

> We will proceed no further in this business,

[1] *Ibid.* I. vii. 2.

and he offers perfunctorily a recital of the considerations which, he is persuading himself, have led to this decision:

> He hath honour'd me of late; and I have bought
> Golden opinions from all sorts of people,
> Which would be worn now in their newest gloss,
> Not cast aside so soon.

But these, to Lady Macbeth, are considerations of little weight. She suspects that it is his cowardice which is cloaking itself in their name. She assails him with a direct accusation:

> Was the hope drunk
> Wherein you dress'd yourself? Hath it slept since?
> And wakes it now, to look so green and pale
> At what it did so freely?

and she adds a particular sting to the charge by threatening that his craven heart will forfeit her love for him: 'From this time such I account thy love.' She goes on forthwith to heap further scorn on his apparent cowardice:

> Art thou afeard
> To be the same in thine own act and valour
> As thou art in desire? Wouldst thou have that
> Which thou esteem'st the ornament of life
> And live a coward in thine own esteem?

Macbeth feels overpowered: 'prithee, peace', and in half-daunted defence he adds:

> I dare do all that may become a man;
> Who dares do more is none.

Lady Macbeth counters this by reminding him that he had previously pledged himself to all the hazards of the project, and, doing that, had proved himself a valiant man:

> When you durst do it, then you were a man;
> And, to be more than what you were, you would
> Be so much more the man. Nor time nor place
> Did then adhere, and yet you would make both.

And now when time and place have made themselves, Macbeth collapses like a craven weakling. She, a woman, would have been strong enough to undertake whatever measures might have proved necessary to secure that to which her whole being had so ardently pledged itself:

> I have given suck, and know
> How tender 'tis to love the babe that milks me:
> I would, while it was smiling in my face,
> Have pluck'd my nipple from his boneless gums,
> And dash'd the brains out, had I so sworn as you
> Have done to this.

And under the strain of her assault, Macbeth reveals what consciously, but unconfessed, is the strongest constraint he feels: 'If we should fail?' At once Lady Macbeth seizes the means to reassure him. There will be no failure. She puts forward a plan which she has devised to make everything easy of achievement. The scheme is simple, and she blunts the crucial point of the execution of it, the actual murder, by hinting that, even in that, her hand will strengthen his: when they have drugged the chamberlains into a swinish sleep,

> What cannot you and I perform upon
> The unguarded Duncan?

Macbeth is immediately restored to self-possession and to adoption of the plan. He is transfixed in admiration of his wife's undaunted mettle, her valour, her superb 'man-ness':

> Bring forth men-children only;
> For thy undaunted mettle should compose
> Nothing but males.

In effect, he is satisfied now that the project may be safely done. As the scene closes his wife reveals her instinctive sense of the real needs of the occasion. Macbeth must be nerved to the task. This must be the way of it: he must 'bend up each corporal agent to the terrible feat'. He must 'screw his courage to the sticking-place' so that it will withstand the unnerving act which must be performed. In the meantime he must practise this self-discipline, assume the fairest show, and contrive by self-control to display a false face which will 'hide what the false heart doth know'.

But in the interim between the recovery of this determination and the doing of the deed which it determines, Macbeth's self-confidence is shaken again. The composure had been but momentary; and shortly, when he should have been abed, he is nervously wandering in the courtyard of his castle. It is after midnight—'the moon is down...and she goes down at twelve'—and Banquo, having attended the king in Macbeth's house until he had retired, is belatedly departing through the courtyard with torches lighted for the homeward journey. He encounters Macbeth at this hour in his own courtyard: and his surprise is the greater because Macbeth had withdrawn from the royal presence before the king had signified his own intention to retire. In this encounter, Banquo recalls an earlier occasion when strange things had happened in the night to both of them. He reminds Macbeth of the witches on the heath, and of their prophecies. But Macbeth, obsessed by his wife's immediate plan, has lost his eagerness to discuss the matter with the man whom yesterday he had regarded as a necessary accomplice. In the new circumstances, Banquo may not be needed at all: the discussion can be put off to a time 'when we can entreat an hour to serve'. But in saying this, Macbeth is led to display his inability to keep circumstance in hand; and he ends by blurting out damning evidence of what is in his mind. 'I think not of them', he had said when Banquo mentioned the witches. But, immediately, remembering that earlier he had invited Banquo to further talk about the prophecies, he adds a foolishly inept remark which discloses just what he is trying to conceal: if, he tells Banquo, in the conversation which at some future date shall take place,

> you shall cleave to my consent, when 'tis,
> It shall make honour for you.

No bribe was ever more flagrantly confessed.

When Banquo goes, he leaves Macbeth with a mind distracted once more by all the terrors which his earlier imaginative premonitions had excited. He feels the need of a sedative. But whilst he awaits the drink, his excited imagination exposes him to intense strain. He suffers the torment of an hallucination. His eyes are made 'the fools o' the other senses'—that is, in fact, his eyes befool his other senses. They make him seem to see in form as palpable as any real dagger, a blood-stained weapon, just such an instrument as he is committed in a moment to use. But his hands cannot grasp it: for in fact there is no such thing. It is merely an hallucination which proceeds from his heat-oppressed brain. It springs from his obsession by the bloody business now in this very moment to be done. It fills his present time with horror; and renders him still more incapable of doing the deed effectively. Before he can recover himself, the signal bell sounds. All is set for the murder: even now, he must go to the royal chamber and perform the dreadful deed. He goes, and does it. But the moment it is done, he gives way, and causes an uncovenanted commotion by crying aloud, 'Who's there? what, ho!'[1]

The cry is heard by Lady Macbeth. She is waiting in the room beneath, her spirits also heated by a more than customary share of wine which she has allowed herself to drink for this special purpose:

> That which hath made them drunk hath made me bold;
> What hath quench'd them hath given me fire.[2]

She becomes still further excited as, straining to catch audible signs that the act is afoot, she hears the ominous shriek of the owl:

> It was the owl that shriek'd, the fatal bellman,
> Which gives the stern'st good-night.

Stretched in this tense apprehensiveness lest Macbeth may even

---

[1] *Macbeth* II. ii. 9.   [2] *Ibid.* II. ii. 1.

yet falter in the attempt, she hears his cry. Fears that he has failed surge through her:

> Alack, I am afraid they have awaked
> And 'tis not done.

She imagines the worst, for all along she knew that it was the attempt and not the deed which might confound them. Yet her preparations had seemed to make success infallible. In this state of consternation, she sees her husband enter, and hears his blunt announcement, 'I have done the deed'. But he is plainly unsure of himself. Did she hear a noise? he asks. She acknowledges that she had caught the owl's scream and the cricket's cry, but she does not directly disclose the other sound which had perturbed her far more than owl's or cricket's, the sound of her husband's voice. She asks Macbeth if he had not also heard a voice, did he himself not speak? Confusedly and without ordered recollection of what had happened in those terrible moments which he had just endured, he asks 'When?'. Was it after he left the royal chamber? Recalling in his anxiety what rooms he had passed on his way down, and whether noises might have issued from them which might mean disclosure of his acts, his mind is more powerfully caught and held by the sight of blood on his own hands. 'This is a sorry sight.' Lady Macbeth has recovered her composure, and seeks to calm her husband by remarking in the tone of casual conversation

> A foolish thought, to say a sorry sight.

But Macbeth's immediate memory is clinging to him. He goes over the horrible incidents again. In the dead silence as he crept stealthily from Duncan's chamber, he had been startled by a voice. From an adjacent room, the one in which Duncan's sons were sleeping, 'one did laugh in's sleep, and one cried "Murder",' and both awoke, but, muttering their prayers, they fell back into sleep. When Lady Macbeth hears of this, she is not in the least perturbed; it is exactly what might normally happen when two guests are lodged together in one room. But

Macbeth cannot put the incident so easily aside. Praying, the guests had uttered the traditional terms 'God bless us!' and 'Amen'. But his own lips had remained functionless. It is another sign that his single state of man is disintegrating. Earlier, his eyes made fools of his other senses, and now his throat and tongue and lips decline their normal office. Lady Macbeth warns him that in allowing his mind to dwell so curiously on these unimportant matters, he is heading straight for madness, straight to a complete breach between mind and body in the state of man. But Macbeth cannot put his feelings aside at will. His unrest suggests to him with vivid imaginative reinforcements that from henceforth he has surrendered peace and quiet, and, above all, the natural rest and quietude of sleep, the blissful repose which by its restorative oblivion preserves the life-force of mind and of body.

> Methought I heard a voice cry 'Sleep no more!
> Macbeth does murder sleep', the innocent sleep,
> Sleep that knits up the ravell'd sleave of care,
> The death of each day's life, sore labour's bath,
> Balm of hurt minds, great nature's second course,
> Chief nourisher in life's feast.[1]

Lady Macbeth would dismiss all this as mere weakness, 'to think so brainsickly of things'. There are easy means of escape. Macbeth must at once wash from his hands the incriminating blood. Suddenly she realises that in another detail Macbeth had bungled in the doing of the deed. He had brought the chamberlains' daggers away with him, and they should be found lying near the corpse. She tells Macbeth to take them back, and to smear the sleeping grooms with blood. But the thought of returning to the scene of the murder awakens paroxysms of terror in Macbeth:

> I'll go no more:
> I am afraid to think what I have done;
> Look on't again, I dare not.

[1] *Macbeth* II. ii. 35.

Lady Macbeth despises such fears: but she has apparently forgotten that a little time before it was another such 'compunctious visting of nature', not exactly the same as Macbeth's but close akin to it, which had made her unable to do the deed herself:

> Had he not resembled
> My father as he slept, I had done't.[1]

The deed now done, however, she resumes sufficient self-control to promise gaily that she will carry back the daggers herself, and if there is blood still flowing from Duncan, she'll 'gild the faces of the grooms withal'. She goes to return the daggers. Whilst she is away, Macbeth's agitation is increased by the knocking on the outer gate. It is as if everything will for ever remind him of the horror of his deed:

> How is't with me, when every noise appals me?...
> Will all great Neptune's ocean wash this blood
> Clean from my hand? No, this my hand will rather
> The multitudinous seas incarnadine,
> Making the green one red.

As he is sunk in this morbid terror, Lady Macbeth comes back. Brusquely, and even angrily, she chides him for his childishness, and proceeds briskly to make all arrangements to avoid arousing suspicions in the newcomer's mind.

So the scene ends with the gruesome clanging on the gate, the gate which will soon be opened by the strangest figure Shakespeare ever used to speak with choric voice, the drunken porter, whose key will turn indifferently the locks of hell's gate and those of Macbeth's castle.

But there is no longer any need here to follow the course of the play in so much detail. It continues directly along the line already made plain; it traces step by step the progressive disintegration of the man Macbeth. In the process, he becomes, in a literal sense, a nervous wreck, a distracted mortal possessed more and more by more and more terrors which haunt his days and turn his nights to sleepless torments. His mind is full of

[1] *Macbeth* II. ii. 13.

scorpions. He eats his meals in fear, and sleeps in the affliction of terrible dreams. Hallucinations grip him more intensely, and reach their harrowing climax with the ghost of Banquo. The mere experience of contentment, the feeling of ease and the sense of substantial integrity perpetually escape him. No matter what he achieves, to be thus is nothing: the unruffled calm of feeling himself to be safely thus is what he longs for, and it is this which he never attains. In his longing for it, he envies the unfeeling oblivion of the dead. But living, and driven by life as he is driven, the 'fit' comes on to him with quick recurrence. It forbids for him the feeling which he seeks, the sense of conscious integrity in his single state of man:

> Then comes my fit again: I had else been perfect,
> Whole as the marble, founded as the rock,
> As broad and general as the casing air.[1]

Instead, he feels himself 'cabin'd, cribb'd, confined, bound in to saucy doubts and fears'. Occasionally, and then but fitfully, he seems to recover some power to link his will with those of his corporal agents which must execute it. But such specious control comes now only when his mental anguish has excited him to desperate projects and his mind in grasping them only does so in the false quietude of despair. He inures himself to the sight of blood, blood shed by his own deeds; but it is a conquest attained only when murder has become a habit with him.

> I am in blood
> Stepp'd in so far that, should I wade no more,
> Returning were as tedious as go o'er.[2]

He is brutalising himself into a mere animal automaton; and the human spirit which was once Macbeth lies within him dying of exhaustion, harrowed by incessant fears, and utterly worn out by the torments of its restless ecstasies. The spark within him by which the flame of living is kept alight is extinguished: he loses the mere desire to live. He is sunk in

---

[1] *Ibid.* III. iv. 21.   [2] *Ibid.* III. iv. 136.

'the sere, the yellow leaf'. He begins to be 'aweary of the sun'.
He is ready for the 'inescapable mortal end'. In a last desperate
encounter with circumstance, he is tied to the stake, and, bear-
like, he must fight the course. The stringency of the situation
inspires him to a last rally of the spirit which once had 'manned'
him. He scorns the easy way-out of Roman fools:

> Why should I play the Roman fool, and die
> On mine own sword? whiles I see lives, the gashes
> Do better upon them.[1]

Though for a moment shattered on hearing that Macduff
fulfils the terms of the witches' prophecy, he recovers: 'I will
not yield', and he dies fighting with the instinctive vital energy
with which he had always fought.

The breakdown of Lady Macbeth is exhibited from a similar
angle of vision. Once more it is the disintegration of the single
state of flesh and spirit which had made her the being which
she was. The presentation of her dissolution is kept in the same
range of pathological and physiological observation which had
formed the record of Macbeth's own case. As with his, her
malady exhibits outward and physical symptoms which compel
a fatal prognosis. Far less endowed than he with imaginative
energy, at first she seems immune to fears of what may come.
She is ready to meet circumstance as it arises, and as far as she
can foresee it. Before the murder she is generally and quickly
self-possessed, and can make light of contingent and speculative
after-effects. But something she has overlooked, though in
other circumstances she had experienced it; and the weight of
it, the pressure of primal human 'kindness', begins to break
her even as Macbeth the waverer seems to be hardening himself
to events more readily. Almost immediately after the murder
the first hint of her collapse appears. When Duncan's corpse had
been discovered, and as Macbeth is telling his tale to Duncan's
sons, she first learns that foolishly and not in accord with her

---

[1] *Macbeth* v. viii. 1.

carefully contrived plans, he has murdered the chamberlains. The shock is momentarily too much for her: she faints, but even doing so, clings to consciousness: 'Help me hence, ho!' It is the first sign, however: circumstance and 'compunctious visitings of nature' in the end will break her too. Yet she has still large store of rallying power. She can still take charge of such situations as are brought about by Macbeth's disordered acts and gestures. She assumes control in the scene where Macbeth is unnerved or unmanned by Banquo's ghost. Yet finally she too pays full toll. Rest and unperturbed sleep flee from her even as they have deserted Macbeth. In her case, however, the condition is even more palpably pathological. She becomes the victim of somnambulism. Thick-coming fancies keep her from her rest; for nature, which she has so effectively subdued in her conscious mind, breaks through from her subconsciousness. The disease is beyond cure. Her life is forfeit. And, even to her husband, her death is no more, beyond the suspicion of irritation at its inopportune incidence, than another of the uncountable chances which make fools of man's bemused efforts to find a purpose in life. The speech is the culmination of Macbeth's spiritual tragedy:

> She should have died hereafter;
> There would have been a time for such a word.
> To-morrow, and to-morrow, and to-morrow,
> Creeps in this petty pace from day to day
> To the last syllable of recorded time,
> And all our yesterdays have lighted fools
> The way to dusty death. Out, out, brief candle!
> Life's but a walking shadow, a poor player
> That struts and frets his hour upon the stage
> And then is heard no more: it is a tale
> Told by an idiot, full of sound and fury,
> Signifying nothing.[1]

In such a mood, Macbeth reaches the nadir of his tragedy. There is nothing left remarkable beneath the visiting moon,

[1] *Ibid.* v. v. 17.

nothing any longer serious in mortality. Life is entirely emptied of every conceivable meaning. The mystery of Shakespeare's genius admits us into Macbeth's consciousness; we share with Macbeth the imaginative experience which seems to seize on life's tragic fact as something more absolute and more universal than hitherto it had been found to be.

In some degree, this absoluteness and this universality appear to spring from the sheer simplicity of Shakespeare's handling of the human situation disclosed. The tale he tells is consistently cabin'd, cribb'd and confined to mortality, to man as man, to things human and of the earth, to the tangible realm of time and of space. But, clinging resolutely to time, Shakespeare seems to see it merge into timelessness; holding firmly on to the body of man, he watches it at work in the shaping of its own spirit. The bare raw matter of *Macbeth* can be put in terms so simple as to appear almost ludicrous. Macbeth is a human being, just one, but a significant one, just one example of that complicated organism, the familiar and representative human animal called man. He kills another man, destroys, that is, another piece of human nature. But, doing so, he destroys the human nature in himself. It is all as simple as that. There is no need for recondite metaphysics, nor, immediately, for any particular theology. Macbeth is just a mortal making in his own experience one of the most momentous discoveries in human history. He is discovering what in its nature evil is. By the same act, he is initiating the great spiritual adventure of mankind, its search for goodness. Indeed, gripped by the sensation of simple naturalness which the play induces, it seems even more accurate to talk not merely of man's search for goodness, but of his making of it. Macbeth appears to stand as the symbol of a crucial moment in human history, the moment at which mankind discovered itself to be possessed of capacities for entering on unending vistas of spiritual progress. Yet throughout it all, he feels and thinks and acts in terms of direct and immediate experience; and the succession of these experiences, all, in fact, that constitutes his life and his fate, follows as with the sheer compulsion of natural law. Through Macbeth, man appears to be discovering human nature and the principles or laws which are its very essence. In the end, these laws emerge as something not hostile to, but as it were, precedent to all and every contemporary formulation of them in terms of religious dogma. Constrast, for instance, *Macbeth* with *Richard III*. In *Richard III* the alleged motive power rests entirely in 'conscience'; but in *Macbeth*, crucial events occur in the more general and more rudimentary realm of consciousness itself, and the theological sanctions of the earlier play are somehow transmuted into more universal compulsions. There is here, of course, no question of dismissing or of denying conscience. It is rather a sense that the roots of it are being discovered somewhere more deeply hidden in sheer human nature. It is all as if Shakespeare saw truth more clearly when he unwrapped it from the traditional phrases in which from time to time man in his spiritual conflicts had tried to formulate it.

The artistic situation has a parallel in the imaginative processes of another English poet, whose main interest, like Shakespeare's, was in men and women and in their quest for goodness. Browning had a marked preference for trying to catch man's spirit at the crucial moments of its experience. His preferred themes are taken from two of the world's such moments, the time of the birth of Christ, and that century of the later renewal of the human spirit which Browning and most of us up to thirty years ago would intelligently have called the Renaissance. It is for this reason that Browning chooses Cleon and Karshish and the St John who died in the desert; for this reason, too, that Italian artists push themselves so frequently into his *Men and Women*. Macbeth has a similar significance for human morality to that which Browning's Cleon and Karshish have for man's religious history. But Shakespeare's divinations break farther back through ideal time than do Browning's.

Indeed, some of the most pertinent commentaries on *Macbeth* and its significance in man's spiritual history can be drawn from observations in Plutarch's *Moralia*. Plutarch himself belonged to the spiritual epoch of Cleon and of Karshish, an epoch like that so pathetically and sentimentally described by Matthew Arnold as standing between two worlds, one dead, the other powerless to be born, just such an epoch, in fact, as provides mankind's highest joy, a time when the mind, free from fixed opinion, is at liberty to wander through eternity in its quest for truth. Plutarch had, of course, as an intelligent man, taken sides in the philosophic partisanship of his own time, but somehow, confronted with examples of human behaviour, he saw and recorded the phenomena in a manner which carries the conviction of direct intuition.

Take, for instance, in its rawness the human stuff out of which in *Macbeth* Shakespeare makes his pattern of mortal life. Take the primary postulates of it, and remember that postulates were perceptions which experience proved to be true. One has in mind such notions, for instance, as that of human kindness, of the single state of man, of evil as something fundamentally unnatural, or rather, as un-humannatural and not merely in the accepted sense unrighteous, and a score of the many other ideas which have helped or deluded man in his exhilarating search for goodness. There are phrases in Plutarch which seem to fall squarely into Shakespeare's diagnosis of the human mystery. Read them, not in Plutarch's own Greek, but as Philemon Holland put them to Shakespeare and to Shakespeare's contemporaries. As Plutarch's translator, Holland naturally tried to dress him in true English idiom, with the result that not infrequently Holland's English imports ideas which, though post-Plutarchian, are felt by Holland to have substantial equivalence in the philosophic terminology of his own day. There are, of course, real cruces; *sunesis*, for example, and *philostorgia*, *metameleia* and *philanthropia*. But these are so intimate to experience that everyone will make his appropriate accommodation of their sense.

These are the excerpts one finds from Plutarch in Holland's English. They give his notion of man's place in creation, of his partnership with, and his difference from, other animals, of his discovery of the moral sense, and of the consequences of his deeds when he defies his humanity. They can be given as a mere series of quotations from different essays; for in all of them, Plutarch's interest was in man and in. man's search for what could be called the good. Hear him first on that singleness of state which at once allies man with and separates him from the rest of the animal kingdom.

And verily this is that which doth frame and dispose the nature of wilde beasts to divers passions: for it is not long of any opiniòns good or bad which arise in them, that some of them are strong, venterous and fearelesse, yea and ready to withstand any perils presented before them: others againe be so surprised with feare and fright, that they dare not stirre or do any thing: but the force and power which lieth in the bloud, in the spirits and in the whole bodie, is that which causeth this diversitie of passions, by reason that the passible part growing out of the flesh as from a roote, doeth bud foorth and bring with it a qualitie and pronenesse semblable. But in man that there is a sympathie and fellow mooving of the body, together with the motions of the passions, may be prooved by the pale colour, the red flushing of the face, the trembling of the joints, and panting and leaping of the heart in feare and anger: And again on the contrary side by the dilations of the arteries, heart and colour, in hope and expectation of some pleasures.[1]

The 'single state' of man is the idea behind this quotation:

That this is so, it appeareth by the breath, spirits, sinewes, bones and other parts of the body, which be altogether void of reason: howbeit so soone as there ariseth any motion of the will, which shaketh (as it were) the reines of reason never so little, all of them keepe their order, they agree together, and yield obedience. As for example if the minde and will be disposed to run, the feet are quickly stretched out and ready for a course; the hands likewise settle to their businesse, if there be a motion of the minde to throw, or take holde of any thing.[2]

---

[1] *The Philosophie commonlie called The Morals* by Plutarch, translated by Philemon Holland, 1603. 'Of Morall vertue', p. 76.
[2] *Ibid.* p. 66.

But the human organism is not only part of the animal kingdom: he is a particular part of it, and the significant thing generically is that which gives him his specific differentiation: as one species of the animal kingdom, he has as his own his human nature, the moral quality which Aristotle called *philanthropia*.

Neither is man able by any meanes (would he never so faine) to separate from true friendship, naturall indulgence, and kind affection; nor from humanitie, commiseration and pitie; ne yet from perfect benevolence and good will, the fellowship in joy and sorrow.[1]

Plutarch's Greek text of this passage ought to be inscribed on the lintel of any future home of Leagues of United Nations.

The lot of the human animal, however, is not always a sense of satisfaction. Some of its impulses bring immediate joy, paid for later by what seem exorbitant prices of pain. Wherein lies its own good?

Wherein lieth then, the pleasure and delight of sinne, if it be so, that in no place nor at any time it be void of pensivenesse, care and griefe? if it never have contentment, but alwaies in molestation and trouble, without repose?...But in the soule it is not possible that there should bee engendred anie mirth, joy and contentment, unlesse the first foundation be laied in peace of conscience, and tranquillitie of spirit, void of feare, and enjoying a setled calme in all assurance and confidence.[2]

There, before Macbeth was born in the real or in the imaginative world, is Macbeth's tragedy. The course of it, in Shakespeare's own presentation, follows a path which Plutarch had already realised as the road which for humans is their 'primrose way to the everlasting bonfire', or, as he would have said it, without pyrotechnics, to their own destruction.

Plutarch is even more explicit on the way of the sinner, if by sin one means, as did Plutarch, offences against the nature of man. To offend against that is sheer annihilation.

---

[1] Plutarch, *op. cit.* 'Of Morall vertue', p. 77.
[2] *Ibid.* 'Of Vertue and Vice', pp. 79–80.

For mine owne part, I am of this opinion (if it be lawfull so to say) [The bracket is Holland's but the idea in it is pure Plutarch] that all those who commit such impieties and misdemeanors, have no need either of God or man to punish them; for their owne life onely being so corrupt, and wholy depraved and troubled with all kind of wickedness, is sufficient to plague and torment them to the full.[1]

The doctrine, or apprehension, underlying this is more fully expressed in another passage:

Thus much (I say) have we related, that it may be held as a confessed trueth and supposition, that wicked men otherwhiles have some delay of their punishment: as for the rest, you are to thinke that you ought to hearken unto *Hesiodus* the Poet, who saith not as Plato did, that the punishment of sinne doth follow sinne hard at heeles, but is of the same time and age, as borne and bred in one place with it, and springing out of the very same root and stocke: for these be his words in one place:...

> Who doth for others mischiefe frame,
> To his owne heart contrives the same.

The venimous flies Cantharides are said to conteine in themselves a certeine remedie, made and compounded by a contrarietie or antipathie in nature, which serveth for their owne counter-poison; but wickednesse ingendering within it selfe (I wot not what) displeasure and punishment, not after a sinfull act is committed, but even at the very instant of committing, it beginneth to suffer the paine due to the offence: neither is there a malefactour, but when he seeth others like himselfe punished in their bodies, beareth forth his owne crosse; whereas mischievous wickednesse frameth of her selfe, the engines of her owne torment, as being a wonderfull artisan of a miserable life, which (together with shame and reproch) hath in it lamentable calamities, many terrible frights, fearefull perturbations and passions of the spirit, remorse of conscience, desperate repentance, and continuall troubles and unquietnesse.[2]

That is Plutarch's diagnosis of the way of evil. Shakespeare's tracing of Macbeth's fate is even closer to Plutarch than at first appears from Holland's Englishing of the Greek. For instance,

[1] *Ibid.* 'Why divine justice deferreth punishment', p. 548.
[2] *Ibid.* p. 545.

in the last sentence cited, 'remorse of conscience' and 'desperate repentance' are sixteenth-century phrases for experiences which in Plutarch are literally 'lamentations accompanied by shame, multitudinous fears and grievous sufferings, and regrets and ceaseless tumults within'. The human sense of humanity's tragedy is common to Plutarch and to Shakespeare. Evil is unhuman; sin is unnaturalness rather than unrighteousness.

CHAPTER VII

KING LEAR

King Lear is the last of the four supreme tragedies. Before it Shakespeare had certainly written *Hamlet* and *Othello*, and probably *Macbeth*. *Hamlet* is incontestably the first of these, and though there is no firm opinion whether *Macbeth* or *Lear* be last in time of writing, the majority of scholars put *Macbeth* a little before *Lear*. Our general argument, however, which comes to *Lear* as the last of the four, does not depend on absolute conformity with chronological sequence: the way of genius is not strictly tied to stop-watch and to calendar.

All four tragedies are projections of the tragic fate of man in the universe of which he is a part. But as between the first and the last of these projections there are striking differences in the sort of man whose tragic fate is followed, and in the sort of universe within which he is seen. Hamlet is one with ourselves of today, equipped with the nicely discriminating sensitiveness, the finer emotional susceptibilities, and the complex intellectual faculties of modern man. Appropriately, he lives in an extensively conventionalised and highly organised universe whose civilisation borders on sophistication in its elaborateness. Lear, on the other hand, as far as *homo sapiens* can be, is almost devoid of those human instrumentalities whose strength is drawn from the brain's intellectual capacity in discourse of reason. Indeed, through part of the play, Lear is demonstrably insane. Lear's world, too, is that of a human society hardly emerged from the law of the jungle, living in a state wherein mysterious deities and men and beasts are almost indistinguishable in nature's fellowship. Between *Hamlet* and *Lear* the contrast is stupendous, and the intervening plays seem to have caught human beings at significant intermediate stages in the incalculable stretch of space-time between these two extreme limits in the history of mankind's spiritual progress. It is perhaps not to allow conjecture an undue authority, if one imagines that Shakespeare himself was conscious of this wide differentiation between primitive and modern as the respective stages in the growth of moral perception which characterise the world of his Hamlet on the one hand, and that of his Lear on the other. For it is a striking fact that he deliberately lifts Hamlet into modernity out of a source which is crudely primitive in its moral sense, and that even more patently, he throws Lear back from the modernised world, with which Shakespeare's immediate source had invested him, into farthest backward reaches of time and culture.

There must indeed be a settled intent in Shakespeare's heavy stressing of the primitive both in the people and in the world of *King Lear*, though, of course, the intent may have been mainly realised in his artistic subconsciousness rather than excogitated as a deliberate purpose. The most striking feature of Shakespeare's version of the Lear story is that, compared with earlier versions, some of them very much earlier versions, it generally throws up the primitive elements of the story into far greater prominence. To do this, indeed, it appears to put at hazard even the simpler demands of dramatic credibility. For instance, Shakespeare's immediate source, the contemporary anonymous play, *The True Chronicle History of King Leir* [1] (entered in Stationers' Register 1594, published 1602), is a mere journeyman's production, but in its mechanical crafts for securing theatrical plausibility, it is superficially much superior to Shakespeare's play in one or two major features. For one thing, it provides its incidental circumstances with an everyday Elizabethan colour, and often with its colloquial domestic idiom. Gonorill and Ragan are commonplace in their littlenesses. They regard Cordella as a 'proud pert Peat', [2] mainly

[1] *Leir*, Malone Society Reprint (1907).
[2] *Ibid.* l. 98.

because she copies the cut of all the new frocks which they put
on so that they may compete with her greater natural prettiness:

> We cannot have a quaynt device so soone,
> Or new made fashion, of our choyce invention,
> But if she like it, she will have the same,
> Or study newer to exceed us both.[1]

Cambria (as Albany is called in this play[2]) during a talk with
Cornwall, which he seasons with typical Elizabethan bawdry,
says that Leir will perhaps make his disinherited daughter a nun.
Ragan thinks Cordella 'right fit to make a Parsons wife';[3] but
Gonorill, after showing herself as familiar as is her husband
with bawdy talk, says that such a marriage would not be a good
match:

> she is far too stately for the Church;
> Sheele lay her husbands Benefice on her back
> Even in one gowne, if she may have her will.[4]

In stuff like this there is contemporary Elizabethan flavour, as
there is also in the coastal beacon-watchers, slobbering over
their pots of ale until it is too late to fire the beacon warning.

But in an even more important respect, the old dramatist
shows insight and technical skill in handling a real difficulty in
the plot: he displays technical astuteness in coping with the
plot's strain on credulity in its initial scene, the scene of Lear's
incredible folly when he plans to divide the kingdom and to
stage a love-trial as an effective measure for determining the
parts of the division. In *King Leir*, the old king is in bitter
grief for his '(too late) deceast and dearest Queen'.[5] He is left
with three unmarried daughters and no male heir. He must
seek sons-in-law to care for his daughters and to inherit him
when he is dead. He is getting so old that he would even now
like to resign his earthly cares, and 'thinke upon the welfare of

---

[1] *Ibid.* ll. 101–4.
[2] See note on nomenclature, p. 199, n. 2.
[3] *Leir,* l. 488.
[4] *Ibid.* ll. 494–6.   [5] *Ibid.* l. 2.

his soule'. He could do this if he resigned the crown in equal tripartite dowry to his three daughters. A courtier suggests that he should choose the most suitable three from the suitors to his children, and give to the three daughters on marriage a jointure 'more or less, as is their worth, to them that love professe'. In such casual and natural way, the idea of a love-trial enters. Leir, however, does not jump to the proposed expedient: his mind is that they should, all three, have a like share. But another counseller commends the marriage suggestions on sound political grounds: let Leir prepare for the soon-impending future by marrying his three daughters to three neighbour kings, and so secure the confederate integrity of his realm. Leir accepts the suggestion. Gonorill and Ragan are being wooed by the kings of Cornwall and of Cambria, and the wooers seem to be finding favour.[1] But Cordella vows that she will not marry a king 'unlesse love allowes'. So Leir, seeing the political wisdom of the plan suggested, says that he will persuade or cajole Cordella into marrying some king whose realm lies within this isle, and thus the British dominion will be triply assured:

> I am resolv'd, and even now my mind
> Doth meditate a sudden stratagem,
> To try which of my daughters loves me best.[2]

In this way, the dramatist gives simple dramatic credibility to the incident of the love-trial. Moreover, the motive not only justifies a trial; it suggests, with full credibility, the particular terms of the trial clause. It is a real test, not for verbal profession, but for practical proof of the extent of his daughters' love for

---

[1] The Leir play will confuse the Shakespeare reader in these conjugal unions. It distributes husbands to wives conversely from the scheme of Shakespeare's domestic households. Shakespeare puts Goneril and Albany into wedlock and Regan and Cornwall. Here, Ragan marries Cambria, and Gonorill marries Cornwall. See note, p. 199, n. 2.

[2] *Leir*, ll. 77–9.

him. The question is not to be answered by protestation but by promise. This is the question. Leir is choosing husbands for his three daughters: two of them, he knows already, will accept the mate he has chosen for them; he will therefore ask Cordella to prove her love as great as theirs by being willing to do what they will be willing to do, that is, to marry according to their father's choice. The crucial test is:

> Which of you three to me would prove most kind;
> Which loves me most, and which at my request
> Will soonest yeeld unto their fathers hest.[1]

Cordella does not give the promise. She simply says she loves him:

> I cannot paynt my duty forth in words,
> I hope my deeds shall make report for me:
> But looke what love the child doth owe the father,
> The same to you I beare, my gracious Lord.[2]

This, as Gonorill says, is from Leir's point of view, an 'answere answerlesse'. It does not serve the purpose which had caused Leir to set up the test. In fury, he disowns Cordella; and if the disowning is as apparently unreasonable as it is in Shakespeare, it had at least sprung from more intelligible circumstance. Remember, too, that in *Leir*, the device is primarily a means to secure a reasonable political scheme, the intelligible desire of a sonless king to find sons-in-law from whom he might wisely choose an heir to inherit him politically when his time should come. But there is no talk of immediate abdication. It is in fact curious to note this first entrance of abdication into the stuff of the story: for in Shakespeare's *Lear* the abdication is an item hard to hammer into dramatic probability. In all forms of the story before the anonymous *Leir*, the king had nominally retained supreme monarchical authority. He had appointed their ultimate moieties to his two sons-in-law: but their entry into full possession was deferred to await Leir's demise. In the

---

[1] *Ibid.* ll. 233–5.   [2] *Ibid.* ll. 277–80,

meantime, they were to take over, each only some part, generally a half, of his ultimate heritage, the overriding authority remaining in Leir's own hands.[1] As the story goes on in pre-Elizabethan versions, the dispossession of Leir is an act of rebellion with violence. The anonymous dramatist is the first to make abdication a free act of Leir himself.[2] He introduces it, too, as a means of giving greater dramatic plausibility to the whole set of circumstances. It is only when Leir is stung

---

[1] Geoffrey of Monmouth's version puts off the complete distribution until after Lear shall have died. 'Consilio procerum regni dedit predictas duas puellas duobus ducibus cornubie videlicet & albanie cum medietate tantum insule dum ipse viveret. Post obitum autem eius totam monarchiam brittannie concessit habendam' (*Historia Regum Britanniae*, ed. Griscom, p. 264). Holinshed is equally clear: 'betwixt whome [his sons-in-law] he willed and ordeined that his land should be divided after his death, and the one halfe thereof immediatlie should be assigned to them in hand' (Boswell Stone, p. 3). The situation is slightly obscured by the phrase in which Geoffrey puts Lear's answer to Cordelia's wooer. The French king is told 'as for anie dower he could have none, for all was promised and assured to her other sisters alreadie'. So it is put in Holinshed and there could hardly be misunderstanding. But Geoffrey has Lear's answer thus: 'regnum namque suum cum omni auro & argento goriorille & ragau puelle sororibus distribuerat' (p. 265) as if the distribution had actually been completed. However in both Geoffrey and Holinshed it is clear that Lear continued to hold power and authority, for both add that after a long time, when Lear had fallen into age, his sons-in-law rose against him in armed rebellion and seized his kingdom and his royal authority which up to that time he had held with strength and with renown. Wace's version, however, obscures the circumstance somewhat. He only tacitly assumes that the division of the kingdom is not carried out forthwith, 'Que emprés lui le regne avreient' (l. 1783), and he slurs over the later dispossession of Lear, making it seem as much by consent as by force. In Layamon's retelling of Wace, it is not brought about by armed rebellion at all. The sons-in-law cajole Lear into the plan by the promise of retinue and sustenance: they do so very soon after Lear has made his promise to make them his heirs, and not, as in Geoffrey, a long time after.

[2] See note above for some slight qualification of this in respect of Layamon's version.

to sudden fury by Cordella's answer that he resolves on immediate division and an abdication forthwith:

> Shift as thou wilt, and trust unto thy selfe:
> My Kingdome will I equally devide
> 'Twixt thy two sisters to their royall dowre,
> And will bestow them worthy their deserts:
> This done, because thou shalt not have the hope,
> To have a childs part in the time to come,
> I presently will dispossesse my selfe,
> And set up these upon my princely throne.[1]

On the face of it, the old playwright makes a plausible picture of the whole episode. At least, he gives a greater show of reason to Leir's proceedings than did Shakespeare, who found the love-trial and the abdication somewhat heavy going. Indeed Shakespeare only reached partial success by exercising his poetic capacity to give apparent reality to the substance of Lear's passion. The passion of the older dramatist's Leir has more ground but far less substance; and the framework of external action in Shakespeare's staging of the episode is less deftly built than is that of the older journeyman dramatist. In Shakespeare's form of the story, Lear has already provided his two elder daughters with husbands before any thought of dividing the kingdom has entered his head. It is only now when the third daughter is wooed by two suitors that the provision of a proper dowry for her suggests a division into three even but unequal portions of which Cordelia may have the richest third. To give the occasion greater grace, the division will not await testamentary disposal, but will be by immediate deed of gift. Lear will abdicate. This, and no more than this, as the sign of the depth of his affection for Cordelia is all that the scene offers as ground for the stupendous unreason of Lear's anger when he is incensed at Cordelia's obtuse answer to his easy and merely formal question. For his question, unlike

[1] *Leir*, ll. 318–24.

Leir's, had neither political nor rational purpose behind it; it was merely sentimental. Hence many critics take the scene as a deliberate indication that dotage had already got the better of Lear's reason and judgement, and that already he was heading straight for the madness which was soon to overtake him. But Coleridge had surer insight into the scope of Shakespeare's intention. Lear's anger was less the outburst of occasioning circumstance than of those elements which were deep within his nature.

The strange, yet by no means unnatural, mixture of selfishness, sensibility, and habit of feeling derived from and fostered by the particular rank and usages of the individual; the intense desire to be intensely beloved, selfish, and yet characteristic of the selfishness of a loving and kindly nature—a feeble selfishness, self-supportless and leaning for all pleasure on another's breast; the selfish craving after a sympathy with a prodigal disinterestedness, contradicted by its own ostentation and the mode and nature of its claims; the anxiety, the distrust, the jealousy, which more or less accompany all selfish affections, and one among the surest contradistinctions of mere fondness from love, and which originate Lear's eager wish to enjoy his daughters' violent professions, while the inveterate habits of sovereignty convert the wish into claim and positive right, and the incompliance with it into crime and treason; these facts, these passions, these moral verities, on which the whole tragedy is founded, are all prepared for, and will to retrospect be found implied in, these first four or five lines of the play.[1]

Yet for most of us, even accepting Coleridge's account of Shakespeare's purpose, there remains some doubt as to whether Shakespeare's means realise his intention in this scene. Coleridge continues: these lines

let us know that the trial is but a trick, and that the grossness of the old king's rage is in part the natural result of a silly trick suddenly and most unexpectedly baffled and disappointed.

---

[1] *Coleridge's Shakespearean Criticism*, ed. T. M. Raysor, vol. 1, p. 55.

'In part', says Coleridge. But the partially natural cannot be relied on to secure full dramatic credibility. Coleridge himself admits that

> *Lear* is the only serious performance of Shakespeare the interest and situations of which are derived from the assumption of a gross improbability.[1]

Perhaps Shakespeare himself felt that he had relied too much on the sheer weight of poetry, and that to give Lear a firm dramatic identity there was immediate need to provide such supports as drama traditionally uses. The most effective of these, however, he could not at once employ, for his story had not at that point an incident from which all the strands of Lear's character could emerge clearly and distinctly in action. He went another way about it, less directly dramatic in itself, but established in dramatic practice. Immediately following the scene of the frenzy, he introduced a brief and crowded passage of conversation between Goneril and Regan [2] which is entirely made up of descriptive portraiture, hoping thereby, perhaps, to give psychological support to the poetic impression, and in that way to give to it not only the momentary reality it had won for itself, but the enduring acceptance of retrospect.

> *Goneril.* You see how full of changes his age is...he always loved our sister most, and with what poor judgement he hath now cast her off appears too grossly.
> *Regan.* 'Tis the infirmity of his age; yet he hath ever but slenderly known himself.
> *Goneril.* The best and soundest of his time hath been but rash; then must we look to receive from his age, not alone the imperfections of long-engraffed condition, but therewithal the unruly waywardness that infirm and choleric years bring with them.

Yet if the first scene manages to hint, rather than with conviction to depict intelligibly, the majestic limbs of Lear's spiritual stature, the rest of the play fills in the whole structure.

[1] *Ibid.* p. 59.　　　　[2] *King Lear* I. i. 286 seq.

Lear becomes 'every inch a king'; and the old play's Leir
remains nothing more than a pathetic, and sometimes testy,
old man whose 'senceless senses' are easily played on by his
scheming daughters, and who takes their ill-treatment of him
meekly, with many tears, and with all Christian resignation:

> Come let us go, and see what God will send;
> When all meanes faile, he is the surest friend.[1]

Such a Leir can obviously be dismissed from tragedy, and
allowed, as the old dramatist and all previous tellers of the
story of Lear properly allow him, to pass his remaining days in
the comfort of reconciliation with a Cordella who is now fully
reinstated in her royal honours.

Coleridge thought that Shakespeare, risking all that the old
dramatist's skilful handicraft had cleared out of his simpler
way, could with confidence hope to foist on his audience the
improbability of his plot because it retold a tale already rooted
in the popular faith. It certainly was an old story: but in all
older forms it ended happily. Shakespeare's inversion of this
has consequences of its own. But, unrelated to that vital change,
Shakespeare's version has more improbabilities in it than has
any of the older versions. Some of these improbabilities have
been noted above in a comparison with their counterparts in
the old play. There were, however, other versions of the story
which were equally accessible to Shakespeare, and may very
well have been seen by him. The earliest is in the twelfth-
century Latin of Geoffrey of Monmouth's *Historia Regum
Britanniae*. The tale recurs in the *Gesta Romanorum*, of which
fifteenth-century English translations were current. It is frequently retold by historians and poets in the sixteenth century:
by John Higgins in *The Mirror for Magistrates* (1574), by Warner
in *Albion's England* (1586), by Spenser in his *Faerie Queene*
(1590), and, of course, by Holinshed (1577).[2] There is no

---

[1] *Leir*, ll. 2089–90.

[2] Certain points of difference between the versions will be found in
notes to pp. 199, 209.

certain evidence, however, for thinking that Shakespeare had more than two of these accounts in his mind when he wrote *King Lear*. The two were the very brief account in Holinshed, and the full length dramatic version in *The True Chronicle of King Leir*.

Perhaps the first sentence of Holinshed's tale reminded Shakespeare of the remote antiquity of its matter:

Leir…was admitted ruler over the Britaines in the yeare of the world 3105 at what time Joas reigned in Juda[1]

—a tale obviously moving in places consecrated to a far more ancient time than that in which the nuns and the parsons' wives and the beer-drinking beacon-watchers of *Leir* could be at home. In substance, however, the Lear saga is the same in all these pre-Shakespearian records.[2] The middle stuff of it is given succinctly by Holinshed thus:

When this Leir therefore was come to great yeres, and began to waxe unweldie through age, he thought to understand the affections of his daughters towards him, and preferre hir whome he best loved to the succession over the kingdome,

---

[1] Holinshed *apud* Boswell Stone, p. 1.

[2] The essential sameness of early versions of the Lear story is obscured by variations in nomenclature, both of persons and of places. Welsh forms of the daughters' names, as Geoffrey of Monmouth may have known them, appear to be Koronilla (the eldest), Rragaw and Kordalia. Geoffrey of Monmouth has them as Goriorilla, Regau, Cordeilla. In Wace, they are Gonorille, Ragaü, Cordeille; in Layamon's *Brut*, Gornoille, Ragau, Cordoille. Confusion starts however with the names of their husbands, and the early versions sometimes vary the pairing in the marriage schemes. Geoffrey of Monmouth states that Lear gave his two daughters to the dukes of Cornwall and Albany ('duobus ducibus cornubie videlicet et albanie', ed. Griscom, p. 264), and the order in which he names them seems to have caused later confusion, the assumption being that he names the elder first, whereas it is clear from later parts of his narrative, that it was the second daughter whom he gave to Cornwall. He later calls Goneril's husband Maglaurus, duke of Albany, and says that after Goneril had objected to the size of Lear's retinue, Lear left her and sought Henninus, duke of

whereupon he set about the love-trial. Gonorilla 'calling hir gods to record, protested that she loved him more than hir

---

Cornwall who had married Regau. Holinshed follows Geoffrey closely and repeats Geoffrey's order in first naming the bridal pairs; so, like Geoffrey, he helped later confusion. 'The father... married his two eldest daughters, the one unto Henninus the duke of Cornewall, and the other unto Maglanus the duke of Albania' (Boswell Stone, p. 3). But Holinshed keeps his account so brief that nowhere does he need to specify which daughter had which husband. Confusion has started however, before the tale gets to Holinshed's days. In *Le Roman de Brut*, Wace, like Geoffrey, first states that the two daughters were married to two dukes; but though he names the younger first, it would appear that he makes it quite clear that the second is the elder:

> Al duc de Cornoaille l'une,
> E al rei d'Escoce l'ainz nee.
>
> (ed. Arnold, ll. 1780–1)

Later he calls the King of Scotland Manglanus, and the Duke of Cornwall Hennim:

> Hennim, ki Ragaü aveit,
> Ki en Cornoaille maneit.   (*Ibid*. ll. 1891–2)

But Layamon, following Wace, in his Middle English *Brut*, is confused. He marries the sisters to the wrong men.

> Þe duc of Cornwaile
> scal habbe Gornoille,
> & þe Scottene king
> Regau þ scone.   (ed. Madden, p. 131)

Later however, telling of Lear's domicile after the division of the kingdom, he says that the king went first to Scotland, to his eldest daughter and her husband Maglaune (*ibid*. p. 139), a version which, of course, fits with Wace's and with Geoffrey's, but not with Layamon's own passage cited above. The confusion of husbands and wives by Laymon recurs in Shakespeare's source, the anonymous sixteenth-century play, where Goneril is Cornwall's wife, and Regan's husband is called Cambria: this particular confusion is curious, for Cornwall and Cambria were parts of one dukedom, and in *The Mirror for Magistrates*, Regan's husband, Hinnine, is prince of Cornwall and Camber. Shakespeare, has, of course, Cornwall for Regan's husband, and Goneril's is called Albany, as he had been in Geoffrey. (Formerly, owne life, which by right and reason should be most deere unto hir'. The second daughter Regan, 'confirming hir saiengs with great othes, [said] that she loved him more than toong could expresse, and farre above all other creatures of the world'. In her turn, Cordeilla 'made this answer as followeth':

knowing the great love and fatherlie zeale that you have alwaies borne towards me (for the which I maie not answere you otherwise than I thinke, and as my conscience leadeth me) I protest unto you, that I have loved you ever, and will continuallie (while I live) love you as my naturall father. And if you would more understand of the love that I beare you, assertaine your selfe, that so much as you have, so much you are worth, and so much I love you, and no more.[1]

Holinshed bluntly goes on:

The father being nothing content with this answer, married his two eldest daughters, the one unto Henninus the duke of Cornewall, and the other unto Maglanus the duke of Albania, betwixt whome he willed and ordained that his land should be divided after his death, and the one halfe thereof immediatelie should be assigned to them in hand: but for the third daughter Cordeilla he reserved nothing.

However, a prince of Gallia took the dowerless daughter in marriage. In due course, as Leir was still further fallen into age,

---

Albany geographically included Scotland.) Spenser has the whole thing right, as Shakespeare had: Goneril's husband is Maglan of Scotland, and they lived in Albany. But *The Mirror for Magistrates* adds to the confusion by curiously inverting Layamon's form of it. Layamon in the first place married them wrongly. But *The Mirror* is right in this: Goneril is married to Maglaurus of Albany and Regan to Hinnine of Cornwall and Camber. But at the point where Layamon gets back to the orthodox version—the departure of Lear from the eldest to the younger daughter's—*The Mirror* goes astray. Lear leaves Goneril and Albany to go to Cornwall, 'Raganes love to trye', and there he is well-received at first both by Regan and by Prince Maglaurus (who, of course, is not Regan's husband, but is Goneril's Maglaurus of Albany). (*Parts added to The Mirror for Magistrates*, ed. L. B. Campbell (1946), pp. 149–151.)

[1] Holinshed *apud* Boswell Stone, p. 3.

his two elder sons-in-law, tired of waiting for their full heritage
(Leir had only given them half of it as yet), rose in arms and
reft from him the governance of the land, upon conditions to be
continued for terme of life: by the which he was put to his portion,
that is, to live after a rate assigned to him for the maintenance of his
estate, which in processe of time was diminished as well by Maglanus
as by Henninus.[1]

As these conditions were thus being whittled down, Leir fled
to Gallia and was joyfully received by Cordeilla and her
husband. They gathered an army, invaded Britain, slew their
brothers-in-law (nothing is said of the sisters), and restored
Leir to his throne. After his death, Cordeilla ruled in his place
for five years.

The poetic versions in *The Mirror for Magistrates*, *Albion's
England*, and *The Faerie Queene*, are even shorter than Holinshed's. Warner and Spenser follow him in time and find in
him all they want. *The Mirror* is independent, but its details are
like his, with but very slight and immaterial differences. *The
Mirror*, for instance, is the first account which includes in
Cordelia's reply to her father's love-trial, the reservation of
a possible sharer of her love if she should marry:

> Yet shortely I may chaunce, if Fortune will,
> To finde in heart to beare another more good will.[2]

Only Shakespeare's Cordelia makes a similar reservation:

> Haply, when I shall wed,
> That lord whose hand must take my plight shall carry
> Half my love with him, half my care and duty.[3]

Though the old play's Cordella makes no such remark, it is
unnecessary to imagine that Shakespeare must be copying *The
Mirror*. Shakespeare's Cordelia was soon to marry; and the
Cordella of the old play helped to fill out its matter by her

---

[1] Holinshed *apud* Boswell Stone, p. 4.
[2] Only from the 1587 ed. See Campbell *ed. cit.* p. 148.
[3] *King Lear* I. i. 102.

theatrically romantic courtship of the French king in disguise. But Shakespeare surely did not need even so much of a hint to give his very marriageable Cordelia, so soon to be a bride, the spontaneous and natural reservation from her father's share in her love.

It is plain that all these varieties of the story have one inherent difficulty in the way of their being accepted as plausible human tales. They have a father who prefers one of his three daughters, but who, when he devises a plan for a spectacular confirmation of his happiness, is frustrated by the ambiguous terms of his favoured daughter's reply and is at once driven into wild frenzy by it. In the main, the tellers of the tale try to carry the difficulty by rushing it: such answer, they imply, must naturally enrage a father to such a frenzy. The mechanical recorder, Holinshed, is not susceptible to artistic perturbation: enough for him merely to record 'the father being nothing content with this answer...'; but this is a curtailed summary which neither indicates the weight of the impact on the father's sentiment, nor justifies his drastic retaliation. Holinshed the narrator was merely retelling Geoffrey of Monmouth's story, whether at first or at fifth hand hardly concerns us here. Geoffrey baldly made Cordelia say 'Etenim quantum habes, tantum vales tantumque te diligo',[1] and this seems sufficiently mercenary in a daughter to arouse any father's furious disgust; yet because of its mercenary sufficiency, it is inadequate to make Lear's love of Cordelia and Cordelia's later care for him either 'probable or necessary' in Aristotle's sense. The quandary is regularly side-tracked by the later poetic narrators. *The Mirror* merely gives Cordelia's answer as

> No cause (quod I) there is I should your grace despise:
> For nature so doth binde and duty mee compell
> To love you, as I ought my father, well.[2]

---

[1] *Historia Regum Britanniae*, ed. Griscom, p. 264.
[2] Only from the 1587 ed. See Campbell, *ed. cit.* p. 148.

Spenser disposes of the situation even more succinctly:

> But Cordeill said she lov'd him as behoov'd:
> Whose simple answere, wanting colours fayre
> To painte it forth, him to displeasaunce moved.[1]

But the poet's needs are not the dramatist's. When the dramatist begins to use the material for his dramatic purposes, he encounters problems of aesthetic plausibility which must either be silenced by poetic power or be met by psychological congruities. The first dramatist of the Lear tale, the author of *The True Chronicle*, was palpably concerned to fit the protestations of the love-trial into a plausible dramatic pattern. He gave Leir an intelligible motive for the trial and an intelligible reaction to such reply as his Cordella made to her father. But what rendered the motive intelligible was the conformity of Leir's desire for such trial with a normal man's reaction to its circumstances; what, however, made Leir's particular reaction to his daughter's answer intelligible was the assumption that Leir was a man very different from the average reasonable man; and the anonymous dramatist of Leir was incapable of investing his Leir with the passionate potentialities which would give convincing reality to this indispensable differentiation. His Leir could have planned the trial; but his Leir could not have emerged from it as the story made him emerge. Yet the old dramatist had done his dramatic best to overcome the difficulty in his story. He had sought dramatic probability for Leir himself, making dramatically possible the Leir who devises the love-trial and the Leir who responds to it as Leir does. But he fails to convert the dramatically possible into the dramatically probable. His Leir could be what he wants him to be; but in fact he fails to become it. One of the crucial details in the original story which challenges the dramatic imagination is a particular term in Cordelia's answer at the love-trial; and his dramatic genius is not sufficient to meet it. The first teller, Geoffrey of Monmouth, made Cordelia

[1] *The Faerie Queene*, Book II, Canto x. 28.

say 'quantum habes, tantum vales tantumque te diligo', a phrase
of which the meaning may be taken to lie at any point between
two wide extremes. In its most literal sense, it is brutal, 'you
are worth as much as you have'; in its most charitable extension
it may almost be 'you are entitled to all the love your great
worthiness assures for you'. But the ambiguity is wide, and
the baldly mercenary interpretation is the one which springs
first to mind. It has been suggested that the phrase was taken
by Geoffrey from his unknown French source.[1] There is an
early medieval French proverb, 'tant as, tant vaus', or, in
another variant, 'tant a home, tant est prise'. Its clear meaning
is that a man is esteemed according to his wealth, and wealth is
clearly thought of in a material measure. The 'tant vaus' may
perhaps in a mild way mitigate the too material limitation of
'tant as' by suggesting dignity in the world in place of mere
cash in hand. It looks as if the literary lure of the proverb were
considered by Geoffrey to be a sufficient excuse for risking the
incongruous psychological consequences of the ambiguity.
Such a merely stylistic justification is more obviously required
by the best-known French medieval version of the tale, that
told in Wace's twelfth-century *Roman de Brut*. Wace gives the
relevant sentence of Cordelia's reply in this form:

> Tant as, tant vals, e jo tant t'aim.[2]

Up to this last sentence of her reply, Cordelia has spoken in
a high moral tone, unemotional, of course, but unexceptionable
in sentiment:

> U ad nule fille qui die
> A sun pere par presoncie
> Qu'ele l'aint plus qu'ele ne deit?
> Ne sai que plus grant amur seit
> Que entre enfanz e entre pere
> U entre enfanz e entre mere.
> Mes peres ies, jo aim tant tei
> Come jo mun pere amer dei.[3]

---

[1] These suggestions were put to me by my colleague, Dr F.
Whitehead.   [2] Wace, ed. Arnold, l. 1742.   [3] *Ibid.* ll. 1733–40.

Translated somewhat freely this becomes:

Where is there a daughter who would show such presumption as to tell her father that she loves him more than in fact she ought to love him? I cannot conceive greater love than that which binds a child to its father or to its mother. You are my father. I love you as much as it is right that I should love you.

The high-mindedness of this touches the acme of spiritual austerity. But then comes the summary proverbial conclusion; and the moral pitch drops at once to a discordant flat:

> E pur faire tei plus certein,
> Tant as, tant vals, e jo tant t'aim.

Saying this, Cordelia would not add another word. 'A tant se tout, ne volt plus dire.' Perhaps Wace's Cordeille, like Wace himself, was lured by her stylistic conscience: throughout her speech, she showed a high-brow fondness for rhetorical finesse. Perhaps, too, there was sufficient range of ambiguity in the proverbial phrase to make it cover both the sense in which Cordeille should surely mean it, and the other sense which Leir most certainly found in it.[1] For a dramatist, however, a literary crux of this kind becomes a problem.[2] But it was a problem which the Elizabethan dramatists settled in their

---

[1] See Orr, 'On Homonymics' in *Studies in French Language* etc. presented to Professor Pope. Manchester University Press, 1939.

[2] Layamon had felt a need to soften Cordelia's reply even in his poem, perhaps because he was less susceptible to the charms of the verbal artistry which attracted Geoffrey and Wace. He renders Wace's 'Tant as, tant vals, e jo tant t'aim' by adding a gloss which dulls it into proverbial generality:

> al swa muchel þu bist woruh:
> swa þu velden ært.
> & al swa muchel swa þu hauest:
> men þe wllet luuien.
> for sone heo bið ilazeð
> þe mon þe lutel ah.

> (*Brut*, ed. Madden, p. 129–30)

own way. Neither the author of *The True Chronicle* nor Shakespeare relied on merely verbal ambiguity to explain Lear's frenzy. The anonymous dramatist set the whole scene in an atmosphere of everyday reasonable probability. Shakespeare makes the substance and not the form of Cordelia's reply the motive of Lear's frenzy: and doing so, is thrown back on the resources of poetry for transmitting Lear's passion so as to sweep us into momentary oblivion of the human unreasonableness of his outburst. From the very beginning, Shakespeare's Lear is unreasonable, unreasonable in his deliberate plans for the love-trial, and even more unreasonable in his response to it. His anger has no *double-entendre* to justify it. It can only exist by its own warrant, and that warrant must come from poetry rather than from drama.

But in *Lear*, poetry and drama, existing each in its own right, come so near together that, if they do not completely coalesce, they are nevertheless in closer imaginative co-operation than in any other of Shakespeare's plays, a co-operation compared with which the lyric contribution to the drama of *Richard II* and even that to *Romeo and Juliet* are of little and even extraneous moment. Shakespeare the dramatist chooses the arena in which Shakespeare the poet can be dramatically himself in the fullness of his poetic power. The dramatist calls up his human characters, strips them of all perquisites but the primitive strands of human life, and releases them to live in a dramatic cosmos which is little more than stark nature's universe. In creative energy of this order, poet and dramatist are leagued in intimate concord. The poet is expending his poetic resources to create a sense of universality and of ultimacy in the imaging of a tragic action: and that is a dramatic end.

To secure the end, however, the first requisite is the conjuring of a circumambient atmosphere from and within which an elemental human world may have its being, a rude and simple universe wherein life and man are both at their beginnings,

fresh from nature's moulds, a universe of nature whose turbu-
lent winds and flashing lightnings are macrocosmic passions
resurgent in the anger and the lust of its aboriginal human
denizens. The storm scene is the most superb instance in drama
of the complete imaginative fusion of poetry and of drama.
There is no storm in the story as the Middle Ages knew it. But
the author of *The True Chronicle* had mechanically used his
mechanical stage-properties to supply 'thunder and lightning'
for marking the moment when the suborned assassin, swearing
'by hell and all the devils' that Leir's daughters themselves
had commissioned him to murder Leir, is nonplussed for an
instant by Leir's retort:

> Sweare not by hell, for that stands gaping wide
> To swallow thee.[1]

—words mechanically reinforced by the professional stage
direction 'thunder and lightning'. The hint, however, must
have fired Shakespeare's imagination. The storm becomes the
dynamic symbol of the energy which vitalises the play's
universe. Creatively it fuses nature and human nature, the
macrocosm and the microcosm. Imaginatively, it identifies
the passions of men with the elemental powers of nature's
universe.

The world of Lear is a world set solely in the imagination,
and the pillars of it are the immaterial stuff of poetry. But
though poetry be the breath of its existence, it animates
a structure which dramatically is linked more tangibly together
within the framework of a firmament and all that must be
therein. It has its heavens and its earth, and man is groping
towards a sense of their interdependence. In the might of the
heavens, in the elements and in the sacred radiance of the sun
and the operation of the orbs, men are dimly descrying superhuman powers, gods and goddesses of nature, in a confused

[1] *Leir*, l. 1632.

hierarchy of dominion, Hecate, Apollo, Juno, and Jupiter,[1] wreaking their will on man, and guessed sometimes as ministers of avenging justice or even for a fleeting moment as dispensers of a divine benevolence. But in general the heavens of *King Lear* are dwelling-places of vaguely apprehended pagan deities, dimly separating themselves from the formless forces of nature into faintly discerned and half-personalised beings who are felt most intimately through the terror of their common and collective almightiness. They are clearest as gods when they make their honours of men's impossibilities: their great opposeless wills determine man's happiness and his afflictions. They are to be feared and endured, and sometimes they may be propitiated by prayer. Within such wide limits of half-conscious and half-articulated belief, the people of the play have frequently their own distinctive attitudes, though these are scarcely so positive as to become a peculiar creed. Lear's own is typical. Life and death is at the disposal of the heavens, of the stars,

---

[1] Much has been written of the 'gods' in *King Lear*. They have already established themselves in the earliest versions of the story. Geoffrey tells how Leir's father Bladud was expert in necromancy and skilled in magic. Meeting his death in an attempt to fly by mechanical aids, he fell on to the temple of Apollo in Trinovant, 'ceciditque super templum appollinis infra urbem trinovantum in multa frustra contritus (Geoffrey, *op. cit*. p. 262). Regan swore 'per numina caeli' that she would reduce Lear's retinue (p. 266), and Lear, in the ensuing distress, invoked the 'irrevocabilia seria fatorum' (p. 267). When Lear died, Cordelia buried him in a cave which was then consecrated to Janus Bifrons (p. 270). In his turn, Holinshed records that Bladud, Leir's father, 'tooke suche pleasure in artificiall practices and magike, that he taught this rite throughout all his Realm', and that, having taken it upon him 'to flie in the ayre', 'he fell upon the temple of Apollo which stoode in the Citie of Troynovant' (ed. 1577, p. 18). In the Leir story itself, he records that in the trial of love, Goneril, invited to attest her love, called 'upon hir Gods to record', etc. (p. 19). In the centuries between Geoffrey and Holinshed, Wace had kept to the substance of Geoffrey's account, adding minor variants such as these: that Bladud fell on the temple of Apolin which was in Londres

'the operation of the orbs, by whom we do exist and cease to be'. He feels his deities most convincingly in nature, which imaginatively impresses him by its force in creation and in generation:

> Hear, nature, hear; dear goddess, hear![1]

But his simplest visual sense of deity is in beings assuming the shapes of godhead, Apollo, Minerva, Juno and Jupiter, as later they were to be named, and as Lear is here proleptically allowed to name them, for to Shakespeare's day they were deities of elder time. He searches from the gods for some witness of a moral purpose in their wills. But 'gods', 'heavens', and 'elements' are so confusedly identified in his consciousness that he is mainly aware of their hostility to man. Perhaps the gods themselves have stirred his daughters' hearts against their

---

(*ed. cit.* l. 1648), and that Cordelia was buried in the crypt of the temple of Janus (l. 2050). But the medieval English tradition must have amplified these pagan elements in the background of the story. Even so soon after Wace as was his translator Layamon, there are noticeable additions of detail and of stress. For example, when Layamon records that Bladud fell on 'Appollones temple', he adds 'þe wes þe tirfulle feond' 'who was the mighty fiend' (*ed. cit.* p. 123). He had previously described Bladud's occultism:

> he cuðe þene vuele craft:
> þat he wið þene wurse spæc.
> & al þat ever he wolde:
> þe wurse him talde. (p. 120)

He was, in fact, a real worker in black magic. He made a temple to Minerva, a 'heathenish name' (p. 121). In the Lear story, he makes Goneril swear by Apollin, on whom is her whole trust:

> Swa helpe me Apollin:
> for min ilaefe is al on him. (p. 126)

And further, he lets Lear invoke Appolin (p. 129); and most significant of all, lets Cordelia give Apollo thanks as her lord:

> Appollin mi lauer ich þankie þe. (p. 150)

[1] *King Lear* I. iv. 297.

father; and, as 'the elements', wreaking their wrath on him, they are plain yoke-fellows in wickedness:

> I call you servile ministers,
> That have with two pernicious daughters join'd
> Your high-engender'd battles 'gainst a head
> So old and white as this.[1]

Yet some inner thrusting-on drives him to catch at a hope that the great gods will find that their enemies are those whom men on earth have cause to call the wicked:

> Let the great gods
> That keep this dreadful pother o'er our heads
> Find out their enemies now.[2]

For 'this dreadful pother' which they keep over our heads may even be a fearful summoner to 'pent-up guilts', calling the wicked to put off their wickedness and to submit to the will of the gods.

There are other people in *King Lear*, however, who have a surer feeling than has Lear himself that the gods incline to justice and even sometimes to benevolence. But in the main, this sentiment is a colour from their temperaments, and what kindliness they themselves are disposed to they see reflected in their deities. Cordelia supplicates them as 'kind gods', gods, that is, at least accessible to pity. Few, however, even of these better and kinder men dare go beyond a hope that the gods are just. In his own horror at Goneril's inhumanity, Albany cries:

> If that the heavens do not their visible spirits
> Send quickly down to tame these vile offences,
> It will come,
> Humanity must perforce prey on itself,
> Like monsters of the deep,[3]

and he eagerly casts about for confirmation of his hope:

> This shows you are above,
> You justicers, that these our nether crimes
> So speedily can venge.[4]

[1] *Ibid.* III. ii. 21. [2] *Ibid.* III. ii. 49.
[3] *Ibid.* IV. ii. 46. [4] *Ibid.* IV. ii. 78.

For Edgar, too, it is the demonstrable operativeness of deity in the punishment of wickedness which gives him confidence in their moral nature:

> The gods are just, and of our pleasant vices
> Make instruments to plague us.[1]

But the very phrasing of his faith suggests a belief not essentially different from Gloucester's 'As flies are we to the gods'; for Edgar's picture of divine justice in operation has hints of gods whose hedonism is comparable to that of the deities in Tennyson's *Lotos Eaters*. In the end, too, for Edgar, 'men must endure their going hence even as their coming hither; ripeness is all'.

Perhaps most typical of the 'religious' atmosphere of the play are the attitudes represented on the one hand by Gloucester, and, on the other, by Kent. In each case, the attitude is part of the character. Gloucester is a simple, easy-going, good-natured, sentimental, conventional fellow, whose thoughts are not so much the outcome of his thinking as the utterances of his momentary mood. He is superstitious, prone to the occultism of sectaries astronomical: 'these late eclipses in the sun and moon portend no good to us'.[2] But he holds nothing profoundly. His temperament and his fears give him the sensation that 'as flies to wanton boys are we to the gods'. Yet on another occasion the same temperamental disposition makes him seek solace in prayer to 'the ever-gentle gods'. But Kent is a different man entirely. He is a sort of primitive Stoic agnostic. 'Thou swears't thy gods in vain', he tells Lear. For himself, a casual and placid recognition of Fortune and the turning of her wheel is man's safest guess at the power which controls his destiny:

> Fortune, good night: smile once more; turn thy wheel![3]

[1] *King Lear* v. iii. 170.
[2] *Ibid.* I. ii. 112.
[3] *Ibid.* II. ii. 180.

But he has no deep concern in these mysteries: it is sufficient for him to follow his impulse and to render services of help and kindness, or, when occasion requires, of blunt resistance to evil. He is not a fatalist by conviction. He finds strength and self-reliance in the consciousness of good works; beyond that he neither has nor needs apparent certainties. Hence, when he says,

> It is the stars,
> The stars above us, govern our conditions,

he is not declaring a positive faith in planetary influence: he is using that form of words as an emphatic way of asserting that there is an infinity of things in life which flatly defy all intelligible explanation, as, for instance, the fact that Cordelia should be sister in blood to Regan and Goneril:

> It is the stars,
> The stars above us, govern our conditions;
> Else one self mate and mate could not beget
> Such different issues.[1]

The most explicitly philosophic exponent of the body of theological opinions expressed in *King Lear*, Edmund, has been deferred until the last, for the plain reason that he represents, not the climate of opinion prevalent in the play, but the rebel's rejection of it. His notions are valid, but only obversely valid, in an assessment of the intellectual universe of *King Lear*. In the consciousness of all its other people, there is a sense of inscrutable mysteries which they try to formulate in beliefs which range from the crass occultism of superstition to the faint adumbrations of an emergent religious and moral system. But Edmund has the rationalist's contempt for everything which escapes, or transcends, the strict categories of rational validity. He offers casual recognition to the gods, but claims autonomous authority to make them deities of his own shaping. 'Thou, nature, art my goddess.'[2] He professes that to her

---

[1] *Ibid.* iv. iii. 34.   [2] *Ibid.* i. ii. i.

divine law all his services are bound. But this formal submission is merely his opportunity to impose on nature his own
will. He tells her what, in his own instance, her regulations are
or should be. She must erect her own authority against such
laws as the 'curiosity of nations' have incorporated in public
custom and in popular habit. She must exalt the products of
her 'lusty stealth' above the issue of law-abiding and custom-
loving wives and husbands. Nature and all her fellow gods
must stand up firmly for bastards.

Of course, in Edmund's scrutiny of the foolish consequences
which ensue when recognition of the mystery of life takes on
the positive forms of superstitious belief, there is cogent critical
sense: it is the excellent foppery of the world, when we are sick
in fortune, to make the stars guilty of our disasters,

as if we were villains by necessity; fools by heavenly compulsion;
knaves, thieves, and treachers by spherical predominance; drunkards,
liars, and adulterers by an enforced obedience of planetary influence;
and all that we are evil in, by a divine thrusting on: an admirable
evasion of whoremaster man, to lay his goatish disposition to the
charge of a star.[1]

But it is criticism which turns back on its exponent. It is,
moreover, valid only within the range of its own moral
implications, and touches neither the religious nor the metaphysical props on one or other or both of which an ethic must
be built. For our immediate purpose the very blatancy of
Edmund's onslaught on superstition is a piece of indirect
evidence which establishes the climate of vague philosophic
and religious opinion prevailing in the essential structure of
King Lear.

Such, then, is the universe which is inhabited by the people
of Shakespeare's play. Perhaps the most summary sense of its
moral quality emerges from the instinctive responses which are
made at decisive moments by the unimportant ordinary folk

[1] *King Lear* I. ii. 132.

who complete the cast of the play as nameless agents of some piece or other of its formal action. Their visible motives display their unreasoned feeling that in some way man's destiny is not unconnected with his goodness, and that the arbiters of fate are gods whose general will is goodness. There are, for instance, the three servants of Cornwall. The first of them, though he has served Cornwall since he was a child,[1] is so incensed at the sight of Regan's and Cornwall's mutilation of Gloucester that he draws his sword on them and mortally wounds his master, though he himself is slain in the act, a sacrifice to the might of some irresistible inner impulse. The second servant, seeing Cornwall the apparent victor and not knowing of his fatal wound, utters his protest in simple theological amazement:

> I'll never care what wickedness I do
> If this man come to good:

and the third, in similar mind, adds of Regan:

> If she live long
> And in the end meet the old course of death,
> Women will all turn monsters.

The incident which has moved the three of them is related shortly afterwards by a messenger in these terms:

> A servant that he bred, thrill'd with remorse,
> Opposed against the act, bending his sword
> To his great master; who, thereat enraged,
> Flew on him, and amongst them fell'd him dead,
> But not without that harmful stroke, which since
> Hath pluck'd him after.[2]

In this account, there is the same underlying assumption that goodness somehow triumphs over evil, even though, doing so, it pays a mortal price. But the messenger finds that the instrument which effectually asserts and enforces goodness lies in moral and in human attributes rather than in any clear policy

---

[1] *Ibid.* III. vii. 73.   [2] *Ibid.* IV. ii. 74.

of the gods. The retributory servant is impelled by compassion, for that is what 'thrill'd with remorse' can only mean in this context. It is something which the messenger recognises as a power in the heart of human nature, its *philanthropia*, its human kindness, its 'love'. Even the dying villain Edmund, strangely struck by the thought that, though it were only by Goneril and Regan, he has been 'beloved', is blindly moved to plan from his death-bed some deed of good in despite of his own nature.

The examination of this metaphysical world of Lear has been pursued at some length for more than one reason. One of the reasons is this. As a universe, its outstanding features and its dominant outlines must have impressed Shakespeare and Shakespeare's audience by their striking difference from the corresponding elements in the universe which Shakespeare was reconstructing, that, namely, of *The True Chronicle of King Leir*, the play which must have been in his memory, if not on his desk, as his own *Lear* unfolded itself in his dramatic imagination.

The outstanding feature of the older Leir's world is its pervading and even obtruding Christianism. Its opening lines strike a distinctive note of Christian belief:

> Thus to our griefe the obsequies performd
> Of our (too late) deceast and dearest Queen,
> Whose soule I hope, possest of heavenly joyes,
> Doth ride in triumph 'mongst the Cherubins.[1]

It adopts the whole institution of Christian practice, its offices, its sacraments, its liturgy and its creed. It knows not the gods; it has God alone. Its worship is through the ecclesiastical system of holy church. Leir longs for relief from the ties of monarchical duty, so that he may betake him to his prayers and to his beads.[2] Cordella blames herself for neglecting strict attendance in the temple of her God, and therein rendering thanks for all his

[1] *Leir*, ll. 1–4.   [2] *Ibid.* l. 557.

benefits. If she could achieve again the love of her father, she would endure the harshest austerities of penitential discipline, and

> would abstayne from any nutryment,
> And pyne my body to the very bones.[1]

Barefoot,

> I would on pilgrimage set forth
> Unto the furthest quarters of the earth,
> And all my lifetime would I sackcloth weare
> And mourning-wise powre dust upon my head.[2]

In the meantime, 'I will to Church and pray unto my Saviour'.[3]

In a universe like this of Leir's, the Christian King of Heaven is lord of the human world. As Jehovah he is omnipotent:

> Oh just *Jehova*, whose almighty power
> Doth governe all things in this spacious world.[4]

His law is absolute. It is his pleasure that his subjects should submit:

> it is the pleasure of my God
> And I do willingly embrace the rod.[5]

It is impious for man to question God's will:

> Let us submit us to the will of God:
> Things past all sence, let us not seeke to know;
> It is God's will, and therefore must be so.[6]

But the will of God is justice: the heavens are just, and God will always succour his obedient flock:

> Come, let us go, and see what God will send;
> When all meanes faile, he is the surest friend.[7]

This is a God who, first of all, is the God of justice. His vengeance falls on those who sin against him. He has set conscience in mankind to prompt in men remorse that their wickedness

---

[1] *Ibid.* ll. 1078–9.   [2] *Ibid.* ll. 1080–2.
[3] *Ibid.* l. 1092.   [4] *Ibid.* ll. 1649–50.
[5] *Ibid.* ll. 610–11.   [6] *Ibid.* ll. 1656–8.
[7] *Ibid.* ll. 2089–90.

has earned for them: 'heavens hate, earths scorne, and paynes of hell'.[1]   In the end, to compensate for the severity of this rigid moral discipline, God promises the joys of immortality:

> Now, Lord, receyve me, for I come to thee
> And dye, I hope, in perfit charity.[2]

This, then, was the universe enveloping the life of the Leir whom Shakespeare transmuted into his own Lear. Clearly, he had at the same time to transmute the things of its earth. To do so, he threw the whole story back into the dim recesses of a pagan cult which even as such had hardly grown to conscious articulation of its pagan creed. As is the metaphysical world of *King Lear*, so perforce are its earthly institutions, its material furnishings, and so perforce are its people in their nature and their habits.

King Lear's is a church-less and a priest-less world. Its political organisation is a simple scheme of monarchy wherein the king's authority is uncontrolled and unlimited in its absoluteness. A robed man of justice may appear sporadically, but he is a mere appendage of the regal household and an interpreter of the royal will. The few geographical and historical references would help the Elizabethans to thrust Lear's world backwards into the remote past. It belongs to the age of the barbarous Scythians and of others who made their generation messes to gorge their appetite. Its accredited wise men are Thebans;[3] its more gorgeously dressed are apers of Persian fashions in their attire.[4] It lived its life in days long before the mythical Merlin prophesied, and at a time when Albion was not a literary archaism for England but its regular everyday name. Its material furniture is of the sparsest, a bare minimum for the maintenance of life and government. Its people are courtiers, warriors, farmers and fishermen; and its instruments and arts are as primitive as its needs. Government has its prisons,

---

[1] *Leir* l. 1648.   [2] *Ibid.* ll. 1670–1.
[3] *King Lear* III. iv. 162.   [4] *Ibid.* III. vi. 85.

its halters, its whips, its stocks and, more widely, its arms. Its
subject, man, has his house or his hovel, his clothes and his food.
There are tailors and stone-masons; there are sheep-cotes, mills
and pinfolds, pins and pricks and red-burning spits,—and of all
of it one remembers a mere button [1] better than anything else.
In such a primitive society, even houses are but solid tents
wherein to eat, to sleep and to take shelter from wind and cold
and rain, to seek cover from the pelting of the pitiless storm. [2]
A larger house may pile itself into a steeple, and thereby have
a means of throwing up a weathercock, for with this as a kind of
radar prognostication, man may know and counter the powers
which are the real stuff and furniture of his universe, the wind,
the cold, the rain and the storm. The least enviable of mortals is
he with houseless head and unfed sides. Of all the arts of human
society, the kitchen ones alone are those that have grown into
techniques; the knapping of eels on their coxcombs with
a stick as they are put into the paste alive is an accomplished
skill. [3] But the life of these people in *King Lear* (omitting the
anomaly of the cultured tradition of chivalric duel which is
thrust into the play as a means of its *dénouement*) has not yet
done more than open the machine age, and that only for its least
dispensable artisan; the builder has invented his primitive lever
for shifting massive blocks, and this contrivance is so re-
cognisably unique that for its label it has the bare name, 'an
engine'. [4] This nomenclature is a reminder that, though *King
Lear*'s is a world of the rudest material simplicity, there is
a remarkable dearth in it of names for even the commonest
objects of domestic life and day-to-day existence. Stools,
couches, tables and so forth: but little else. Indeed, in such
a world, the animal kingdom is nearer to men than are the
forms and implements of social practice. Hence, the Fool
doubly underlines his prophecy: it is twice-removed from
contemporary reference, and it will still be a prophecy when in

[1] *Ibid.* v. iii. 309.   [2] *Ibid.* iii. iv. 29.
[3] *Ibid.* ii. iv. 123.   [4] *Ibid.* i. iv. 290.

ages to come Merlin shall first pronounce it, for the Fool lives before Merlin's time.[1] The prophecy envisages a world far different from Lear's, inhabited by types of men as yet undreamed of—priests, brewers, heretics, cutpurses, usurers, bawds and so forth, and each with all of his new-fangled impedimenta.

Given this kind of physical world, the men who are Lear's contemporaries must fit into it; as indeed they do. In outward and in inward habit, they are of a very ancient time. Like earliest humankind, their occupation is in hunting, though now its motive is as much for pleasure as for food. After the hunt, they feast; and after that, they may throw the dice. Sometimes they are heard to sing, but music comes but once into the tale, and then expressly for a medicinal occasion. In their choice of wardrobe they generally remember that clothes are primarily blankets for the loins, or coverings without which the body would succumb to the extremity of the skies. But having to accommodate himself with clothes, man, and especially woman, is beginning to trick himself in borrowings from beasts of field and forest, silk and wool, and civet to ensure a pleasant perfume. The vainer sort of men, in their adulterate sophistication to go beyond a utility uniform, search for ornament which does not even serve the primary need for warmth. What Goneril and Regan seek by their factitious gorgeousness of gown is in its way what Oswald also seeks in his futile artificialities of precious speech. But Goneril and Regan and Oswald are markedly exceptional in their fashions. The general norm is the contrary of theirs.

Of greater dramatic importance than the outward manner of the people of *King Lear* is their inward habit. In their passions, their modes of thought, their moral axioms and their responses to life's occasions, they are similarly primitive. They act on impulse and on instinct more than by excogitated intent and planned purpose. Intellectual forethought is largely re-

[1] *King Lear* III. ii. 81.

served for the schemers of evil doings, and for such villains the simple-natured are an easy prey; 'on honesty their practices ride easily'. Lear is easily deceived by Goneril and Regan; Goneril and Regan each by the other; Gloucester and Edgar by Edmund; and so on. When those of better nature encounter what they take to be evil, they retort in passionate vituperation or, perhaps, in passionate appeal, but seldom by reasoned argument. In this way, Lear reacts to Cordelia's reply; in this way, he makes answer to his other daughters; in one of these ways, too, Kent disposes of Oswald. Their normal manner of countering evil is by action, and not by speech./ They are, indeed, creatures of passion and of instinct; and this links them closely with their extra-human world, and particularly with its other animate occupants, the beasts of field and forest. No play of Shakespeare's turns more often to the animal kingdom, and summons so many of its varied species. But when they are cited, it is no wise to give stylistic colour to a metaphor; it is the speaker's natural way of putting his consciousness of life into his verbal idiom. The men and the women of *King Lear* are and feel themselves to be near companions of the beasts. They are dragons in their wrath, wolves and tigers in their cruelty, fitchews in their lust. Their passions are simple and emphatic. Their anger is rage, their love is adoration, their appetite is lust. In their simplicity, they have not acquired the nicer discriminations of sentiment. They are tougher skinned; they recoil from signs of softness; Cordelia's cold answer to her father's test is her more gracious form of the habit which led Goneril to despise the milky gentleness and the harmful mildness of her husband. But they have attained a simple yet a strong sense of that characteristic whereby they are the human kind in nature's animate kingdom. Though comrades to the wolf and to the owl, they are nevertheless distinct from these; and in that which marks them men apart from beasts, they seek the firmest sanctions of their way of life. Nature has made and governs all things, man and beast alike. She is the source of universal life. In all her mighty operations, that which is primary, that which is in the beginning, and is behind all else, is her power to create. Amongst her creatures, man and beast are nearest to her in her essential capacity: they share with her that part of the creative activity which is generation, pro-creation. That is their sacred inheritance. But men alone, and not beasts, perceive its sanctity. Man's dawning moral sense, struck by the mysterious majesty of birth, sees parenthood as a holy responsibility. Since, without birth, there can be no life, the relationship of parent to child and child to parent impinges on his consciousness as the most naturally stringent of all moral ties. Shaping his conduct to a system, parental and filial love must be the very corner-stone and even the main pillar of it, and this gives him entry to a higher world wherein beasts have no part. Man's code of conduct separates itself at once from the habit of the beasts. Beasts remain baldly natural, man enters a second nature, human nature and human-natural-ness. Man becomes a moral being, the beast remains a creature of appetite. For man henceforth nature has its ordinations. Nature commands in him respect for origin; and no such com-pulsion urges beasts to mould their behaviour into compelling patterns of this kind:

> The hedge-sparrow fed the cuckoo so long,
> That it had it head bit off by it young.[1]

The law of the human world is different:

> That nature, which contemns it origin,
> Cannot be border'd certain in itself;
> She that herself will sliver and disbranch
> From her material sap, perforce must wither
> And come to deadly use.[2]

Possessing human attributes of conscious intuition, of reason, and of speech, and so transcending the race of beasts, the human being who departs from the natural law of humans to adopt

---

[1] *King Lear* I. iv. 235.　　　　[2] *Ibid.* IV. ii. 32.

the law of the beasts, has become less than a beast. He has proved himself a monster. This word 'monster' and its adjective 'monstrous' recur repeatedly as expressions of horror in the play. Summarily they connote that which contains the nuclear germ of all evil, the viciousness which is otherwise described as the 'unnatural', unnatural, that is, in the sense of unnatural for man though natural to beasts. Within this simple apprehension of ultimate moral criteria, the goodness and the badness of Lear's world establish themselves distinctly. Villainy is 'unnatural, detested, brutish,...worse than brutish',[1] monstrous, in fact. Its most flagrant acts are murder, lechery and filial ingratitude; for each of these in its own way contaminates nature herself in her creative energy; murder frustrates her, lechery befouls her, and filial ingratitude denies her. But on the other hand, virtue knows

> The offices of nature, bond of childhood,
> Effects of courtesy, dues of gratitude;[2]

they form her categorical sanctions of morals and of manners, part indeed, of a code of conduct in which manners identify themselves with morals, for the 'effects of courtesy' are in practice 'the policy and reverence of age'. If man denies or neglects these offices of nature, mankind is lost: then

> Humanity must perforce prey on itself
> Like monsters of the deep.[3]

To prevent such calamity, to save humanity, to punish its monsters, the gods must deprive the wicked of their true 'naturalness'. It is a prayer of this kind which Lear hurls as an imprecation on Goneril's head:

> Hear, nature, hear; dear goddess, hear!
> Suspend thy purpose, if thou didst intend
> To make this creature fruitful!
> Into her womb convey sterility!

[1] *Ibid.* I. ii. 81.
[2] *Ibid.* II. iv. 181.   [3] *Ibid.* IV. ii. 48.

Dry up in her the organs of increase;
And from her derogate body never spring
A babe to honour her! If she must teem
Create her child of spleen; that it may live,
And be a thwart disnatured torment to her!
...that she may feel
How sharper than a serpent's tooth it is
To have a thankless child![1]

It is in this sort of world and with people like this that the
drama of *King Lear* enacts itself. The generic community of its
population is plain to be seen, with one possible exception,
Lear's Fool. It is not that he does not fit easily into the material
structure of the society in Lear's realm. He is the traditional
royal retainer whose licensed task is to entertain the king in
such ways as the king finds entertaining. But he grows beyond
his privileged and covenanted function, and, doing so, he
sometimes seems to be breaking beyond the confines of his
allotted universe. In the most measurable assessment of his
professional rôle, he pushes licence to the limit of allowable
commentary on his master's doings. He points his remarks on
Lear's projects with a sting which pierces to the quick, and he
knows how near the edge he is thrusting:

Thou wast a pretty fellow when thou hadst no need to care for her
frowning; now thou art an O without a figure: I am better than thou
art now; I am a fool, thou art nothing.[2]

Commanded by Goneril's grimaces to desist, he promises that
he will do so, 'I will hold my tongue', but he goes on to say
his pertinent say. As he does so, although his affection for
Lear and for Cordelia links him morally with the human
society to which he belongs, he assumes a dramatic significance
which puts him above the conventionally dramatic obligation
to be no more than the person required by the plot and to be
that person consistently. He is for the most part in the play;
but, as occasion serves, he contracts out of the groupings of its

[1] *King Lear* I. iv. 297.   [2] *Ibid.* I. iv. 210.

humanly dramatic types and out of their impacts on circumstance and on each other, in order to speak in the voice of that disembodied wisdom with which the Ironies and the Gods review the deeds and the fates of mortal men, the voice which ancient dramatists gave to the figure they also made part of, but not always part in, their plays, the Chorus. Like his choric prototype, the Fool has second sight: his talk has in it many of the names of things not yet in use in the households of Lear's contemporaries. But to think his prophetic utterances mystically inspired would be to mistake them utterly. The foresight he has is the cumulative product of mankind's human experiences. It phrases itself in the terms of popular adage; it is the judgement of man's common sense. The Fool knows that when the candle goes out, we are left darkling; he knows, too, the reason why the seven stars are no more than seven, it is for the pretty reason that they are not eight. Just as the fools, and the heroes, of Shakespearian comedy know a church by daylight, just as they never forget that an hour after nine o'clock it is ten o'clock, so Lear's fool accepts as an immutable fact of nature that a crab will taste like a crab. His wisdom is the horse-sense of the world corroborated into man's common sense. Even in cruder apprehensions of it, such as a Costard's or a Bottom's, it has proved itself a potent aid to life. Its worth is greatest, however, when its intellectual content, its common sense, is mingled with its emotional counterpart, the common sentiment of human kindness. This is the way in which Lear's Fool has it. He expresses an attitude to life in which Shakespeare finds a promising clue to man's mortal happiness. In the play of *King Lear* the part of the Fool limits the power of his benevolence for shaping the happiness of his lord and master. He can only thrust his sympathy into the sufferings brought about by neglect of his simple admonitions. It is his lot to have been born into a tragic universe: in a different world, an Illyria or a forest of Arden, he would have been a promoter of widespread gaiety and of general well-being. But the tragic world discovers abysses deeper than his plummet can sound. He passes from the action of his play before it ends, uttering the mingled voice of irony and pathos in a choric summary of the lot of human kind.

As the heavens and the earth of it, as its men and its women, so is the theme of *King Lear*. It is resolved into elemental simplicity. Its plot is a simple domestic circumstance; and of all such circumstances, the most intimately personal, the breaking of the bond between parent and child. Such an episode is within the imaginative capacity of all mankind; and the emotions which it will excite are within the range of common experience. The particular plot grows easily into a more general theme of equal simplicity: life assaulted by the impact of sheer evil. So by its very simplification, *King Lear* universalises the tragedy which it represents. It involves all humanity in the tragic conflict of life. It achieves this largely by the prevailing primitiveness of its realm and the inhabitants of it. It maintains as its persistent impression a sense of the nearness of man and beast. In one family and of one blood, man and beast are born; Cordelia is own sister to Goneril; Edmund is half-brother to Edgar. But the nearness is even more intimate; in the single state of man, beast and human dwell intermittently together. That is, of course, a mere truism. Shakespeare gives it vital and urgent reality. In his scenes, human nature is palpably a part of nature. The line dividing man from beast is a tenuous thread, and common to both in these elemental conditions are all the impulses of appetite and all passions of the blood. The thin dividing line, however, is the consciousness within man of his human nature. This sense in him of human kindness, recognisable in divergent urgings towards gratifications refining on or transcending the mere satisfaction of appetite, is beginning to flower as a sentiment of human kindliness, and so it is establishing a simple moral ideal of 'man-ness' or virtue. But even as he is growing to this self-consciousness of his human kindness, man does not discard his natural attributes: they lurk within him, ready to break through whenever the constraint of his human kindliness relaxes. Hence the fragility of man; the beast is strong within him, more violent, more thrustful than the frail and faint promptings of his humanity. But at least the beast is becoming clearly recognised as the beast. What *King Lear* throws into such impressive prominence is the ever-present sense of the universality of evil and of its power; of its dwelling amongst men and within man; of the plight of poor naked mortals under its onslaught; of the vast and expensive ravages which it makes on life; of the hardness of the conflict to repel it, the pain and the suffering entailed, and the apparent uncertainty of victory. In no other play is evil made so human; in no other play are there humans so evil. And in none is a deeper human pain exacted by this human evil. Behind the darkness of the foreground, human kindliness is strengthening itself into habit; and habit is stoutly corroborating itself as custom. A spiritual civilisation is dimly emerging and man is making or discovering a morality. But the price of it is heavy in blood and tears; and the picture of Lear paying this price is the main stuff of the drama. The essential substance of the piece is the presentation of his successive sufferings, his moods, his passions, his feelings as his pain is intensified by the succeeding blows of his daughters' cruelty. They are dramatically the core of the play; they are precisely the very matter of poetry, the ideal material for the poet-dramatist who was Shakespeare.

But as the quality of this material is emotional rather than intellectual, *King Lear* is a harder play to discuss than is, say, *Hamlet*. Indeed, it is not a play to talk about; it is a play imaginatively to live through either in the theatres of the world or in the inner theatre of the mind. Hamlet translates his awareness of life into the idiom of thought; Lear's awareness is spontaneously expressed directly from his feelings. It is nevertheless possible with him as with Hamlet to follow the successive waves of his emotion and watch them falling into a shape recognisable as the psychological pattern of a human being. But there is no need to go over the ground which Bradley explored with his fine critical insight, and where he traced the compulsive sequence of moods in a man of Lear's character. Being the particular man which Lear is, and inhabiting the particular world in which he lives, his tragic fate is as inevitable as anything in mortal history could be. But the particulars which make Lear's compounded character what it is are the simplest elements of human nature at large; and the particular conjunction of external circumstance in his own particular world from which his tragedy springs is a human relationship which is shared by all humanity. The tragic requirement of inevitability is assured; and to it is joined the impressiveness of a universality wider than in all Shakespeare's other plays. *King Lear* exhausts the world to extract from it its heaped-up tale of human pain; but then it brings the essence of the agony home to the bosoms of all who watch the tragedy.

It may appear as if at certain times men have not felt the entire inevitability of Lear's story. The eighteenth century provided an alternative ending to it, and left Lear living in the comfort of reconciliation with Cordelia, just as the earliest tellers of the tale, Geoffrey and Wace and Layamon had done. The current sentiment of its human kindliness had run to sentimentality, and its complacent rationalism had demanded poetic justice. But Lear is not to be plucked back into the pettinesses of domesticity, nor to the memory of life's whips and scorns:

> Vex not his ghost: O, let him pass! he hates him
> That would upon the rack of this tough world
> Stretch him out longer.[1]

It is more likely that the happy ending which Tate gave to the play was not mainly meant to provide comfort for Lear; it was probably a device to save Cordelia. Even Dr Johnson, not

[1] *King Lear* v. iii. 313.

normally a wallower in his century's sentimentality, felt an impulse to rescue her from death. He approved Tate's alteration of the plot.

A play in which the wicked prosper, and the virtuous miscarry, may doubtless be good because it is a just representation of the common events of human life: but since all reasonable beings naturally love justice, I cannot easily be persuaded that the observation of justice makes a play worse: or, that if other excellences are equal, the audience will not always rise better pleased from the final triumph of persecuted virtue.... I was many years ago so shocked by Cordelia's death, that I know not whether I have endured to read again the last scenes of the play till I undertook to revise them as an editor.[1]

But the play is the tragedy of King Lear, not that of Cordelia; and Lear only realises and exhibits the bottommost depth of life's tragedy when Cordelia is snatched from him for ever. Only by this stroke is the menace of evil shown in its utmost power. Nothing less worthy than Cordelia could so worthily reveal the price which man must pay in discovering the worth of goodness. Her death is sacrificial, and upon such sacrifices whatever gods there may be pour their incense.

[1] *The Critical Opinions of Samuel Johnson*, ed. J. E. Brown, p. 80.

CHAPTER VIII

CONCLUSION

For Shakespeare, his tragedies were experiences, things apprehended through the whole of his sentient nature. They were
not merely ideas. Yet it is not improper that his readers, trying
to fit the tragic experience which he communicates to them
into the system of their own apprehension of life, should endeavour to translate that experience into the discursive idiom
within which they are trying to make their own sense of life
intellectually coherent. This is what they mean when they talk
of Shakespeare's idea of tragedy. They mean the idea which,
though never explicit in Shakespeare, seems to them to be
implicit in his imaginative presentations of tragedy. Shakespeare himself has a sense for tragedy, and not a philosophy of
it. From play to play, he presents, in each of them, particular
sets of particular men confronting the circumstances peculiar
to that play. In each, his insight seems to perceive and reveal
the moral ulcer whose malignancy destroys the fabric of the
physical and the spiritual life of his protagonist. But in the
greater tragedies, he sees more deeply. There is first the diagnosis
of the illness. But generally he hits on a familiar and even
a common disease, and reserves his imaginative energy for
recreating each successive stage in the progress of the malady
so that in the end we, the watchers, are completely rapt with
the sensible conviction of its relentless fatality and of its
irreparable devastation.

As we have been following the course of his tragedies from
play to play, our main interest has been to observe the particular
manner in which the tragic action propels itself to its tragic
ending, assuring itself of its own inevitability, and gathering
round it the added weight of universality and momentousness.

With each one, however, something, sometimes more, sometimes less, has been said about the notions of tragedy which seem to be implicit in it, and about the extent to which such notions seem common to the other tragedies. In this concluding review there will be no pretence to formulate a theory or a philosophy of Shakespearian tragedy. Such attempts have been made again and again in the last two hundred years; seldom without profit, but never with entire success, for Shakespearian tragedy breaks through language and escapes into the outer darkness, just as does the life which it reflects. We shall do no more than hazard a few generalisations built on the impressions which are left strongest within us by the reading of his plays and especially by the reading of the greater ones amongst them. Naturally, the generalisations may be merely such as suggest themselves to one particular person; to others, they may be nothing more than remarks peculiar to that particular person.

First and foremost of these impressions is this. Shakespearian tragedy is profoundly spiritual, and yet in no real sense is it at all religious. To say that it is entirely humanist is to invite a misunderstanding of its scope. It is almost completely confined to life as the human experience of living. In its whole ambit, it takes life as a manifestation of the phenomena which are the substance of morality. But it is occupied with life as life is lived in a universe wherein mightier forces than those of man are perpetually exerting their powers in shaping the lot of mankind. These are the vast circumambient mysteries. In their ways, they are too inscrutable to be resolved into any but the simplest and vaguest theological formulary, and their complicity in making man's destiny is so indirect and so remote that, as divinities, they have no assessable or definable rôle in the overt plan of Shakespeare's tragedies. Nor does that plan presuppose or promise ampler and more gratifying revelation of the nature of God or of the gods. At farthest, it vaguely apprehends that the ultimate arbiters cannot be hostile to man's search for goodness, though they leave to man himself the immense rigour of the strife. Shakespeare's abiding interest is in the absorbing spectacle of this effort. His preoccupation is moral, and not religious. In his normal day-to-day existence, there is no reason to suspect that Shakespeare was not a good Elizabethan Anglican: but the ideal world in which he moved when he was imaginatively excited was the world of man and of morality, not that of the gods and of theology.

Yet Shakespeare's moral world is not inconsistent with a universe capable of being apprehended religiously. At all events, and without distorting its outlines, hosts of men have fitted it into their own sectarian dogmas. Predominantly, however, Shakespeare's major concern is that of the humanist. But it is that of a humanist whose imaginative grasp is wider than his rational comprehension, and who therefore is always too conscious of the elusive mystery of things ever to be a consistent rationalist or even to be professedly an agnostic. For he has an unswerving faith. It is faith in the mysterious spirit of man.

In Shakespeare there is no hard and fast dichotomy between body and soul. He appears to find the spirit of man as the characteristic functioning of the complex organism of flesh, blood, nerve, heart and brain, as in each man it manifests itself distinctively through a form of conduct which is the outcome of that particular man's instinct, passion, reason and will. In his tragedies, physical death involves a cessation of the spirit within the body. But bodily death is only tragic when it entails, or follows, or occasions mutilation of the individual and, thereby, of the general spirit. The death of the human spirit is the extermination of man. Hence the note which marks the final depth of tragedy is often the voice which cries that no longer is there anything serious in mortality, that life is no longer worth the living. For this annihilates the spiritual universe into which mankind seems to be arduously ascending. The expression of this utter defeat may be directly phrased, as it is in the despair of a Macbeth when he finds that life is a tale told by an idiot, signifying nothing: or in the pathetic recognition by a Lear when he realises the inscrutable but final destruction of what for him as an individual was the only hope of happiness:

> No, no, no life!
> Why should a dog, a horse, a rat have life,
> And thou no breath at all?[1]

or in the terrible clarity of Othello's despondent resignation:

> O vain boast!
> Who can control his fate?...
> O Desdemona! Desdemona! dead![2]

Indirectly, it is no less devastatingly tragic in Hamlet's abject surrender of his moral nature, when, abandoning himself to the disposal of chance, he tries to foist the abnegation on to his conscience as the acceptance of a benign providence: 'we defy augury; there's a special providence in the fall of a sparrow'.[3]

For man, and for Shakespeare contemplating man, the true tragedy of life is a conviction of its futility. This might well be, of course, the voice of despair uttered by one who hitherto had been exalted with an exhilarating sense of the infinite richness of life. In his comedies Shakespeare had revelled amongst his men and women with an exuberant confidence in the spirit of man. Are, then, Shakespeare's tragedies a recantation, a denial of his trust in human nature, and in the capacities of human life? Our own view is that there is no fundamental contradiction between the Shakespeare of the comedies and the Shakespeare of the tragedies. In the tragedies, of course, one participates in the unutterable sorrows of mortal existence; they are felt, too, as more bitter and more prevalent than

[1] *King Lear* v. iii. 305.
[2] *Othello* v. ii. 264.
[3] *Hamlet* v. ii. 230.

hitherto they had seemed: and escape from them appears less likely than an easier optimism had perceived. For tragedy comes on man not only and not mainly through evil and sin: it relentlessly pursues the virtuous-minded, and often they seem to fall to the unforeseen outcome of their good intentions. The tragic *peripeteia* is, in F. L. Lucas' brilliant phrasing of the Aristotelian formula,[1] the working in blindness to one's own defeat, and the *anagnorisis* is the realisation of the truth, the opening of the eyes, the sudden lightning flash in darkness. For the victims, the tragic heroes, the ensuing extinction is absolute and unrelieved.

But for us, human beings who are kin to them, there is something which survives through, and even by reason of, the very agony. It is the longer view, and perhaps the larger view, that man indeed perishes, but that mankind is progressively revealing transcendent potentiality for higher and higher attainments in the realm of the spirit. Within its own dominion, the spirit of man is indomitable. When, in the individual, it is overborne by powers outside it and alien to it, its very defeat and his destruction are a new access of strength to the spirit itself. In its simplest display this indomitability shows itself in the instinctive energy which compels even the weaker or the more vicious of tragic heroes, a Richard II, a Richard III, or a Macbeth, to some gesture of nobility in his final overthrow. But in the larger sense, the very groundwork of the idea of tragedy is an assumption of the potential nobility of mere man. It is a sentiment which inheres in the whole body of traditional tragedy, ancient and modern. Tragedy, as an art-form, is the shape in which it comes to its most perfect utterance. But the note it echoes is the burden which resounds as one of the most compelling and most recurrent intuitions in primitive and in later literature. In our earliest Anglo-Saxon poems, the heroic spirit becomes most heroic and nearest to tragedy in the voice of the old warrior at the battle of Maldon, who, seeing his leader slain

[1] F. L. Lucas, *Tragedy* (Hogarth Press), p. 95.

and himself and his comrades likely to be overwhelmed, exhorts them to steadfastness:

> Hyge sceal þe hearde heorte þe cenre
> Mod sceal þe mare swa ure maegen lytlaþ;

'our courage must be still harder, our hearts still keener, the spirit the greater, as the strength of our bodies grows less'. Different in circumstance, but not in substance, is the hymn to man sung by the chorus in *Antigone*:

> πολλὰ τὰ δεινὰ κοὐδὲν ἀν-
> θρώπου δεινότερον πέλει.[1]

Man, mere man, is here invested with the dread awfulness which hitherto had been the attribute of gods alone. Indeed a vital chapter in the record of man's spiritual progress could be written from the semantic history of the Greek δεινός and the English 'kindness'. The Sophoclean awe recurs in *Hamlet*.

What a piece of work is a man! how noble in reason! how infinite in faculty! in form and moving how express and admirable! in action how like an angel! in apprehension how like a god![2]

But both Sophocles and Shakespeare, without bating their reverence for the spirit of man and their wonder at its incalculable capacity, knew also how precarious is its nature and how fragile it could be. 'The beauty of the world', yet but 'the paragon of animals', and oftentimes no more than 'the quintessence of dust'; or, as Gilbert Murray puts the Sophoclean lines:

> Speech he hath taught him and wind-swift thought,
>> And the temper that buildeth a city's wall,
> Till the arrows of winter he sets at naught,
>> The sleepless cold and the long rainfall.
> All-armèd he; Unarmèd never
>> To front new peril he journeyeth;
> His craft assuageth Each pest that rageth
>> And defence he hath gotten gainst all save Death.
> With craft of engines beyond all dream
>> He speedeth—is it to good or ill?[3]

[1] Sophocles, *Antigone*, 332.   [2] *Hamlet* II. ii. 315.
[3] *The Antigone* translated by Gilbert Murray (1941), p. 33.

Yet in spite of this, illimitable nobility is within man's compass, though it may lie dormant or even be perverted to evil.

It is perhaps the prevalence of such sentiments as this which helps to explain the apparent paradox that human beings find pleasure in the most tragic works of the tragedians. In 1824, one M'Dermot published a treatise, *A Philosophical Inquiry into the Source of the Pleasures derived from Tragic Spectacles*. He prefaced it with an examination of various explanations advanced by English, French and German thinkers, reviewing the opinions of Dubos, Fontenelle, Helvetius, Lessing, Schlegel, Hume, Burke, Kaimes, Blair, Knight and Hazlitt. These suggestions range widely. Tragic pleasure is an escape from pain: 'better than the insipid languor which rises from perfect tranquillity and repose'. Or pleasure and pain are near each other; sorrow can be soft and agreeable, and tragic pain is mitigated to pleasure because there is a dimly-lurking consciousness that the spectacle is mere fiction. Or pain causes a prerequisite perturbation and sensation, and the magic of artistic presentation transmutes the pain to pleasure. Or again, our pleasure is the contemplation of our own freedom from the evils which we see represented. More bluntly, our pleasure springs from our inherited delight in cruelty. Less unkindly, we rejoice in the energies and violent efforts displayed in feats of strength, courage and dexterity, and also in the calm energies of virtue called forth by the exertions of passive fortitude. Tritest of all, tragic pleasure arises from the influence on us of virtuous impressions.

So varied, and so contradictory, and so unsatisfactory are the theories reviewed. But none of the critics denies that pleasure undoubtedly does arise from the witnessing of tragedy. Of all M'Dermot's philosophers, the one whose notions seem to go a considerable way towards meeting the problem in its application to Shakespeare is Schlegel. Schlegel suggests that tragic pleasure springs from 'a feeling of the dignity of human nature' and from 'the traces of a higher order of things impressed upon the apparently irregular progress of events and secretly revealed in them'. Yet in one particular, these propositions seem to need extension to include, even in their own kind, the highest gratification offered by Shakespeare's presentation of human tragedy.

The mainspring is Shakespeare's sense of what life is. Life begins in mystery, both in beast and in man. But all living creatures have one capacity which is godlike in its nature: they have the power to create their own kind as out of nothing, to bring something new into the world. Procreation, however, is the prerogative both of beast and of man. On the one hand, it is this common and magic creative gift which perpetually reminds Shakespeare of the close and primary link between the human and the animal kingdom. Yet on the other hand, it is in the differences subsequent to the production of their offspring that Shakespeare sees the essential differentiation between man and beast. The reproductive impulse in beasts may impel them for a brief moment to instinctive protection of their offspring. But the human animal has the added gift of self-consciousness. His paternal protective instinct becomes an emotion, and his recognition of mere kind begins to emerge as the sentiment of kindness. Once the sentiment is familiarly and consciously experienced, it takes on far-reaching implications. It impels behaviour which will come to be recognised as obligatory. The idea of duty is beginning, and as it slowly grows, man is becoming more and more of a moral being, more and more distinct from the animal. Kindness will grow to human kindliness, as the sense of obligation extends itself beyond the ties of immediate paternity. Yet the initiatory impulse is the nuclear and peculiar instinct which is specific to the human kind. The first great stage of this discovery is lived through in *King Lear*, and the second in *Macbeth*. In *Othello* and in *Hamlet*, man has travelled much farther along the way by which he is moralising his nature. He has become more and more aware of a larger and a still larger good. In a merely human relationship, through instinct and emotion, Othello and Desdemona are discovering for themselves and for us a way in which man may shape a higher good in life than he has hitherto dreamed of as possible. In *Hamlet*, the mind of man has a sense that it is almost able to make goodness itself. At moments it would appear, and in no cynical mood, that 'there's nothing either good or bad, but thinking makes it so'.

It is in this moral creative power of man when his instinctive nature has grown to the disciplined awareness of his spiritual consciousness that Shakespeare sees the sanctity of human life. It is the developed expression of the impulse which is the primary activity by which man becomes man and by which he is distinct from all other forms of life. No achievement of the spirit is beyond its reach. There is high significance in the fact that the chronological order of Shakespeare's greater tragedies is from *Hamlet* to *King Lear*. The wonder of man and the marvel of his spiritual potentiality is unmistakable in the first: but in the last, the miracle has been traced back to its very rudiments, and is discovered in the primary nucleus or gene of the human species. Hence Shakespeare's faith in mankind; for man's essential nature and his distinctive property is a specific something or other which makes predominantly and progressively for good; and when he sets himself against his own kindness, he fordoes himself.

Yet throughout his existence, he remains, as man, a part of the animal kindom. Moreover, physically, he is subject to a material universe. The beast is always within himself; and often the universe about him appears like an un-moral power which stimulates the beast more than the man in him, and which, even when less apparently hostile, shows no obvious preference to assist the higher as against the lower of his efforts. Happiness is seldom apportioned to degrees of worthiness for it. Suffering is more certain than joy. Yet somehow or other, the bad and the good, each in their way, are extending and deepening the sense of goodness. Though the progress involves immense pain and irreparable loss, and the process is heartbreakingly slow, the things of the spirit are gradually gaining on the inheritance of the beast. Mankind is realising more and more the nature of human kindness. The individual passes, aware of the destructiveness of his evil; or, on the other hand, though painfully failing to reach the good for which he strove, he manifests, in his ripeness to accept his fate, his own fellowship in the human kind, for whom the common or general good is the highest good. It is this faith in the nature of man which permeates Shakespeare's poetry. Even in its agonies, human life is worthwhile; for the instinctive sense of human kindness not only impels man to live, it impels him no less certainly to suffer and to die for the spiritual enrichment of his kind. Ultimately therefore it is no longer merely a question of personal happiness. It is a matter of spiritual progress in the well-being of humanity at large. To Shakespeare evil is inhumanity, not only in the sense that evil is the source of the cruelty which man inflicts on other men, but in the deeper sense that evil is a distortion of the essential nature of man. For to Shakespeare, man is the human kind, and the vitalising element of the human kind is human kindness, and human kindness is fellowship, and fellowship is love, and love is the means by which man perceives or makes the goodness on which the happiness of his kind depends.

But all these assertions, of course, are not obviously an intellectual transmission of the immediate response which our whole sentient nature makes to Shakespeare's tragic plays. They are merely attempts to see the plays dispassionately when they have receded, as do all other facts of our experience, into that body of awareness which cumulatively is for each one of us what he means by his life. We endeavour to build this mass of material into some sort of shape which will satisfy the mind's thirst for order. But what we are really handling are not direct and immediate perceptions, they are afterthoughts succeeding those perceptions. Yet there would appear to be some sort of evidence that Shakespeare's own afterthoughts tended in the same direction. After his tragedies, he wrote his romances,

The Winter's Tale and *The Tempest*. Their imaginative and dramatic inferiority to the tragedies is very likely due to the premature oncoming of the dramatist's old-age. His hand preserves its cunning, but his imaginative insight is less penetrating. Evil and pain have lost much of the destructiveness and of the agony which in his tragedies he had found them to have. He is still aware of their rifeness, but they do not press themselves so urgently on his consciousness. He feels and finds benignity in old-age, a benignity which grew in him in a similar way and through similar causes as it had grown in his own Countess of Rousillon. In his romances, with their depiction of kindly charity, reconciliation, forgiveness and tolerant sympathy, he expresses the serene calmness of a mind which accepts life trustfully in the confidence that it is primarily and naturally an embodied impulse toward human goodness. In these last plays, as in his tragedies, the foundation of the faith is the same. It is incarnated plainly in the natural spirit of a Perdita and of a Miranda, who are human nature in its simplest, most natural and unsophisticated essence, the instinctive simplicity of girlhood. It is a trust which the greatest English tragedian shares with other great tragedians. There is much of it in the Antigone of Sophocles; it is even more closely Shakespearian in the Iphigenia of Euripides.

It remains, however, that the romances are afterthoughts to the tragedies, and neither rebuttals nor denials of the agony and the waste which the tragedies have revealed. As afterthoughts, even their efficacy, and maybe their validity, is diminished unless one perpetually goes back directly and frequently into the imaginative world of the tragedies, goes back, too, with the conviction that the tragedies are the plays in which Shakespeare's apprehension of the experience of living is at its keenest. There is no escape from their direct sense of the sorrow and of the evil which may, and for most mortals, must afflict mankind. But even in the deepest gloom of the tragedies there emerges from moment to moment, and endures to the very end, the austere but heartening sense that to be part of the life of man is in itself an exalting experience. In the most harrowing of their situations, when the individual human being is oppressed by torments unwarranted and undeserved by any code of human justice, and is facing what seems like utter annihilation, he still retains some inner consciousness of a mastery of the soul, which, though yet unreached, is within the prospect of a remoter future time. He and we, his watchers, endure an austere, even a sombre, but yet an exhilarating experience. The sense of human dignity which it evinces is an attitude to life very similar to the one put into words some seventy years ago by a distinguished Cambridge and Trinity man, FitzJames Stephen, in a volume the main purport of which was to expound a doctrine in many respects completely hostile to all that Shakespeare felt in his bones:

What do you think of yourself? What do you think of the world?... These are questions with which all must deal as it seems good to them. They are riddles of the Sphinx, and in some way or other we must deal with them....In all important transactions of life we have to take a leap in the dark....If we decide to leave the riddles unanswered, that is a choice; if we waver in our answer, that, too, is a choice: but whatever choice we make, we make it at our peril. If a man chooses to turn his back altogether on God and the future, no one can prevent him; no one can show beyond reasonable doubt that he is mistaken. If a man thinks otherwise and acts as he thinks, I do not see that anyone can prove that he is mistaken. Each must act as he thinks best; and if he is wrong, so much the worse for him. We stand on a mountain pass in the midst of whirling snow and blinding mist, through which we get glimpses now and then of paths which may be deceptive. If we stand still we shall be frozen to death. If we take the wrong road we shall be dashed to pieces. We do not certainly know whether there is any right one. What must we do? 'Be strong and of good courage.' Act for the best, and take what comes. Above all, let us dream no dreams, and tell no lies, but go our way, wherever it may lead, with our eyes open and our heads erect. If death ends all, we cannot meet it better. If not, let us enter whatever may be the next scene like honest men, with no sophistry in our mouths and no mask on our faces.[1]

[1] F. Stephen, *Liberty, Equality, Fraternity* (2 ed. 1874), pp. 353-4.

To have attained the moral temper thus described by FitzJames Stephen is to have armed oneself to face life and all its consequences with calm and with courage. It is humanity's great spiritual conquest. It is sheer nobility, and it is sheerly human. It is the attitude to life which inspires all the heroic tales of man's greater triumphs throughout the ages. That some such spirit as this is the specific and peculiar nature of man is the groundwork of Shakespearian tragedy. To FitzJames Stephen, whose acute mind was more legalist than philosophic, the metaphysical implications of this moral nobility were narrowed within an honest, yet for man at large, an austere and cold philosophy. To Shakespeare, who was not a philosopher but a poet, a similar apprehension of human worth was irradiated with the warmth of living, and in his imaginative experiences of it he wrung from this earth and from man's flesh some intimation of the spiritual destiny towards which mankind has slowly but surely moved in the inevitable course of its natural growth. So Shakespeare clings eagerly and joyfully to the earth and to man. Doing so, he finds man in life, or man and life, are experiences which, despite their cost, broaden and deepen the sense in man of his true nature, his human kindness, his *philanthropia*. Even Timon's tirades are but explicable distortions which confirm the foundation of his faith in the essential nature of the human genus. So Shakespeare's faith is humanist, an unconquerable trust in the nature of man. After all, the sense of life as it is apprehended by living men is what really matters to them. When, in that apprehension, they invoke God, it is as the complementary necessity of man's universe; He is invoked to satisfy the needs of the universe such as he, man, conceives it to be, to complete a cosmos which is universal because it fulfils man's conception of the essential elements which are requisite to constitute a chaos into a universe. Shakespeare, realising life in actual and imaginative experience, found sufficient substance for his trust in life in his direct experience of living men as individual embodiments of a human kindness which spontaneously generates human kindliness, and, doing so, produces a nobility which is the measure of human worth. The primary and specific instinct of humanity is thus creating, and then perpetually widening the moral substance of man's spiritual life.

The Shakespearian sense of man and of life is a value which has been accepted by men of almost every creed. Humanist in essence as its structure is, it has been found not incompatible, though not co-extensive, with profoundly religious beliefs about the nature of man, of his ideals, and of his destiny. For instance, William James, perhaps in our time a typical representative of the philosopher whose main concern has been to explore the psychology of religion, and thence to build up a complete philosophy on the foundation of a Christian belief, quotes approvingly as the conclusion of his essay *The Will To Believe* the very extract from FitzJames Stephen which has been cited above as an expression of the sense of life which lies at the heart of Shakespearian tragedy.

INDEX

Aeschylus, 35, 151
Albion's England, 198, 202
All's Well That Ends Well, 70, 240
Antigone, 20, 235, 240
Antony and Cleopatra, 15
Aristotle, 7, 8, 19, 22, 39, 40, 45, 50, 84, 186, 203
Arnold, Matthew, 4
As You Like It, 69, 78–9, 225

Bacon, Francis, 8
Bandello, M., 51
Barker, Granville, 133
Battle of Maldon, 234–5
Beard, T., 33–4
Belleforest, F., 105–9, 114
Beowulf, 148
Blair, H., 236
Boccaccio, G., 50
Boswell Stone, W. G., 155–6, 169, 194, 199–202
Bradley, A. C., 1, 4, 5, 15, 16, 161, 228
Broke, A., 51, 53–4, 62–3
Brown, J. E., 5, 229
Browning, R., 152, 183
Burke, E., 236

Campbell, L. B., 34, 201–3
Castelvetro, L., 45
Chappuys, G., 114, 117, 135
Cinthio, G. B., 49, 50, 114–17, 125–6, 130–40
Cleopatra, 50
Coleridge, S. T., 4, 76, 118, 139, 196–8
Coriolanus, 15
Corneille, P., 50
Cotgrave, R., 167

Dante, 77
Darwin, C., 3
De Nores, Jason, 50
Dido, 50

Dryden, J., 4
Dubos, J. B., 236

Euripides, 83, 151, 240

Fabyan, R., 42
Faerie Queene, 198, 202, 204
Fontenelle, B., 236

Galsworthy, J., 45
Geoffrey of Monmouth, 194, 198–200, 203–6, 209, 228
Gesta Romanorum, 198
Goethe, 4
Gollancz, Israel, 105–9

Hall, R., 29–31, 33–4, 37, 38
Hamlet, 11, 13–14, 77, 79, 81, 83–112, 113–14, 141–3, 169, 189, 190, 233, 235, 237–8
Hazlitt, W., 4, 236
Hecatommithi, 50, 114–17, 125, 130–40
Helvetius, C. A., 236
Henry IV, 69, 70
Henry V, 69, 70
Henry VI, 63
Higgins, J., 198
Holinshed, R., 28–31, 33–4, 37–8, 40–4, 46, 48, 63, 155–60, 167–9, 194, 198–203, 209
Holland, Philemon, 35, 72–4, 184–7
Homer, 31, 148, 151
Horace, 61
Hudson, H. N., 76
Hume, D., 236
Huxley, T. H., 3
Hystorie of Hamblet, 105, 107–9

Iphigenia, 83, 240

James, William, 243
Johnson, Dr, 4, 5, 228–9
Julius Caesar, 15, 69–79, 141

Index

Kaimes (Henry Home, Lord Kames), 236
King John, 15, 63–9
King Lear, 7, 13–14, 189–229, 233, 237–8
Knight, J., 236
Kyd, T., 105

Lamb, C., 118
Layamon, 194, 199–201, 206, 210, 228
Lessing, 236
Lipsius, 5
Lotos-Eaters, 212
Love's Labour's Lost, 225
Lucas, F. L., 234

Macbeth, 13–14, 37, 111, 141–88, 189, 233–4, 237
M'Dermot, M., 236
Marlowe, C., 25, 154
Measure for Measure, 70
Meredith, G., 4
Midsummer Night's Dream, 225
Milton, 154
Mirror for Magistrates, 198, 200–3
More, Thomas, 29, 33, 37–8
Morley, J., 21
Much Ado about Nothing, 69
Murray, Gilbert, 235

Nashe, T., 34
New British Theatre, 24
North, T., 74–5

Oedipus, 10
Orr, J., 206
Othello, 13–14, 113–43, 189, 233, 237

Painter, W., 51
Palace of Pleasure, 51
Petrarch, 152
Phèdre, 20–1
Plutarch, 35, 72–5, 184–8
Polydore Vergil, 29, 34
Prometheus, 10

Racine, 20
Rape of Lucrece, 146
Richard II, 15, 39–48, 50, 66, 71, 124, 207, 234
Richard III, 11, 15, 24–41, 45, 48, 50, 66, 71, 141–2, 167, 169, 183, 234
Richards, I. A., 2
Roman de Brut, 205
Romeo and Juliet, 8, 15, 49–63, 115, 141, 207

Saxo Grammaticus, 104–9
Scaliger, J. C., 50
Schlegel, A. W., 236
Seneca, 33, 49, 52, 60–1
Shaw, G. B., 75
Sonnets, 146
Sophocles, 235, 240
Sources of Hamlet, 105–7
Spencer, E., 198, 201–2, 204
Spencer, H., 3
Stephen, F., 241–3

Tate, Nahum, 228–9
Tempest, The, 240
Tennyson, A., 240
Thyestes, 33
Tillyard, E. M. W., 30
Timon of Athens, 15, 242
Titus Andronicus, 15, 18–24, 50, 118–19
Tragicall Histoire of Romeus and Juliet, 51
Troilus and Cressida, 70
Troublesome Raigne of John King of England, 63–8
True Chronicle History of King Leir, 190–204, 207–8, 216–18
Twelfth Night, 69, 78, 225

Virgil, 61

Wace, 194, 199, 200, 205–6, 209–10, 228
Warner, W., 198, 202
Watson, T., 44
Whitehead, F., 205
Winter's Tale, 240